ANNETTE
CLEWETT

NETWORK MONITORING EXPLAINED
Design and Application

ELLIS HORWOOD SERIES IN COMPUTER COMMUNICATIONS AND NETWORKING

Series Editor: R.J. DEASINGTON, Senior Consultant, PA Consulting Group, Edinburgh

Currie, W.S.	**LANS EXPLAINED**
Chiu, Dah Ming & Sudama, Ram	**NETWORK MONITORING EXPLAINED**
Deasington, R.J.	**A PRACTICAL GUIDE TO COMPUTER COMMUNICATIONS AND NETWORKING, 2nd Edition**
Deasington, R.J.	**X.25 EXPLAINED, 2nd Edition**
Henshall, J. & Shaw, S.	**OSI EXPLAINED, 2nd Edition**
Kauffels, F.-J.	**PRACTICAL LANS ANALYSED**
Kauffels, F.-J.	**PRACTICAL NETWORKS ANALYSED**
Kauffels, F.-J.	**UNDERSTANDING DATA COMMUNICATIONS**
Muftic, S.	**SECURITY MECHANISMS FOR COMPUTER NETWORKS**

NETWORK MONITORING EXPLAINED
Design and Application

DAH MING CHIU and RAM SUDAMA
Digital Equipment Corporation,
Massachusetts, USA

ELLIS HORWOOD
NEW YORK   LONDON   TORONTO   SYDNEY   TOKYO   SINGAPORE

First published in 1992 by
ELLIS HORWOOD LIMITED
Market Cross House, Cooper Street,
Chichester, West Sussex, PO19 1EB, England

 A division of
Simon & Schuster International Group
A Paramount Communications Company

© Ellis Horwood Limited, 1992

All rights reserved. No part of this publication may be reproduced, stored in a retrieval system, or transmitted, in any form, or by any means, electronic, mechanical, photocopying, recording or otherwise, without the prior permission, in writing, of the publisher

Printed and bound in Great Britain

British Library Cataloguing in Publication Data
A catalogue record for this book is available from the the British Library

ISBN 0–13–614710–0

Library of Congress Cataloguing-in-Publication Data
Available from the publisher

Contents

Preface			13
1	***Introduction***		17
	1.1	MONITORING A SYSTEM	17
	1.2	BASICS OF COMPUTER NETWORKING	19
		1.2.1 The Open Systems Interconnection Reference Model	22
		1.2.2 Evolution of networking technology	25
		1.2.3 Examples of networks	26
		1.2.4 Network applications	27
	1.3	NETWORK MONITORING OVERVIEW	29
		1.3.1 Access to monitor information	29
		1.3.2 Design issues	29
		1.3.3 Management applications	32
		1.3.3.1 Fault management	32
		1.3.3.2 Configuration management	33
		1.3.3.3 Performance management	33
		1.3.3.4 Security management	33
		1.3.3.5 Accounting management	34
2	***Access to Monitor Information***		35
	2.1	OVERVIEW OF THE GENERAL MODELS	35
		2.1.1 Functional models for monitoring managed objects	36
		2.1.2 Methods of access to monitoring agents	40
		2.1.3 Naming and addressing	41
		2.1.4 Information models of managed objects	42
		2.1.5 Registration	43
		2.1.5.1 Registration of object identifiers	44
		2.1.5.2 Registration of global names	45
		2.1.6 The management protocol	45
	2.2	INTRODUCTION TO THE MANAGEMENT PROTOCOLS	46

2.3	**Internet SNMP**			**47**
	2.3.1	Background		47
		2.3.1.1	*The Internet and RFCs*	47
		2.3.1.2	*The development of SNMP and related references*	50
	2.3.2	Protocol		51
	2.3.3	Information model		52
		2.3.3.1	*Object types*	52
		2.3.3.2	*Constructed object types*	55
		2.3.3.3	*Object instances*	56
2.4	**ISO/IEC/CCITT CMIP**			**59**
	2.4.1	Background		59
		2.4.1.1	*The ISO/IEC and CCITT standardization process*	59
		2.4.1.2	*References*	61
	2.4.2	Protocol		63
	2.4.3	Information model		64
		2.4.3.1	*Managed object classes*	64
		2.4.3.2	*Managed object class template and other related templates*	65
		2.4.3.3	*Object containment hierarchy*	70
2.5	**IBM SNA MANAGEMENT AND NETVIEW**			**73**
	2.5.1	Background		73
	2.5.2	Protocol		76
	2.5.3	Information model		81
2.6	**DIGITAL'S EMA and DECmcc**			**83**
	2.6.1	Background		83
	2.6.2	Protocol		84
	2.6.3	Information model		85
		2.6.3.1	*Entities*	85
		2.6.3.2	*Agents and Directors*	86

3 *The Design of Network Monitors*   89

3.1	**MONITORING AGENTS**		**89**
3.2	**INTEGRATED VS EXTERNAL MONITORS**		**90**
	3.2.1	Integrated monitoring agents	91
	3.2.2	External monitoring agents	92

		3.2.3	Technological evolution	95
			3.2.3.1 Network bandwidth	96
			3.2.3.2 Shared medium	96
			3.2.3.3 Processor speed and memory cost	97
		3.2.4	State-of-the-art external monitoring agents	98
		3.2.5	Summary	99
	3.3	WHAT LAYER TO MONITOR?		99
	3.4	CASE STUDIES AND EXAMPLES		100
		3.4.1	A datalink monitor	101
			3.4.1.1 Design overview	102
			3.4.1.2 Modes of operation	104
			3.4.1.3 Display formats	104
			3.4.1.4 Sample reports	105
		3.4.2	An event logging monitor	105
			3.4.2.1 Event capacity	106
			3.4.2.2 Design overview	107
			3.4.2.3 Timestamping events	107
			3.4.2.4 Sample reports	108
		3.4.3	A LAN traffic monitor	108
			3.4.3.1 Design overview	109
			3.4.3.2 Sample reports	111
		3.4.4	A network workload monitor	114
			3.4.4.1 Design overview	114
			3.4.4.2 Connection record identification	117
			3.4.4.3 Connection states and termination	118
			3.4.4.4 Connection locality	119
			3.4.4.5 Connection duration	120
			3.4.4.6 Connection activity	121
			3.4.4.7 Performance	121
			3.4.4.8 Sample reports	122

4 *Applications of Network Monitoring*   127

	4.1	INTRODUCTION		127
	4.2	FRAMEWORKS FOR MANAGEMENT APPLICATIONS		127
	4.3	PROTOCOL ANALYSIS AND DESIGN		128
		4.3.1	Examples of protocol design and implementation issues	129
		4.3.2	Review of protocol performance studies	131

		4.3.2.1	A case study of LAN traffic	131
		4.3.2.2	Packet trains - a model of network traffic based on measurement	133
		4.3.2.3	Measurement of network application behavior	134

4.4 TESTING AND DEBUGGING DISTRIBUTED SOFTWARE — 138

- 4.4.1 Distributed vs. non-distributed testing — 140
- 4.4.2 Integrated vs. external monitors for debugging — 140
- 4.4.3 Logging event traces — 141
- 4.4.4 Merging event traces — 142
- 4.4.5 Use of event traces in simulation and testing — 142
- 4.4.6 Related papers — 143

4.5 FAULT AND CONFIGURATION MANAGEMENT — 143

- 4.5.1 Fault management — 143
- 4.5.2 Configuration management — 144

4.6 PERFORMANCE AND CAPACITY MANAGEMENT — 145

- 4.6.1 Network utilization and performance monitoring — 145
- 4.6.2 Examples of capacity planning — 146

4.7 SECURITY — 147

- 4.7.1 Security in monitor information — 147
- 4.7.2 The use of monitors in security applications — 147

4.8 ACCOUNTING — 149

- 4.8.1 Using a LAN monitor for departmental accounting — 150
- 4.8.2 Using an integrated monitor for cost accounting — 150

4.9 RESOURCE MANAGEMENT — 151

- 4.9.1 Load balancing — 151
- 4.9.2 Resource brokering — 152
- 4.9.3 Resource management — 152
- 4.9.4 Static vs. dynamic attributes — 154
- 4.9.5 The use of monitors in resource management — 154
- 4.9.6 Summary — 155

5 Summary and Future Directions — 157

5.1 SUMMARY — 157

	5.2	**FUTURE DIRECTIONS**	158
		5.2.1 Directions in network technology	158
		5.2.1.1 Scale	158
		5.2.1.2 Heterogeneity	159
		5.2.1.3 Bandwidth	160
		5.2.1.4 Network security	160
		5.2.2 Directions in implementation technology	161
		5.2.2.1 Processors, memory and disks	161
		5.2.2.2 Software programming	162
		5.2.2.3 User interface	162
		5.2.3 The use of "intelligent systems" in network monitoring	162
		5.2.4 The impact of standards development on monitors	164
		5.2.5 Integration of network and system management	165

Appendix A - An ASN.1 Primer   167

Appendix B - ISO OSI Standards   177

Appendix C - Internet Standards   179

Abbreviations   183

Glossary   185

Trademarks   195

References   197

List of Figures

Figure 1 -	Monitoring in a feedback system	18
Figure 2 -	Two applications communicate via a path	19
Figure 3 -	The simplest network communication path	20
Figure 4 -	Different network configurations	21
Figure 5 -	More than two systems connected via a subnetwork	22
Figure 6 -	The OSI Reference Model	23

Figure 7 -	Monitoring End and Intermediate Systems in OSI	25
Figure 8 -	Different approaches to external monitoring	31
Figure 9 -	High level model of managed objects	35
Figure 10 -	Basic functional model for monitoring managed objects	37
Figure 11 -	Summarization monitoring agent	38
Figure 12 -	External monitoring agent	39
Figure 13 -	External monitor	40
Figure 14 -	State of standardization for Internet protocols	49
Figure 15 -	Hierarchy of ISO object identifiers	54
Figure 16 -	ISO Standardization Process	60
Figure 17 -	CMIP protocol messages	64
Figure 18 -	Network layer containment hierarchy	71
Figure 19 -	Typical SNA configuration	74
Figure 20 -	SNA management monitoring mechanisms	75
Figure 21 -	NetView/PC as a management gateway	76
Figure 22 -	PUMS protocol boundaries with other components	77
Figure 23 -	The unsolicited flow	79
Figure 24 -	The request/reply flow	79
Figure 25 -	The request/reply flow (multiple resources)	80
Figure 26 -	NMVT Alert subvector types	81
Figure 27 -	Format of the Basic Alert subvector	82
Figure 28 -	NMVT Response Time Monitoring subvector types	82
Figure 29 -	Format of an RTM Data subvector	83
Figure 30 -	A monitoring agent	90
Figure 31 -	Integrated monitoring agents	91
Figure 32 -	External monitoring agents	94
Figure 33 -	Evolution of network monitoring technology	98
Figure 34 -	Installation of a datalink monitor	102
Figure 35 -	Datalink monitor design	103
Figure 36 -	Split-screen monitor display trace	105
Figure 37 -	Event logging trace output	108
Figure 38 -	LAN traffic monitor design	109
Figure 39 -	LAN utilization by segment	111
Figure 40 -	LAN utilization by protocol type	112
Figure 41 -	Top five sources	113
Figure 42 -	Tasks performed by a workload monitor	116
Figure 43 -	Total network connections by application	122
Figure 44 -	Average connection duration by application	123
Figure 45 -	Average data transfer by application	124
Figure 46 -	Total data transfer by application	125
Figure 47 -	Network packet size distribution	126
Figure 48 -	Distribution of packet lengths	132
Figure 49 -	Defining thresholds for fault prevention	144

Figure 50 -   A resource management service   153

List of Tables

Table 1 -   ASN.1 Universal Tags   172

To Kiran, Justin, Stephanie and Mom & Dad

Preface

Data communications networks have evolved into sophisticated and complex systems that affect many aspects of our lives, and are often critical to our work environments. Like other complex systems, they have an internal structure and control mechanisms that require constant attention and management. Systems of this sort are analogous to the human body, in which stimuli are sensed by the nervous system and reported to the brain, which processes the input and takes appropriate action.

In the case of computer networks, the "nervous system" consists of network monitoring agents, and the "brain" consists of network management applications and management information repositories. Collectively, these serve to process and store information that can be used either directly by other management applications, or reported to human administrators for further analysis. One way or the other, these applications allow the network state to be modified in order to correct faults, improve performance, repel attacks, and so on. To the extent that the applications can take action themselves without human intervention, management of the network can be automated.

We first became interested in the automation of network management several years ago, as it related to work we had done in designing distributed applications and distributed algorithms for network protocols. A distributed application can't perform it's function, if there are problems in the underlying network. We sought ways to make networks more reliable for the applications that run on them. Similarly, the design and verification of distributed algorithms require accurate models of the network. These studies demanded that we improve our understanding of how real networks behave.

It became clear early on in our research that the brain can't direct the body unless it is getting timely and accurate input from the nervous system. In our case, the network management applications we wanted to design depended on receiving information about the changing state of the network for their decision-making functions, and the kind of information we required wasn't readily available. This led us directly into the field of network monitoring, and resulted in several papers describing our research on network workload characterization and application-level monitoring.

Subsequently, the publishers contacted us and pointed out that, although network monitoring is a significant and growing area of computer networking, there is very little information on it in the literature. They asked if we would write a comprehensive review of the technology as part of their series on computer communications and networking, which led us to produce this book.

The field of network monitoring is broad, and in many cases obscure. Network management in general has only recently begun to be analyzed and architected, and monitoring, as a subset of management, has not yet received a great deal of attention. An understanding of the basics of network monitoring is needed, however, by anyone who designs, purchases, installs or maintains computer networks. Indeed, it can be very beneficial to those who develop network applications, or even those who only use those applications. We have done our best to put together information on past, present and future trends in the technology, and provide it in a form that is readable to those not fully conversant in this area of specialization. We hope we have struck a reasonable middle ground, neither boring our readers with too much detail, nor ignoring important concepts and examples.

The layout of the book

The book is divided into five chapters. The first chapter, the *Introduction*, describes the general concepts of system monitoring, and provides a brief primer on the basics of computer networking. It then gives an overview of what is to follow in the next three chapters.

Chapter 2, *Access to Monitor Information*, describes how monitor information is communicated to management applications. It goes into some detail on network management standards, and how they apply to monitors. It also gives examples of some of the more popular network architectures in actual use, and how they accommodate monitoring.

Chapter 3, *The Design of Network Monitors,* discusses the design issues for network monitor implementations. It makes the distinction between *integrated* and *external* monitors, and explains how their designs have evolved with changes in the implementation technology. It then describes four specific monitor designs in detail, providing examples of the output of each of the monitors for comparison.

Chapter 4, *Applications of Network Monitor*ing, explains some of the ways that monitor information is used in actual network management. This is not intended to be an exhaustive study, but only to stimulate the reader into thinking of additional uses for this information.

Chapter 5, *Summary and Future Directions,* first reviews briefly what has been covered in the book in the first four chapters. It then goes on to analyze trends in the technology that are likely to influence the development of network monitors over the coming decade.

Acknowledgments

We would like to thank Ellis Horwood Limited for recognizing the lack of educational material available in this important field, and being gracious enough to invite us to attempt to fill that gap.

We would like to thank all of our colleagues in the computer industry, who have contributed their ideas and efforts, not only to this book, but to the development of useful networks and applications that make living life a little easier. We have received valuable advice from Dorothy Cerni, Len Fehskens, Lois Frampton, Tony Lauck, Jeff

Mogul, Linsey O'Brien, Mark Sylor, and Kathrin Winkler, and others, who have also helped us by reviewing the book on their own time.

Most of all, we would like to thank our families, who have stood by us while we undertook this endeavor. Without their patience, we would not have persevered.

1

Introduction

Just like the roads connecting our villages and cities, computer networks are connecting millions of computers and computer users. These networks have become an infrastructure for many applications that now affect the daily lives of many people. For example, electronic mail and document interchange systems that let people exchange multi-media documents; distributed transaction processing systems that automate business transaction involving geographically distant sites; and access to and sharing of remote databases, files, and computing resources.

As such an important infrastructure, the computer network needs to be managed. By management, we mean the functions of both monitoring and controlling the various components of the network. The correct operation of a computer network depends on a great many complex components all working at the same time. Networking technology is also based on a large number of different interfaces and protocols. This distributed and heterogeneous nature of computer networks makes its management very complicated. In this book, we concentrate our study on one aspect of managing a computer network: network monitoring. This is the foundation for solving the more general problem of managing the network.

1.1 MONITORING A SYSTEM

Management of any large and complex system requires monitoring. For example, the economic system is constantly monitored using well-established metrics and methods. Some of the familiar metrics are the GNP, the inflation rate and the employment rate. These indices are based on macro-economic models. The knowledge of these indexes, together with the underlying model, allow economic planners, the government and individual citizens who participate in the economic system to predict near-term directions of the economy, and make decisions accordingly.

Another example is the monitoring of road traffic. Traffic conditions can be constantly monitored to help manage traffic congestion. Knowledge of the road conditions can be applied to help slow down the sources of the traffic (through diversion to other alternatives), and to dispatch traffic regulating forces to avoid a total grid-lock. Road traffic monitoring also helps establish long-term traffic trends. The data that is collected can be used to plan road expansion and maintenance projects.

Yet another example is the telephone system. We have become accustomed to the reliability of the telephone system. The telephone system is built with numerous internal mechanisms that continuously monitor its operation. The instantaneous condition of the telephone network is available at control centers. Automatic mechanisms are built into the telephone switches so that alerts can be triggered when anomalies are detected. The telephone system also is designed with the capability to keep track of all telephone calls for accounting purposes, which is another aspect of monitoring the system.

Finally, the administrators who manage traditional stand-alone time-sharing computer systems are quite familiar with monitoring. Computer operating systems often have facilities to help the systems administrator analyze the activities of the time-sharing system. For example, it is typically possible to examine the number of users on the system, the utilization (usage rate) of the different components of the system (disks, printers, CPUs, and memory), and so on. Since the time-sharing system is an environment that allows users to share resources and store private data, various security management mechanisms are also common. For instance, the frequency of login failures is often recorded, and may trigger an alert if a certain threshold is exceeded so that password-guessing activities can be detected. Depending on the kind of security threats in a particular environment, some systems run even more sophisticated monitoring processes to make sure that the system is secure, much like a policeman patrolling his beat.

Analogous to all these examples, network monitoring is a set of mechanisms that allow network administrators to know the instantaneous state and long-term trends of a complex computer network. The general model is that of a feedback system, as shown in Figure 1. Information about a system (network) is monitored by a monitoring agent (or multiple agents). Management agents can access the information acquired by the monitoring agent and assert control back onto the monitored system.

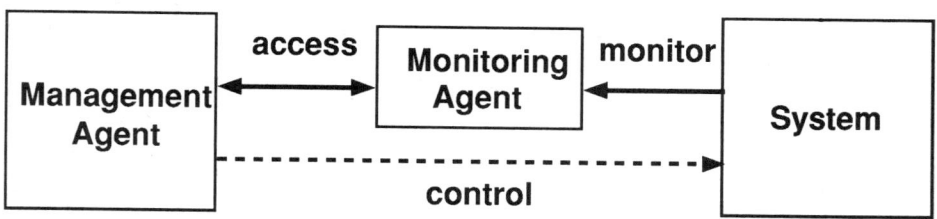

Figure 1 - **Monitoring in a feedback system**

In the remainder of this chapter, we give a basic introduction to each of the components in Figure 1, starting with the *system*, which in this case is a computer network.

1.2 BASICS OF COMPUTER NETWORKING

At the highest level of abstraction, computer communications can be described as two software programs exchanging information through some path of communications (Figure 2). This type of information exchange occurs frequently and at various levels in software systems. For example, data is exchanged through global variables, through shared files, through inter-process communications channels, etc. Computer networking is simply the mechanism that enables the sharing of data between software programs running on systems that are physically separated from one another (*End Systems*).

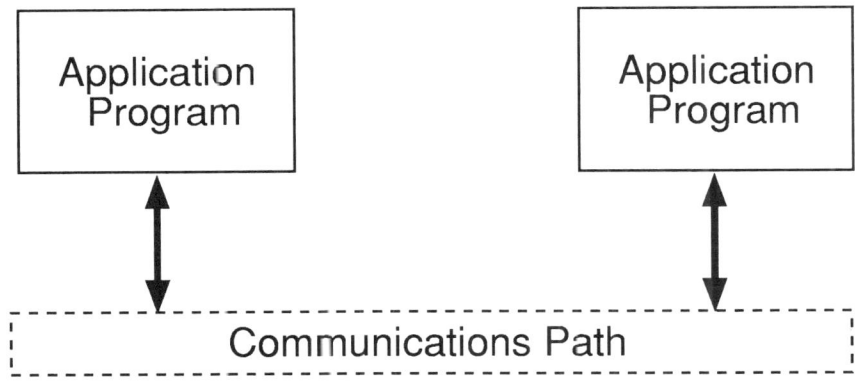

Figure 2 - Two applications communicate via a path

Since, by definition, the End Systems in a network are physically distant, they must be joined by some medium that provides a channel through which data can flow (Figure 3). Many such physical media are actually employed in computer networks, including copper wire, fiber optic cable, radio waves, etc. In most cases, the application software is unaffected by the nature of the underlying physical medium, requiring only the ability to communicate and exchange information. Therefore, an End System invariably contains *networking software* that tries to insulate applications from differences in the physical medium so they will function properly in a wide range of environments.

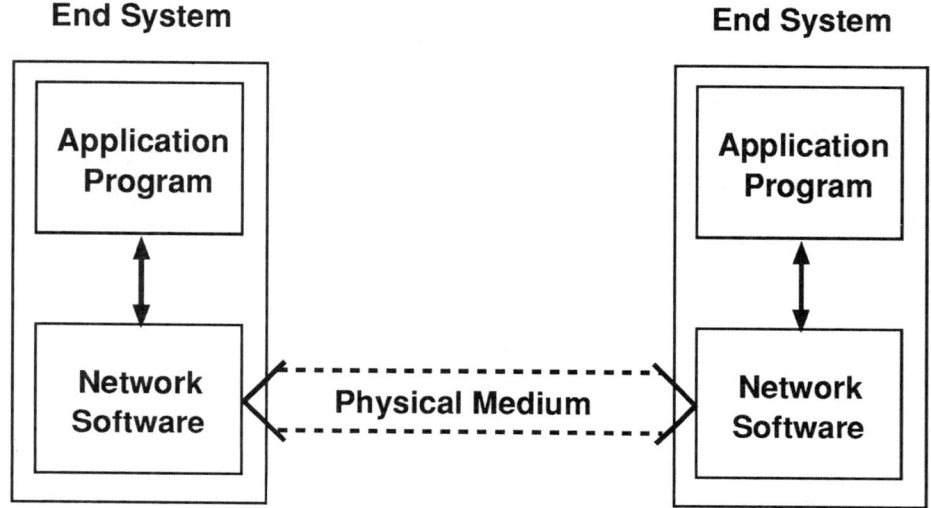

Figure 3 - The simplest network communication path

Most computer networking environments involve communications among more than two End Systems. The simplest way to achieve this would be to provide a direct communications link between every pair of systems. Such a configuration is described as a *fully interconnected* network. This is usually the most costly solution, since for m End Systems, on the order of m^2 links are required. Various configurations can be arranged for systems to share communication links (Figure 4). If a pair of systems do not share a link they may still communicate, as long as there is a third system capable of forwarding messages between them. Therefore, when the systems have forwarding capability, full interconnection at a logical level can be achieved without requiring full physical interconnectivity. This is the essence of *networking*. In some configurations a system can choose multiple paths to do forwarding. This multiplexing function in a forwarder is called *routing*. In larger and more sophisticated networks, some systems may be dedicated entirely to performing this routing function for the End Systems (Figure 5). Such systems are referred to as *Intermediate Systems*.

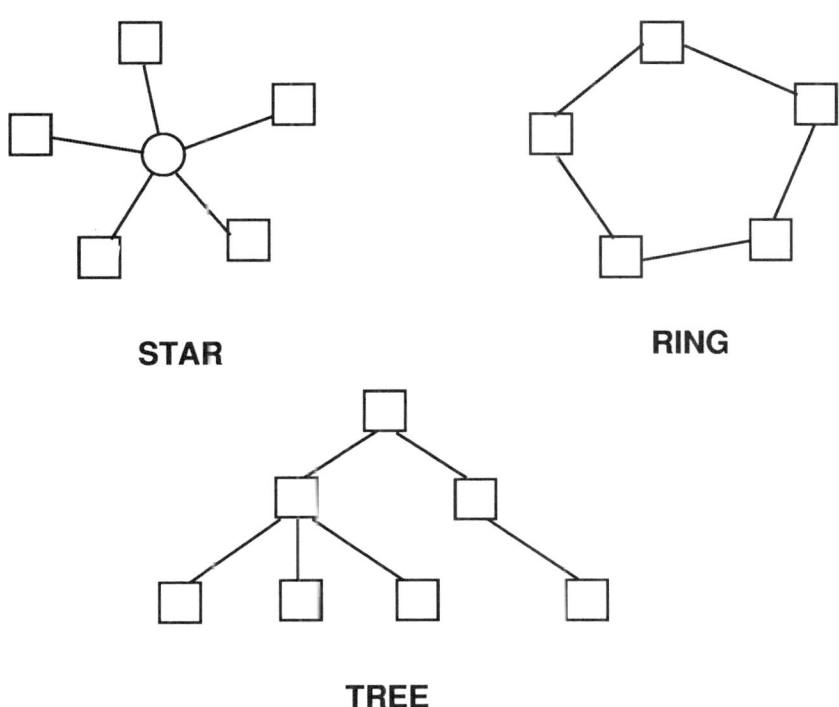

Figure 4 - Different network configurations

22   CHAPTER 1

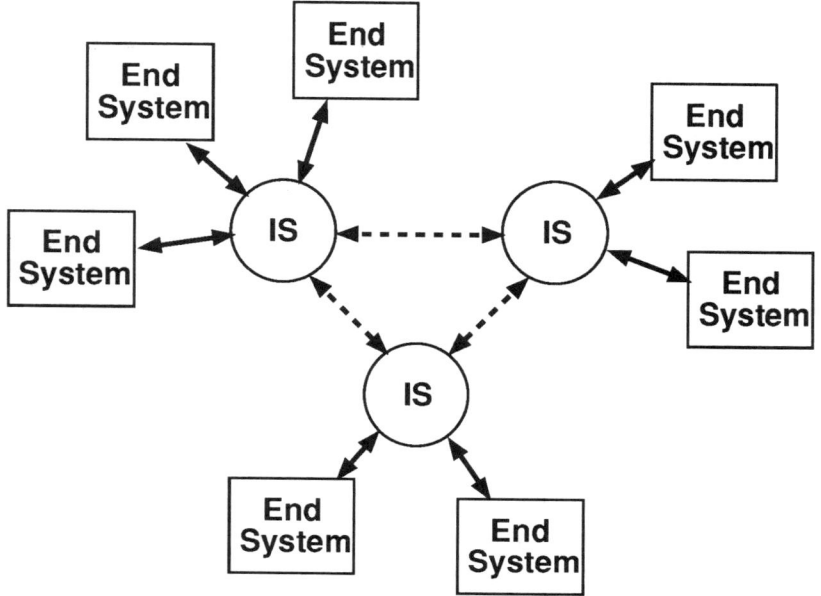

IS = Intermediate System

Figure 5 - More than two systems connected via a subnetwork

1.2.1 The Open Systems Interconnection Reference Model

　　The need to provide communications among the computers supplied by different manufacturers gave rise to an effort in the International Organization for Standardization (ISO) to produce a standard set of network protocols, known as the *Open Systems Interconnection (OSI)*. The first activity undertaken was the definition of an abstract model for the various functions that are provided by the networking software. This model is called the *Open Systems Interconnection Reference Model* (ISO 7498), and is widely considered to be a useful generalization for the design of any networking software, as well as the basis for a set of standards targeted at specific functions of the network.

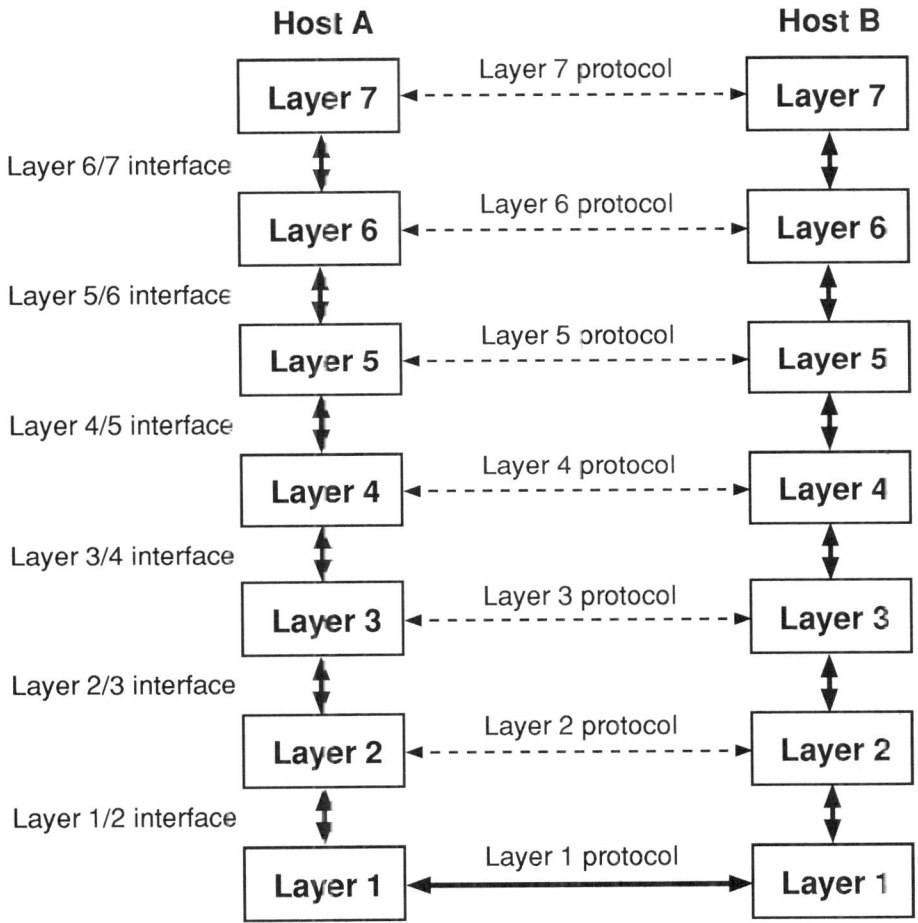

Figure 6 - The OSI Reference Model

The OSI Reference Model makes use of the concepts of *layering, interfaces,* and *protocols* (a good overview can be found in Zimmerman, 1980). A layer is a group of functions which are logically related. Each layer provides an interface to the next layer above, by which its functions can be invoked. By definition, the functions in a layer cannot make use of functions of any higher layer, and if layering is strictly observed they can only directly use the functions of the layer immediately below. This idea of layers and interfaces is common to many large software implementations. In addition, the Reference Model provides protocols, which allow the functions in a layer in one system to communicate with the corresponding functions in their peer layer in another system.

The OSI model defines seven layers in the communications system (Figure 6). These are:

- Layer 1 - The *physical layer* provides the transmission of bits from one system to another. This function is performed by the physical medium itself, including any devices used to interface the system to the communications medium, for example modems.

- Layer 2 - The *data link layer* provides the transmission of a string of bits, called packets, and performs error detection and correction functions to ensure a packet contains the same information received as sent. Sometimes the underlying medium can be simultaneously accessed by multiple systems (called a *multi-access* medium). For example, Ethernet (Metcalfe & Boggs, 1976) is such a medium. For multi-access media, the data link layer also provides the function of media access control (MAC).

- Layer 3 - The *network layer* controls how packets are routed through a network to reach a destination End System. The network layer also controls the rate at which the network accepts packets, to avoid and recover from congestion.

- Layer 4 - The *transport layer* fragments large messages into smaller packets as required by the lower layers, and ensures the reliable delivery of the packets in the correct order. Another function of this layer is to ensure that packets are sent at a rate the receiving End System and application can cope with. At the receiving End System, the transport layer reassembles the packets into messages and delivers them to the next higher layer.

- Layer 5 - The *session layer* assists applications in negotiating the establishment of connections, which may involve locating the destination application, and ensuring that the initiator is authentic and has the access rights to establish a connection.

- Layer 6 - The *presentation layer* performs useful transformations on information, such as compression, encryption, datatype conversion, etc.

- Layer 7 - The *application layer* provides services that may be useful to a large number of user applications, such as file transfer and mail.

Note that there is a well-defined interface between each layer and the layer above it, as well as a protocol permitting each layer to communicate with its peer on other systems.

An Intermediate System typically implements only the lower three layers of the model. The protocol interaction when two End Systems communicate through one or more Intermediate Systems is shown in Figure 7.

INTRODUCTION 25

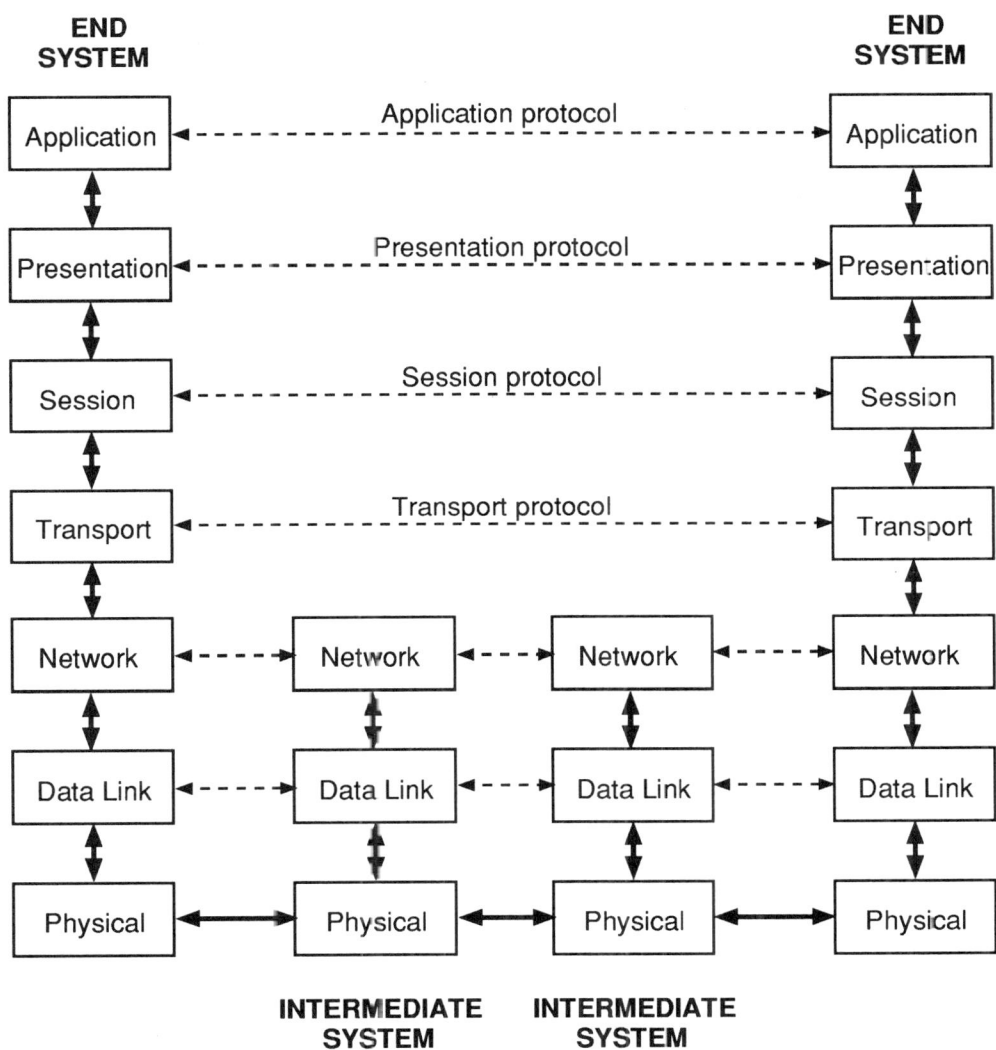

Figure 7 - Monitoring End and Intermediate Systems in OSI

1.2.2 Evolution of networking technology

In the early days of computer networking, it was common to connect systems using physical media that could support communications between only one pair of systems at a time. Such a configuration is described as a *point-to-point* connection. We have already described how various schemes of interconnecting systems have been invented to reduce the number of such point-to-point links in a network, including the use of subnetworks of dedicated routers. The cost and complexity of both the hardware and software (not to mention the bandwidth limitations) severely constrained the deployment of computer networks for many years, and restricted the nature of useful network applications.

Eventually, many of these problems associated with point-to-point connections were solved with a new technology called a *Local Area Network*, or *LAN*. LANs are based on the use of a physical medium which permits many systems to communicate simultaneously over a single interconnect (discussed in Abramson, 1970; Tanenbaum, 1981; Franta & Chlamtac 1981; and Hawe, *et al,* 1984). How this is achieved varies from one LAN technology to another, but all LANs have similar characteristics:

- High performance
- Limited geographical area
- Large numbers of systems interconnected
- Relatively low cost
- Broadcast and multicast capabilities

Because of the limitations in the scaling of most LAN technologies, the point-to-point technologies continue to be used when it is necessary to connect systems that are separated by large distances. This technology has therefore come to be known as a *Wide Area Network*, or *WAN*. These days WANs are often used to connect LANs,
In other words, modern networks are using the most effective technology available to provide the highest level of interconnection, and the highest performance at the lowest possible cost.

1.2.3 Examples of networks

Despite the efforts to standardize the computer networking protocols, the early days of computer networks were primarily based on proprietary architectures. Some notable proprietary architectures are IBM's Systems Network Architecture (SNA), the Digital Network Architecture (DNA), and Apple Computer's AppleTalk. The development of these architectures was very much influenced by the applications and markets that the respective vendors specially cater to.

In SNA, the End Systems connected by a link have asymmetric roles. For example, host-to-terminal_concentrator and terminal_concentrator-to-terminal. This is very natural for older networks that were used to primarily connect terminals to applications on host systems. The networking layer is connection-oriented; the session layer contains synchronization primitives that are used to support transaction processing applications (see for example IBM, 1975).

DNA, on the other hand, models End Systems as symmetric peers. The network layer is connectionless the states for a connection are maintained in the End Systems. The emphasis is to support more general configurations, and provide a more uniform model for different applications. DNA is similar in many ways to the OSI model (see for example DEC, 1987), and incorporates many aspects of the OSI standards.

AppleTalk is a newer network architecture that was developed to interconnect Apple personal computers. The network is well-known for its ease of configuration and use. The architecture takes full advantage of the LAN multi-access and broadcast capabilities to allow the networking software to automatically configure itself as much as possible (see for example Sidhu, *et al* 1990 or Apple Computer, 1985).

In recent years, the Internet protocol suite has become the most popular industrial standard. This family of protocols, also widely referred to as TCP/IP protocols, was developed under the sponsorship of the U.S. Defense Advanced Research Projects Agency (DARPA). The academic community and many other institutions have supported the Internet to foster communication among researchers. Because of its wide deployment, and "openness", a large number of applications have been developed to use this protocol suite (a good reference for TCP/IP is by Comer, 1988).

In the meantime, the OSI protocols are also maturing. OSI has received strong support from the procurement agencies of many governments who defined *Government OSI Profiles* (for example, US - GOSIP, UK - GOSIP) as specifications for equipment purchases. The OSI protocol family is likely to gain more popularity due to its generality. For example, it does not have the address size limitations inherent in many protocols that were designed earlier (including TCP/IP). It also has a more general mail protocol (X.400) and directory service protocol (X.500). Appendix B contains a list of OSI standards documents. Tanenbaum, 1981 and Rose, 1990 provide good coverage of OSI.

In this book, our study of network monitoring will not be based on any particular network architecture. The basic principles, and many of the monitoring techniques, are protocol-independent. For the protocol-dependent discussions, we will always give examples of usage in more than one network architecture.

1.2.4 Network applications

Some of the most basic applications for computer networking are remote terminals and file transfer. These applications came into being with the invention of computer networks.

Since the 1960's, the most basic paradigm of human-computer interaction is the interactive computing model - a computer user interacts with a computer via a terminal. With the advent of computer networks, terminal-computer interaction is modeled as a network application, thus allowing the terminal to be located on a different machine than the computer with which the user is interacting. This application has played an important role in the development of the computer networks by requiring consideration of end-to-end communication delays. Remote terminal protocols have also been evolving. The new breed of terminals are window-based, and support different size displays, color graphics and images. This has led to the acceptance of X-windows (Scheifler & Gettys, 1990) as an advanced kind of terminal protocol.

Another fundamental application is file transfer. A file is one of the most basic abstractions in most computer systems, although different operating systems tend to define file structures slightly differently. File copying is a primitive mechanism for one program to transfer information to another, whether the programs are on the same machine or on different machines. Many other computer network applications can be thought of as extensions to the concept of file transfer; electronic mail is an example.

Mail is probably the most popular network application in current use. Mail represents more than simple file transfer. It is asymmetric, in that there is a sender and a receiver. The receiver gets notification of newly arrived mail. The sender can usually send to one or more destinations in a single action, and get various kinds of notification of delivery.

More recently, there has been a widespread use of networks to provide shared access to databases. In electronic conferencing (or "bulletin-board") applications, multiple users can communicate by writing to a shared database to discuss a topic of common interest. Other databases can be more static. For example, different systems may share a common datatype definition, as well as other network-wide shared information, such as host name-to-address translations.

Another category of applications is transaction processing. These applications typically require synchronization to make multiple actions atomic (either all succeed or all fail). Such applications use computer networks as an infrastructure, and build additional communications mechanisms in the application itself.

In recent years, the trend has been to further distribute all of the resources of any particular machine, so that all machines work together as a *distributed system*. This means users on different machines can transparently share remote files, printers, system environment variables (names) and other application programs, just as if they were local. It remains a challenge, however, to physically distribute systems that can deliver the same level of reliability, performance, availability, and security that a non-distributed system provides.

1.3 NETWORK MONITORING OVERVIEW

The rest of Figure 1 is about monitoring of the network system, and network management applications. This is covered in the remainder of the book in three parts:

- Access to the monitored information: this is concerned with how to define the monitored information, both semantically and syntactically, so that various management agents can access it and interpret it (the *access* arrow in Figure 1).
- The design of the monitoring mechanisms: this is concerned with how best to obtain information regarding the state of the network (the *monitor* arrow and *monitoring agent* box in Figure 1).
- The application of the monitored information: This is concerned with how the monitored information is used in various management functions (the *management agent* box in Figure 1).

1.3.1 Access to monitor information

Designing the management access protocol for a monitoring agent is similar to designing command interfaces for operating systems and databases, which involve a number of user interface issues. The most interesting aspect of this protocol is the semantic modeling of management information. Concepts from object-oriented programming and database design, such as object hierarchies and property inheritance, have been adopted to allow similar objects to share definitions. The design emphasis in the actual access protocols is simplicity; most variations exist in how objects are named, and how information about objects is specified.

To provide consistent and cross-vendor network management, the means of accessing network management information is being standardized. The development of such standards has recently accelerated. Initial efforts have concentrated on standardized definition of the information that can be monitored (and the parameters that can be controlled in a network). This allows managed objects in different vendors' products to be monitored and managed in the same way.

In this book, we will describe several popular standards for accessing the information generated by network monitors.

1.3.2 Design issues

One of the most basic issues in the design of network monitoring is where to locate the monitoring agents.

Based on the OSI Reference Model, it is possible to perform a monitoring function at each layer and in each component of the network. This applies to both the End Systems as well as the Intermediate Systems in Figure 7. Certain states can only be monitored if the monitoring agent is part of (or collocated with) the network component being monitored. We call these *integrated* monitoring agents. The advantage of the integrated monitoring agents is that they can monitor the states of the components as accurately, as immediately, and with as fine a granularity as required.

The mechanism in a network component to collect management information, however, must not be so elaborate that it severely impacts the main function of the network - communicating application information. For example, if 90% of a network's bandwidth is expended in the monitoring function, that function has probably been over-designed. Also, a computer network is a large-scaled system consisting of many components, which can generate a proliferation of management information. In many cases this information is useful only in summary form. Thus, putting monitoring capabilities into each network component tends to create problems in the scalability of a network.

An interesting aspect of LAN technology, from the standpoint of network monitoring, is that it made it possible to insert a single mechanism into the physical medium that is capable of monitoring communications between a large number of systems (Figure 8). These *external* monitoring agents also permit passive monitoring, without any actual intervention into the flow of communications. This approach, while very commonly used for managing LAN-based networks, has several limitations of its own, related to the ability of a monitor to interpret protocol messages between a large number of communicating systems in real-time.

In Chapter 3, we will discuss these issues more fully, and provide examples of how these monitoring agents can be implemented.

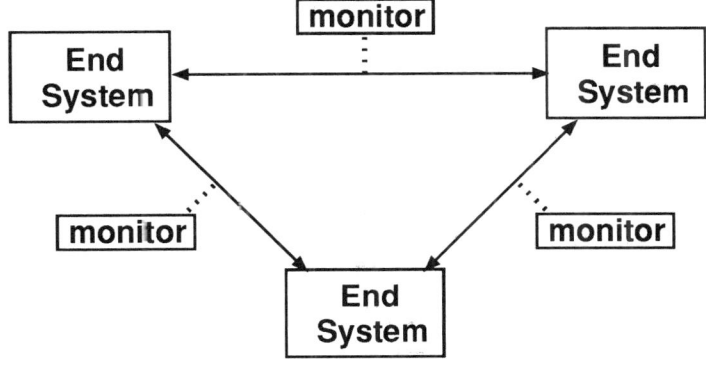

Point-to-Point Medium

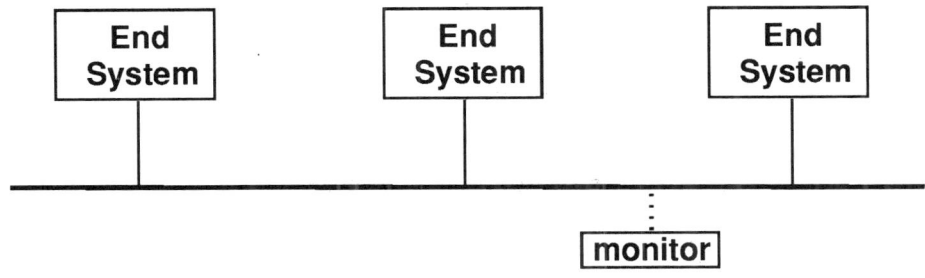

Broadcast Medium

Figure 8 - Different approaches to external monitoring

1.3.3 Management applications

Management applications are the consumers of the monitored information. They set the requirements (e.g., whether statistical information or instantaneous state is needed) that define what to monitor, when to monitor and where to monitor.

The ultimate goal of monitoring the network is to be able to manage the network. To gain a proper perspective of what to monitor, it is essential to understand the requirements for network management. Network management involves the planning, installation, and operation of all the network components to meet the needs of an enterprise. Such needs can be translated into specific levels of performance (bandwidth, response time), reliability, availability, security and accounting.

A substantial effort has been put into characterizing the basic network management functions as part of the definition of management information. The OSI standards divide the network management functions into the following five areas (see ISO 7498-4 OSI Management Framework):

- Fault Management
- Configuration Management
- Performance Management
- Security Management
- Accounting Management

We will briefly examine each area and its requirements for network monitoring.

1.3.3.1 Fault management

Fault management is the most rudimentary function. Users expect to have a reliable computer network. When components malfunction, the network manager must be able to quickly identify the fault and correct the situation. It is often not possible to isolate the fault quickly due to the complexity of the fault; this is especially likely if the fault is caused by the abnormal interaction of multiple components. In these cases, the network may need to be repaired without first diagnosing what caused the fault. The analysis of the fault, however, is still important for preventing it from recurring.

The detection of faults relies on monitoring the states of the network components. Simple fault detection mechanisms are often based on locally monitored states. The faulty states are logged as *errors*. The more critical errors are sent to the attention of network managers as *alarms*. However, it is not always possible to detect more complicated faults based only on locally monitored states. It is often necessary to monitor the aggregate states of multiple network components to diagnose the fault. The technology to monitor aggregate states is possible to a certain extent in multi-access LAN environments. But the ability to comprehensively diagnosis faults automatically based on such global monitors is still beyond the state of the art. This is why the network manager often has to correct the fault first to put the network back into service, and then analyze the cause of the fault later.

1.3.3.2 Configuration management

Configuration management is also a basic management function. It encompasses all the functions of initializing and connecting the network components to provide the network services. This includes assigning names and addresses to the network components, and correctly setting the parameters that control the routine operation of the network. Configuration management also involves capacity planning of the network. This aspect overlaps with the performance management functions.

Configuration management does not depend heavily on network monitoring. However, the planning aspects of configuration management require the network manager to understand the general demand for network resources and connectivity.

1.3.3.3 Performance management

Performance management is concerned with tuning and sizing the network to ensure optimal performance with available network resources. It is important to first establish the performance metrics: for example, the average and standard deviation of response time, the available bandwidth between a pair of systems, the fairness of services to all users (unless the network protocol implements service classes, in which case the different classes of applications should see distinguished level of services when there is contention for network resources). Once the metrics are established, performance management involves monitoring and evaluating the network traffic against the metrics; then changing the network configuration, if necessary, to improve the performance level.

Network monitoring is directly relevant to performance management. The distinctive feature required for performance management is the monitoring of aggregate and statistical information. The aggregation required is both over time (historical) as well as over different resources (spatial). Fortunately, only statistical information is needed, so it is possible to rely on sampling to avoid continuous monitoring of all resources.

1.3.3.4 Security management

Network security mechanisms often have a negative impact on the performance, availability and cost of a network. In many of today's networks, only the crudest security mechanisms (such as passwords and address-based proxies) are employed. This means that security management is largely a matter of auditing and detecting security violations. As more sophisticated authentication and privacy protection mechanisms (based on encryption) are introduced, security management will involve more functions, such as managing and distributing the encryption key databases.

Security auditing and detection of security violations is basically a form of network monitoring. Like fault management, security-related monitoring requires security analysis functions and filters to be collocated with the monitoring functions in order to accurately detect security problems.

1.3.3.5 Accounting management

Accounting management is the function of recording the usage of network resources in order to control the operational cost of the network. The overhead of accounting management is directly correlated to the granularity of accounting. The coarse level of accounting could be based on the apportionment of network resource utilization according to groups of systems connected to the network, each group belonging to a management domain. A finer level accounting would record the usage by each system. A still finer level would be based on usage by each particular user and according to the usage at different times of the day.

Accounting is by far the most demanding application of network monitoring. To support the finer levels of accounting, enormous overheads could be incurred on the network itself. For this reason, network accounting is typically implemented only in commercially operated networks that bill users for network usage. In these applications, the monitoring is often based on the use of specialized hardware and software. As network monitoring technology matures, some coarse-level accounting will likely be based on the more general network monitoring capabilities.

2

Access to Monitor Information

2.1 OVERVIEW OF THE GENERAL MODELS

From the vantage point of a network management application and the network administrator, the physical details of how network resources and activities are monitored are usually hidden. A well-designed network management system presents a logical and user-friendly view of the network, which consists of a large set of managed objects and the states associated with these objects. The network administrator can monitor and often control these states. This is depicted in the following figure.

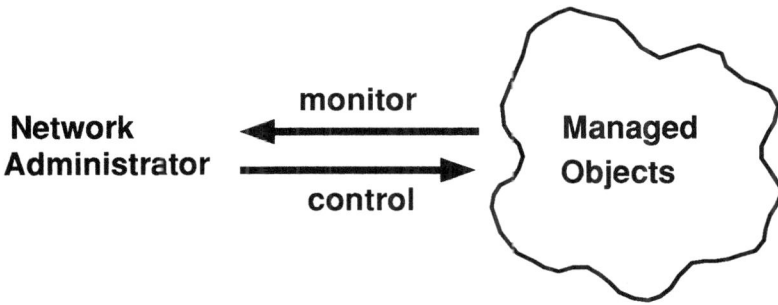

Figure 9 - High level model of managed objects

In reality, the managed objects are distributed all over the network. To further complicate the situation, the managed objects come from a heterogeneous network. The realization of the depicted high level model is based on a large body of concrete definitions of these managed objects, and how they can be accessed. In this chapter, we give a brief review of some of the important models for defining managed objects, and the protocols for accessing them.

In this book, our focus is on the *monitoring* aspect of managing a network. The *control* aspect of how to manage network objects, while closely related to *monitoring*, is significantly complicated by a number of factors, including: how to meet the stronger requirements for access control; how the management *control* interacts with the network object's state transitions driven by its normal functions; and the transactional semantics associated with some of the control functions. In this sense, our review here is only an introduction to multi-protocol network monitoring, and should not be considered as a complete study of all of the network management protocols.

The rest of this section provides a general overview of how distributed managed objects are modeled and accessed. These topics include:

- The models that describe the distribution of functions used to access managed objects,
- The two basic methods of access: polling and event-driven,
- Naming and addressing used to reach the objects,
- The information model of managed objects,
- The process of registration that is needed for naming, addressing and the information types in the information model, and
- The protocol to access managed objects.

This general conceptualization is only useful, however, as a basis for abstractly understanding the monitoring of networks. The realization of these functions is not the same in all networks, accommodating the different histories and capabilities of the networks themselves. We will later describe how network monitoring is done in TCP/IP networks, OSI networks, IBM's SNA networks and Digital's DNA networks, as examples of real networks.

2.1.1 Functional models for monitoring managed objects

There are a number of alternatives in dividing the function of network monitoring into logical modules. Each alternative is described in terms of a functional model. The purpose of reviewing these functional models is to establish a uniform terminology for discussion. These functional models will also be useful in examining how various monitors are designed, which is covered in the next chapter.

The basic components of the functional models model are the *management application*, the *management agent* and the *monitoring agent*. The *management application* is a module of software that implements functions to help the network administrator monitor the network and perform various administrative tasks. The *management agent* accesses information about managed objects and turns the information into a form useful for management application purposes (such as fault, configuration, performance, security or accounting management). The network administrator's access to the management application is via either an interactive user interface, or information recorded in a management information base. The *monitoring agent* is a module of software that provides a management agent access to information about managed objects in the network. These components and their relationships form the basic functional model as illustrated in Figure 10.

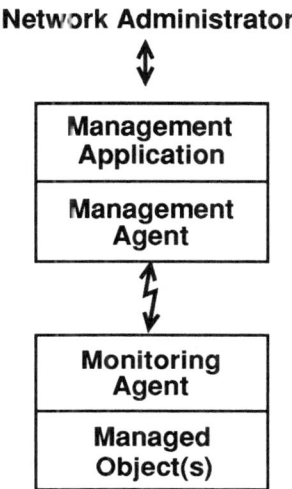

Figure 10 - **Basic functional model for monitoring managed objects**

In this basic scenario, the monitoring agent is collocated with the managed objects. While this is usually the case, it is not necessarily always so.

Generally speaking, a management application needs (and would be able) to access a large number of managed objects. For purposes of flexibility and scalability, an *intermediate* monitoring agent can be defined to provide the function of aggregating the information about managed objects for a management application. We call this intermediate agent a *summarization monitoring agent*. This intermediate agent accesses managed objects via other monitoring agents to obtain information, so it appears to these monitoring agents as a management agent. To a management agent, however, this summarization agent appears as an ordinary monitoring agent. This model is depicted in Figure 11.

The intermediate monitoring agent does not have to acquire its monitored information using a particular access protocol. In fact, the intermediate monitoring agent may obtain the monitored information by traffic analysis. An example of this scenario is shown in Figure 12. The monitoring agent is now *external*, in the sense that it does not collocate and is not integrated with the managed object(s). This external monitoring agent passively observes the traffic generated by a number of communicating objects that share a common communications medium. Based on analysis of the traffic, the external monitor is able to deduce useful management information for the network administrators.

In each of the above functional models, there is a need for the management agent to communicate with one or more monitoring agent to obtain information (as indicated by the wiggly arrows in the respective figures). This chapter is mainly concerned with the protocols used by the management agent and monitoring agent to communicate network monitoring information.

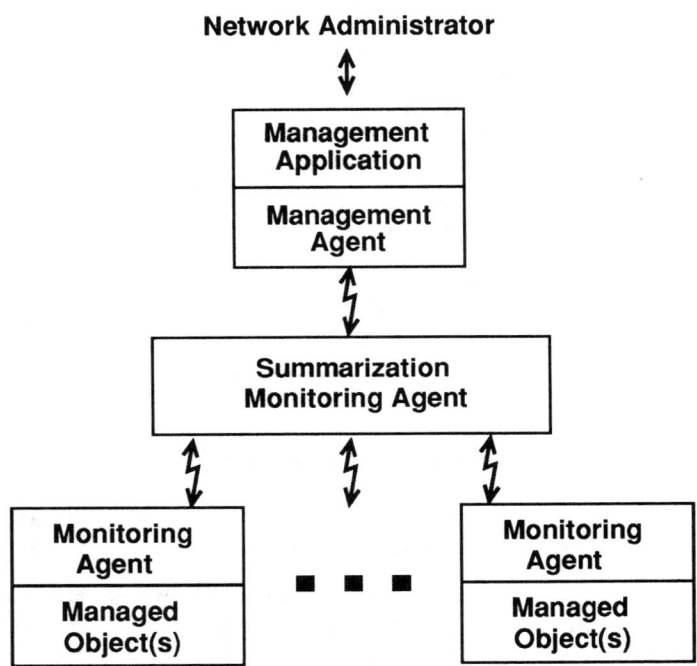

Figure 11 - Summarization monitoring agent

ACCESS TO MONITOR INFORMATION 39

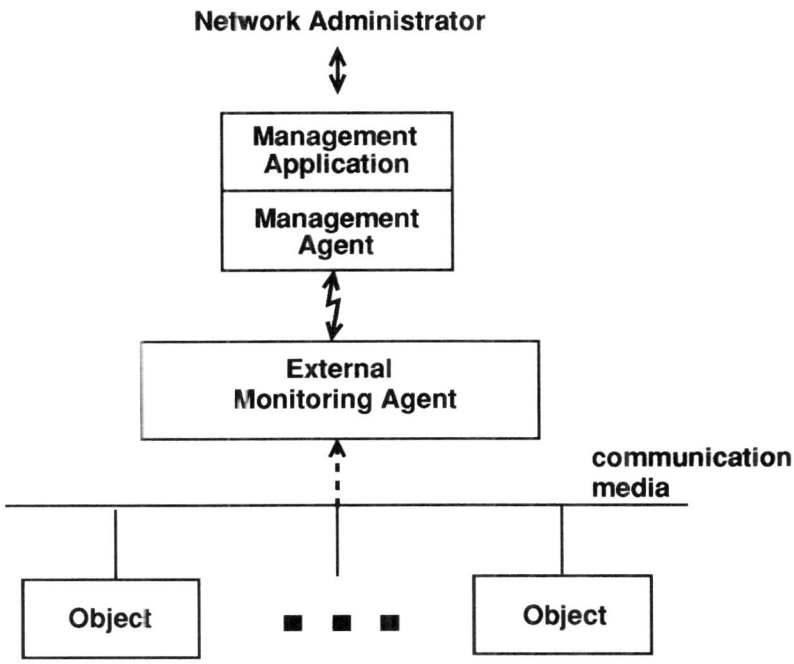

Figure 12 - External monitoring agent

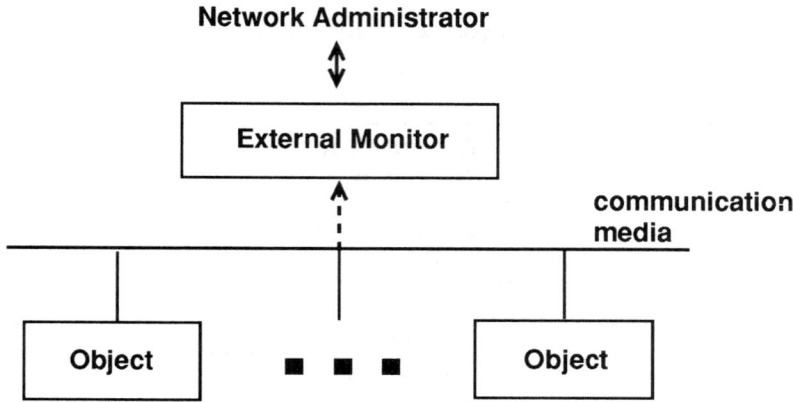

Figure 13 - External monitor

The external monitoring agent may actually be integrated with the management application and the management agent as shown in Figure 13. The combined management application, management agent and external monitoring agent is called an *external monitor*. Because of the collocation of the management and monitoring agents, these external monitors do not require management protocols. As a result, they are relatively easy to build. In practice, they also prove to be very useful and constitute an important type of mechanism for network monitoring. The design of external monitors is discussed in detail in Chapter 3.

2.1.2 Methods of access to monitoring agents

There are two basic methods by which the management agents and monitoring agents exchange information: *polling* and *event-driven*. Each of these methods has useful applications in network monitoring.

In the polling case, the management agent sends a "read" request to the monitoring agent. Usually, there is considerable flexibility in what can be accessed by such a "read" request. In addition to reading a particular piece of state information associated with a managed object, some limited form of search and browsing is usually provided by a management protocol to support the case when the monitoring agent is responsible for a multitude of managed objects and the objects have a multitude of states. After the information is fetched, the monitoring agent returns it to the accessor in a response message. This request/response style of access is useful for diagnosing problems via browsing and searching, for periodically collecting performance and availability information for the purpose of generating reports, and various other management scenarios.

In the event-driven case, the management agent is a pre-configured listener for the monitored information. As events occur (the change of pre-selected states associated with the managed objects), they are observed at the managed object by the monitoring agent, and event reports are forwarded to the listener without the issuance of an explicit "read" request. In some sense, it is as if the listener had issued a long-term, outstanding read for all the specified state changes at the managed object. This method of monitoring is extremely useful for detecting problems as soon as they occur, permitting control of their potential damaging effects. This mechanism is also useful for monitoring objects whose states change relatively infrequently, in which case periodic polling is much less efficient.

Most management protocols support separate protocol messages for these two methods of access. In the event-driven method, the protocol messages are usually relatively simple. The events that can be detected are conveyed in terms of event codes and simple event arguments, in a fashion similar to the way error codes are defined in computer programs. The protocol messages for the polling method of access are invariably more elaborate. The accessible information is modeled as hierarchical objects having attributes with potentially more complicated datatypes. The protocol usually either allows searching, by defining search filters, or browsing, by allowing navigation through the object hierarchy.

This dichotomy in protocol messages stems from the two different access methods, which are often used to solve different management problems. Theoretically, it is possible to have the same protocol messages for both methods of access, and have only the mechanisms that trigger the messages differ. However, in many protocols, different messages are used for historical and other reasons.

2.1.3 Naming and addressing

As we have indicated, a management agent generally needs to communicate with a multitude of monitoring agents. This is a necessity for the management of large networks that span beyond a single LAN. How to name and locate all of the managed objects in such an environment is a key problem.

For the managed objects to be globally accessible, their monitoring agent must have a global address. Each managed object must have a name, or a specified way to be referenced, relative to a monitoring agent, so that a management protocol may connect to the monitoring agent and access the object by its name relative to the monitoring agent. This approach of naming and locating the management objects is very common in practice. The convention for the relative names are different for the different protocols.

Arguably, a short-coming of the above approach is that it effectively makes the identity of a managed object dependent on its address. A more general model is to let the managed objects have globally unique identifiers that are independent of the location of the object, so that when the address of an object changes, it can still be monitored and managed in a transparent manner. This can be accomplished by assigning all objects identifiers that are guaranteed to be unique both spatially and temporally. Features such as this are built into some protocols.

The problem with this type of identifier is that, inherently, it is not very "user-friendly". This motivates the use of names for managed objects. To be location transparent, a managed object would have a global name that was the same everywhere in the network. For scalability, global names need to be organized hierarchically. Network administrators can then specify managed objects in terms of their names, rather than by using addresses or identifiers. The translation from the name to address of the relevant monitoring agent is provided by a name (or directory) service.

A name service can be thought of as a database that holds the mapping from names to addresses, and possibly additional information about the names. In a global network, the name service database is often distributed since there are potentially a large number of objects that need to be registered in the name service. The most critical design requirement for the name service is to provide high availability. Any departure from 100% availability will negatively affect the availability of the object to be accessed. To satisfy this availability requirement, the name service usually highly replicates its database. To achieve this level of replication, the name service generally does not guarantee the name-to-address mapping to be always up-to-date. Some name services rely on manual procedures to maintain the consistency of the replicated data; other, more sophisticated, name services provide automated procedures to maintain data consistency.

In a truly global network, the names need to be registered with a recognized global registration authority to resolve potential conflicts. The registration process may be decentralized by hierarchically delegating registration responsibilities. A separate subsection later is devoted to explaining how some of the global registration processes work.

2.1.4 Information models of managed objects

An information model for managed objects describes how each item of information accessible through a monitoring agent is identified. It also defines the syntax of each item, as well as its semantic relationship to other items. As a crude analogy, this is similar to the way schemas are used in a general-purpose database.

An information model is the crux of the whole management model, and it determines how the actual protocol is defined. This is the area in which most of the differences among the management protocols are found. The main sources of these differences, other than pure historical and arbitrary styling reasons, are the compromises made between generality and simplicity.

An information model *per se* describes only the framework of the management information. The application of a model to the real-world managed objects result in the definition of a Management Information Base[1] (MIB). Since it is impossible to define everything that is ever to be managed in a single MIB, a MIB is defined for each category of objects to be managed. For example, there might be a routing MIB consisting of all managed objects that participate in providing the routing function; or there might be a terminal concentrator MIB, when a management protocol is applied to manage a class of terminal concentrators. What is in the MIB is totally determined by what objects are being managed. If objects in the same network are managed by two protocols based on different management information models, then two MIBs (one for each model) would have to be defined - although they describe the same set of physical objects.

The formal description of a MIB is in terms of a *language*. The language adopted by many management protocols today is the *Abstract Syntax Notation One (ASN.1)*. ASN.1 is an ISO standard (ISO 8824, 1987). Since the language is the means for expressing many of the concepts for managing objects, it is important that readers have at least a cursory familiarity with ASN.1. For this reason, an "ASN.1 Primer" is included in this book as Appendix A, to give a brief review of the basics.

2.1.5 Registration

The process of *registration* is important to enable the global, unequivocal use of addresses, identifiers, names, object types, and syntaxes. Registration ensures the unique assignment of the above identifications. Implicit in the process of registration is the structure of assignment authority - that is, who is allowed to assign the identifications. For reasons of manageability, the structure of assignment authority is usually hierarchical. We will use the terms *registration* and *assignment* interchangeably.

The registration process for addresses is probably the most familiar to the reader. For example, the IEEE (Institute of Electrical and Electronic Engineers) has a procedure for assigning (registering) the MAC (multi-access layer) addresses. The TCP/IP Internet has its counter-part for assigning addresses IP addresses. The OSI network address is based on a diversity of registration authorities under the auspices of both ISO and CCITT (International Telegraph & Telephone Consultative Committee), including the use of telephone numbers and telex numbers, both of which have long-established assignment authority structures (a good description of OSI network address assignments can be found in Martin and Leben, 1992 pp 159-163).

For management information models, the most important registration requirements are for the types and syntaxes of properties (states) of the managed objects, and the relative names (or identifiers) used by the monitoring agent to access them. The process for establishing global names is also relevant if the global names are used to identify

---

[1] This is a term borrowed from the TCP/IP internet community. Here, we have used the term in a generic sense, without referring to a particular family of management protocols.

managed objects, as described earlier.

2.1.5.1 Registration of object identifiers

Traditionally, the type and syntaxes of managed objects are all defined by integer IDs. The registration of the use of specific IDs is done either by the manufacturer (in terms of published specifications), or sometimes by the users. The need for global interoperation and openness has caused more higher-level organizations and processes for registering these IDs to be created. For scalability, this process is hierarchical. The global organization can reserve groups of IDs to be further assigned by the registration authorities at the levels below. Each level's authority can either assign IDs for use in protocols, or reserve some IDs to create an additional level of authority. As a result, the identifier to be used is not just a single integer, but a sequence of integers. This structure forms the OBJECT IDENTIFIER datatype, as defined in ASN.1

For the OBJECT IDENTIFIER datatype, there are three (this is a fixed number) registration authorities at the top level:

```
ccitt (0)
iso (1)
joint-iso-ccitt (2)
```

At the next level, both the CCITT and ISO branches are allowed up to 40 immediate sub-authorities. This limitation is a practical one to allow efficient encoding. After the second level, there are no more bounds on how many sub-authorities each authority may choose to have.

Currently, CCITT has chosen to have four immediate sub-authorities:

```
recommendation (0)
question (1)
administration (2)
network-operator (3)
```

and ISO has also chosen to have four sub-authorities:

```
standards (0)
registration-authority (1)
member-body (2)
identified-organization (3)
```

Each structure reflects the standardization process in the respective standards bodies.

In some of the example protocols, we will see how this global registration process for OBJECT IDENTIFIERs is used, and how the datatype OBJECT IDENTIFIER is used for type, syntax and relative name definitions in the management information models.

2.1.5.2 Registration of global names

There are currently two notable global registration processes for global names. The TCP/IP Internet has a name service called the *Domain Name Service (DNS)*, primarily used for mapping host name to IP addresses (RFC1034-1035, 1987). The host names are hierarchical, similar to the structure for OBJECT IDENTIFIERs. Under the root, the major first level authorities are:

      com   (commercial establishments)
      edu   (education establishments)
      gov   (government establishments)
      one for each country

Then, for example, under "com", "dec" is registered to stand for Digital Equipment Corporation and "ibm" is registered to stand for International Business Machines; under "edu", "mit" is registered to stand for Massachusetts Institute of Technology. A typical IP host name in DNS, therefore, would look something like *myhost.mit.edu* (since the convention is to give the components of the name in the reverse order of the naming hierarchy).

The other global name registration process is that to be used for the CCITT X.500/ISO 9594 standards (commonly referred to simply as the X.500 standard). X.500 is a directory service created through the CCITT and ISO (ISO 9594 & CCITT X.500, 1988) standards processes with much more ambitious goals than DNS. The additional functionality includes attribute-based search (much like a database queries), attribute and structural modifications, and access control. Because of these additional functions, X.500 is emerging as an important mechanism for achieving global directory service.

The X.500 registration process is still under development, as X.500 products have only recently become ready for the market. The top level naming authorities are basically the set of countries of the world. The next level hierarchies for the various countries are not yet fully developed. The current proposals in various countries are to base the directory naming hierarchy on the existing civic (government and commercial) structures; for example, an institution would use the same name that it registered with the government as its name in the directory.

2.1.6 The management protocol

Using the terminology of the OSI reference model, the management protocol is modeled as an application layer protocol. That is to say, the management protocol is usually layered on top of a full stack of lower layer protocols: physical, data link, network, transport, session and presentation.

This layering sometimes proves to be rather heavy-weight for the management of simple devices. For example, a simple-minded bridge or repeater on a LAN may not have the resources to run the full protocol stack.

This tends to cause management protocols to incorporate a number of functions normally handled in the lower layers. By special-casing the design of these functions, the overall protocol stack can be made simpler. For example, the management protocol is often designed to be inherently connectionless, do its own flow and acknowledgment control (by using time-outs and making the protocol inherently request-response styled), and avoid the need for fragmentation and re-assembly. Such division of function allows the management protocol to run directly on top of the datalink layer for managing devices within the scope of a LAN, and to run directly on top of the routing layer for accessing objects in a WAN.

The actual management protocol messages used in network monitoring are typically very simple. It is invariably a variation on a remote *read* request to obtain information defined by the management information model. Examples of these protocols are provided later in this chapter.

2.2 INTRODUCTION TO THE MANAGEMENT PROTOCOLS

The model presented in the last section gives an overview of the general functionality of the management protocols. To appreciate how these protocols work, it helps to review a few important real-world examples.

Network management capabilities are usually offered as an integral part of the networking software. For example, Digital's network management software comes with the associated DECnet software (Lapell et al, 1986; Fehskens, 1989; DEC, 1989); IBM's SNA similarly has its associated network management capability (IBM, 1987; IBM, 1989). In recent years, however, the user requirement for internetworking has dramatically increased the size and heterogeneity of networks. While there is now a strong desire to have standardized network protocols, the need for a standardized network management protocol is sometimes even stronger. In a heterogeneous network, where networking software from different vendors is in use, it is advantageous for an administrator to use a uniform approach in managing the network. To this end, several important network management protocol standards have recently emerged. The most significant of these are the Internet *Simple Network Management Protocol* (SNMP) and the ISO/IEC and CCITT *Common Management Information Protocol* (CMIP).

The ISO network management work started first, in the mid-1980s. As is typical with international standards work, it leans toward generality, and has taken a longer time than the Internet standards to stabilize. The standards work in this area consists of a large number of related specifications: some on the requirements; some on the information model and structure; some on the protocols; and finally, several documents on how to use the protocol for specific management functions. A basic set of specifications have reached the official stable standard status in 1991 (see Appendix B).

The SNMP work started in earnest in 1988, after the Internet Activities Board[1] (IAB) defined the technical direction (RFC1052, 1988). The resultant Internet network management protocol was SNMP. The design principals for SNMP were simplicity and extensibility. Extensibility was achieved by separating the work on the management information model from work on the protocol (SNMP) and the detailed specification of managed objects (MIB). Simplicity was achieved by adopting some constraints on the information datatypes allowed, as well as basing the protocol on a very simple, tested request-response protocol for managing gateways (the Simple Gateway Monitoring Protocol, or SGMP, see RFC1028, 1987). The development of SNMP and the MIB definitions, and their productization have been more speedy (see Appendix C for a set of documents on these standards)

In the following sections, we will review these two standardized management protocols, as well as some of the management protocols in common use in the industry. The emphasis will be on providing an overall understanding of what such protocols do for a network administrator (in terms of monitoring the network), rather than trying to cover all the details of the protocol specifications. To this end, we organize our review as follows: we first give some historical background, as well as the current status of these protocols; we then review some of the details of the design for each protocol (this includes the information models and the protocols themselves).

2.3 Internet SNMP

2.3.1 Background

2.3.1.1 The Internet and RFCs

SNMP is a protocol developed by the Internet Engineering Task Force (IETF). Before we review SNMP, it is useful to first familiarize oneself a little with what is known as the *Internet*, and the protocols and standardization process adopted by the Internet.

From the late 1960s, the U.S. Defense Advanced Research Projects Agency (DARPA) sponsored many research projects on computer networking which led to an operational computer network connecting many research institutions, known originally as ARPANET. Over time, this network expanded significantly, and became known as the Internet..

The Internet community defined a collection of computer communication protocols based on the Transmission Control Protocol (TCP, defined in RFC793, 1981) and its lower level counterpart, the Internet Protocol (IP, defined in RFC791,1981). These

---
[1] Later changed its name to Internet Architecture Board.

protocols, together with many others developed during the course of the research, including FTP (RFC959, 1985) and TELNET (RFC854, 1983), as well as SNMP (RFC1155-1157 1990), are referred to as the *Internet Protocol Suite*, or commonly just as *TCP/IP protocols*.

As the Internet expanded, it was necessary to form an informal committee to guide the technical evolution of the protocol suite. This guiding committee is the Internet Activities Board (IAB). IAB is the coordinating committee for Internet design, engineering and management. Its members are established researchers and professionals with a technical interest in the health and evolution of the Internet system. The IAB has two principal task forces:

1. the *Internet Engineering Task Force,* or *IETF*
2. the *Internet Research Task Force,* or *IRTF*

The IETF arm is generally responsible for resolving all short-term and medium-term protocol and architectural issues required to make the Internet function effectively. The IRTF, on the other hand, is responsible for longer-term research, and for developing new technology for the Internet. The actual work is done by a collection of Working Groups (WGs) under these task forces. Over recent years, these informal task forces and working groups have grown into a large open technical community for developing standards for the Internet. This is usually referred to as the *Internet community*[1].

Any member of the Internet community can design and propose a protocol for use on the Internet. Such proposals are documented in the *Request For Comment* (RFC) series. All Internet standards are published as RFCs, but not all RFCs specify standards. For example, some RFCs are used to document historical and experimental protocols, and others are used only to disseminate general information. In particular, RFC1160, 1990 describes the Internet Activity Board, and its organizations; RFC1250, 1991, describes the IAB Official Protocol Standard, which includes the process of standardization and all the information about RFCs. Most of the background information about Internet and RFCs in this subsection are derived from the above two RFCs.

Generally speaking, protocols are categorized in terms of two characteristics:

1. State of Standardization: A protocol can be in one of the following states: *standard, draft standard, proposed standard, experimental, informational* or *historic*.
2. Status (or requirement level): A protocol can have the following status: *required, recommended, elective, limited use,* or *not recommended*.

Figure 14 depicts the states a protocol goes through as it evolves.

---

[1] As the Internet standards become more and more popular and commercially significant, the constitutions of the IAB is being further formalized under the hospice of a professional society, known as the Internet Society.

ACCESS TO MONITOR INFORMATION 49

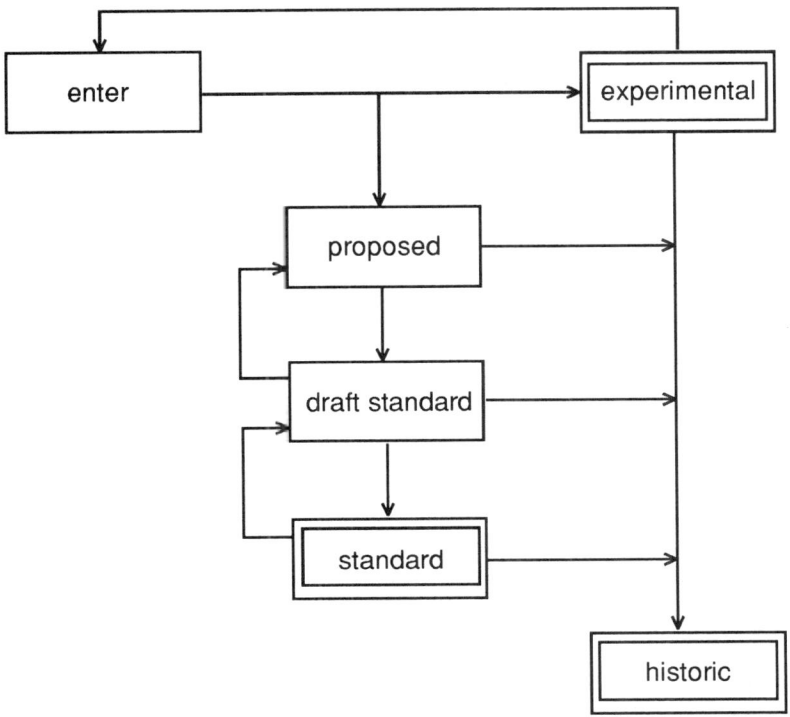

Figure 14 - State of standardization for Internet protocols

The states, illustrated by double boxes, are considered long-term states, which last for years; the single box states are temporary states that last only for a few months. The transition from the proposed state to the draft standard state and from the draft standard state to the standard state follow an approval process in the IAB described in RFC1250. Occasionally, a protocol is not ready for standardization, in which case it is put in the experimental state for some time. Later, experimental protocols can be reconsidered for standardization. Sometimes one protocol is replaced by another and thus becomes historic, or it may happen that a protocol on the standards track is in a sense overtaken by another (or other events occur) and becomes historic before entering actual use on the Internet.

Generally, as a protocol enters the standards track, a decision is made as to the eventual STATUS, the requirement level, or applicability (elective, recommended or required) the protocol will have. At any time, the STATUS decision may be revisited. Again, RFC1250 documents the IAB process of determining the STATUS of its protocols.

2.3.1.2 The development of SNMP and related references

As has been mentioned earlier, the SNMP standard evolved from the Simple Gateway Management Protocol (SGMP). At the time, 1988, when an Internet standard management protocol was sought, several proposals were in contention. SGMP was picked based on a number of reasons[1], including its deployment at the time, and its simplicity.

The development of SNMP has been carefully documented in a series of RFCs related to this effort.

- First, the RFC1052, 1988 and RFC1109, 1989 documented the IAB decisions and guidelines for developing the network management protocols for the Internet.
- The SNMP protocol specification was published in RFC1157, in May 1990.
- RFC1155 was published at the same time frame as RFC1157 to define the structure of the management information for the TCP/IP-based networks. This important RFC laid down the rules for defining the MIBs for TCP/IP networks.
- In the same time frame, RFC1156 was published to define the Management Information Base (MIB) for use by the TCP/IP-based Internet, in the short term. Later, an extended MIB, called MIB-II was published in RFC1158. RFC1158 was later updated again and re-issued as RFC1213, 1991. In addition, RFC1229, 1991 defined some additional (to MIB-II) experimental managed objects.
- Following the above publications, a lot of additional work went into implementing and refining the SNMP protocol, which is discussed in RFC1187, RFC1215, RFC1224, RFC1227, RFC1228, and RFC1283, all published in 1991.
- RFC1212, 1991 defined additional rules for modularizing MIB definitions.
- To use SNMP to manage the objects associated a particular network component, a MIB must be defined for that component. To date, the following MIBs have been published as RFCs. Together with the managed objects defined in the original MIB (MIB-II), there are now more than 500 pages of MIB definitions.
    -- RFC1230, 1991 defined a MIB for objects in the IEEE 802.4 Token Bus.
    -- RFC1231, 1991 defined a MIB for objects in the IEEE 802.5 Token Ring.
    -- RFC1232, 1991 and RFC1233, 1991 defined MIBs for objects in the DS1 and DS3 interfaces for access to T1 and T3 transmission media, respectively.
    -- RFC1238, 1991 defined a MIB for objects in the OSI connectionless network protocol (ISO 8473).

---

[1] The two pages of "soapbox" in Rose, 1990 pp. 593-594 provides an interesting historical perspective.

-- RFC1239, 1991 defined reassignment of experimental MIBs to standard MIBs.
-- RFC1243, 1991 defined a MIB for objects in the AppleTalk protocol.
-- RFC1253, 1991 defined a MIB for objects in the *OSPF* protocol, which is one of the Internet routing protocols.
-- RFC1269, 1991 defined a MIB for objects in the *Border Gateway Protocol*, which is one of the Internet routing protocols.
-- RFC1271, 1991 defined a MIB for objects monitored by a *remote monitor*, which in our terminology corresponds to an external monitor or a summarization monitor.
-- RFC1284, 1991 defined a MIB for objects in Ethernet-like interfaces.
-- RFC1285, 1992 defined a MIB for objects for FDDI.
-- RFC1286, 1991 defined a MIB for objects in bridges.
-- RFC1289, 1991 defined a MIB for objects in DECnet Phase IV.
-- RFC1304, 1992 defined a MIB for objects in the SIP (SMDS Interface Protocol).

Finally, the readers may also find the books by Marshall Rose (Rose, 1990 and Rose, 1991) informative and stimulating. Rose has been a key contributor to the development of the Internet management protocols.

2.3.2 Protocol

SNMP fits quite well into the functional model we have in Section 2.1.1, except that the terminology is somewhat different. What are referred to as the management agent and managed objects in Section 2.1.1 are called *network management stations* and *network elements*. The monitors residing at the network elements are called *management agents*. Network elements are devices such as hosts, gateways, terminal servers, and the like. So SNMP is the protocol used by the network management stations and the management agents in the network elements to communicate management information.

SNMP is an application-level protocol, layered on the TCP/IP stack. The transport service used is the Universal Datagram Protocol (UDP). This datagram transport does not provide sequencing and flow control support, but does give the simplest request-response support, avoiding the three-way handshake.

SNMP supports both access methods described in Section 2.1.2, using the following four protocol messages:

> *get-request*
> *get-response*
> *get-next-request*
> *trap*

SNMP also has a fifth protocol message, a *set-request*. This protocol message is used to change certain attribute values in the management information base that are defined to be modifiable. Since we are concentrating on network monitoring protocols, however, this aspect of the protocol is beyond the scope of our discussions.

The *get-request* and *get-response* pair fits exactly into the request/response paradigm of the polling access method in Section 2.1.2, and the *trap* is the protocol message for the event-driven access method. The *get-next-request* is a unique mechanism in SNMP that allows the network management station to send what is essentially a *get-response* message to the management agent, requesting that the management agent return the next (lexical) value. This function is needed as a result of the management information model adopted with SNMP.

To keep the protocol as simple as possible, the primary method for monitoring information exchange is via the polling, or request/response method. When it is desirable to use the event-driven method, the *trap* protocol message is used by the management agent to trigger an appropriate request/response sequence, to be initiated by the network management station. With this general philosophy, the *trap* protocol message can be reduced to a simple message.

2.3.3 Information model

The modeling of management information is described in two parts:

1. the identification and definition of object types (covered in RFC1155)
2. the identification of object instances (covered in RFC1157)

2.3.3.1 Object types

All objects types are defined using the following template:

Descriptor:	a unique textual (printable string) name
Object Id:	an ISO object identifier
Syntax:	basic ones
Definition:	a textual string defining the semantics
Access:	one of read-only, read-write, write-only or not accessible
Status:	either mandatory, optional, or obsolete

This set of information is packaged using an object definition macro which, formally, has the following ASN.1 definition:

```
OBJECT-TYPE MACRO ::=
    BEGIN
```

```
            TYPE NOTATION ::=
                "SYNTAX" type (Type ObjectSyntax)
                "ACCESS" Access
                "STATUS" Status
            VALUE NOTATION ::= value (VALUE ObjectName)

            Access ::= "read-only" | "read-write" |
                    "write-only" | "not-accessible"
            Status ::= "mandatory" | "optional" |
                    "obsolete"
END
```

The use of this macro to define object types is best illustrated by examples.

```
    OBJECT:  sysUpTime { system 3 }
             Syntax:     TimeTicks
             Definition: The time (in hundredths of a second) since
                         the network management portion of the system
                         was last re-initialized.
             Access:     read-only
             Status:     mandatory
```

In this case, the *Descriptor* of this object is sysUpTime (the time that has elapsed since an active system was last started); the *Object Identifier* is the Object Identifier of system (which is 1.3.6.1.2.1.1) concatenated with 3, as depicted in Figure 15

The top levels of Object Identifiers registration are described in Section 1.1.6. The Internet registers itself under DOD, and registers one branch for the purpose of management protocols. The structure for the management subtree is organized as follows:

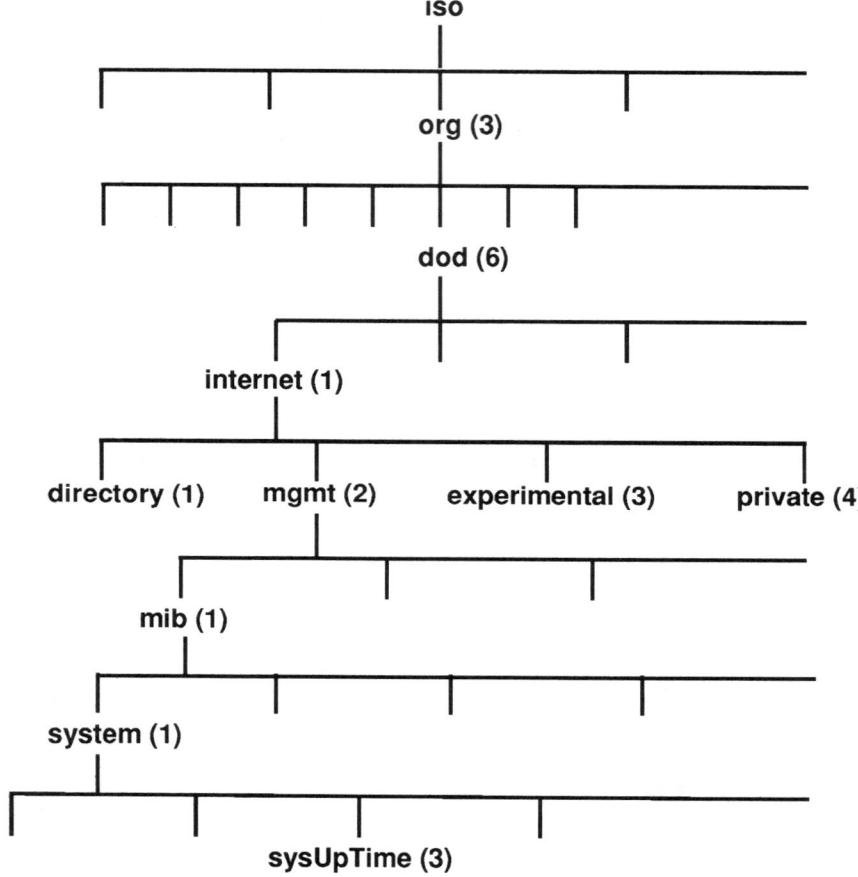

Figure 15 - Hierarchy of ISO object identifiers

So the definition of all the object types actually form a hierarchy in terms of the assigned object identifiers, which is part of the global object identifier tree.

Syntax is used to define the structure corresponding to object types. Syntax is defined in terms of ASN.1 constructs, although not all ASN.1 constructs are allowed in order to control complexity.

The syntaxes currently allowed in RFC1155 are:

ACCESS TO MONITOR INFORMATION

Primitive types (from ASN.1):
> INTEGER, OCTET STRING, OBJECT IDENTIFIER, NULL

Defined types:
> NetworkAddress - a choice of IpAddress or others
> IpAddress - an OCTET STRING of size 4.
> Counter - a 32-bit integer
> Gauge - a 32-bit integer
> TimeTicks - a 32-bit integer
> Opaque - an arbitrary OCTET STRING

The *Definition*, *Access* and *Status* fields are self-explanatory.

2.3.3.2 Constructed object types

Some object types may be constructed from other object types. These constructed object types are called aggregate types. There are two ways to construct aggregate types from more primitive types:

1. the aggregate object type is defined as a list of more primitive types;
2. the aggregate object type is defined as a table of objects of the same (more primitive) type.

As an example of (1), let's consider a type called "atEntry", (or address translation table entry):

```
OBJECT: atEntry { atTable 1 }
    Syntax:    atEntry   ::= SEQUENCE
                          {
                              atIndex INTEGER,
                              atPhysAddress OCTET STRING,
                              atNetAddress NetworkAddress
                          }
    Definition: An entry in the address translation table.
    Access:    read-write
    Status:    mandatory

OBJECT: atIndex { atEntry 1 }
    Syntax:    INTEGER
    Definition: The interface number for the physical address.
    Access:    read-write
```

Status: mandatory

OBJECT: atPhysAddress { atEntry 2 }
Syntax: OCTET STRING
Definition: The media-dependent physical address.
Access: read-write
Status: mandatory

OBJECT: atNetAddress { atEntry 3 }
Syntax: NetworkAddress
Definition: The network address corresponding to the media-dependent physical address.
Access: read-write
Status: mandatory

The aggregate object atEntry is constructed from the primitive objects atIndex, atPhysAddress and atNetAddress. All four types are defined above.

An example for (2) is a table of objects of type atEntry, as defined above. This is defined below:

OBJECT: atTable { at 1 }
Syntax: SEQUENCE OF AtEntry
Definition: The address translation table.
Access: read-write
Status: mandatory

The definition of the MIB for the common objects in the TCP/IP networks can be found in RFC1156 and RFC1158. The MIB in RFC1156 is considered the basic set of managed objects. The objects in RFC1158 were extensions added later on, and are referred to as MIB-II. In fact the above examples can all be found in RFC1156.

With the popularity of SNMP, MIBs for non-Internet protocols are also being defined. For example, RFC1243 defines the MIB for AppleTalk networks.

2.3.3.3 Object instances

Now let us consider how instances of objects are identified. The information model of SNMP only provides systematic identification and definition of object types. Object instances are identified in the SNMP protocol itself.

For each object type, if only one instance can exist, then it is simple. A query for that object type (using the defined object identifier) would yield the corresponding values. There is also a more explicit convention for naming the single instance, by appending a "0" to the end of the object type. For example, the object type for sysUpTime as given in an earlier example is 1.3.6.1.2.1.1.3; the instance (or value) of the type is identified by 1.3.6.1.2.1.1.3.0. If multiple instances can exist for a given object type, then there is a "key' associated with that type. The key's value is always of the form of a sequence of positive integers separated by dots, like the external representation of an object identifier. The general principle for identifying an instance of an object type is by concatenating the Object Identifier of the object's type with a value of the key

> type.value(key)

Usually, the key is simply an index into a table; so the key's value is simply a positive integer. Suppose the table is defined by:

key_type	a_type	b_type
1		
2		

Then the references to the values of the column "a_type" would be:

> type.1
> type.2
> ...

Note, in the general case, the key's type does not have to be of integer syntax, as long as it can be represented as a sequence of integers. A real-world example of this is one given in RFC1157. Suppose there is a routing table with the following entries:

ipRouteDest	ipRouteNextHop	ipRouteMetric1
10.0.0.99	89.1.1.42	5
9.1.2.3	99.0.0.3	3
10.0.0.51	89.1.1.42	5

where the object types are:

ipRouteEntry	OBJECT IDENTIFIER ::= { iso(1) org(3) dod(6) 1 2 1 4 21 1 }
ipRouteDest	Ipaddress ::= { ipRouteEntry 1 }
ipRouteNextHop	Ipaddress ::= { ipRouteEntry 7 }
ipRouteMetric1	INTEGER ::= { ipRouteEntry 3 }

In this case, the key for ipRouteEntry is ipRouteDest. So the three values of the first row are identified respectively as:

1.3.6.1.2.1.4.21.1.1.10.0.0.99 = "10.0.0.99"
1.3.6.1.2.1.4.21.1.7.10.0.0.99 = "89.1.1.42"
1.3.6.1.2.1.4.21.1.3.10.0.0.99 = 5

It is somewhat unfortunate that the keys for accessing instances are not specified in the MIB. Instead, the keys for important managed objects in the Internet are specified in the SNMP specification (RFC1157).

It is not necessary, however, to know the key in order to browse through a table of values. This can be easily accomplished using the GetNext request. Initially, one may perform a GetNext using 0 as the key value. So, for the example table above, the first query would be:

```
GetNextRequest (
        ipRouteDest.0,
        ipRouteNextHop.0,
        ipRouteMetric1.0
        )
```

The response would be:

```
GetResponse (
        ( ipRouteDest.9.1.2.3 = "9.1.2.3" ),
        ( ipRouteNextHop.9.1.2.3 = "99.0.0.3" ),
        ( ipRouteMetric1.9.1.2.3 = 3 )
        )
```

The next query would be:

```
GetNextRequest (
        ipRouteDest.9.1.2.3,
        ipRouteNextHop.9.1.2.3,
        ipRouteMetric1.9.1.2.3
        )
```

with the response:

```
GetResponse (
        ( ipRouteDest.10.0.0.51 = "10.0.0.51" ),
        ( ipRouteNextHop.10.0.0.51 = "89.1.1.42" ),
        ( ipRouteMetric1.10.0.0.51 = 5 )
        )
```

ACCESS TO MONITOR INFORMATION 59

and so on. So, even if one does not know the key, it is possible to derive it from the response and continue from there.

2.4 ISO/IEC/CCITT CMIP

2.4.1 Background

2.4.1.1 The ISO/IEC and CCITT standardization process

ISO (International Organization for Standardization) has a broad focus, making it the leading standards organization in the world. ISO standards range from information-processing systems to almost all industrial products. There are two other international institutions that have product standards that sometimes overlap with the IT standards of ISO:

> IEC   International Electrotechnical Commission
> CCITT   International Telegraph and Telephone Consultative Committee (which is part of the International Telecommunication Union, under the United Nations)

Both IEC and CCITT are older standardization bodies with long histories in their respective fields: IEC is responsible for electrical devices and systems; and CCITT is responsible for the telecommunications systems. To avoid duplication of work, ISO and IEC formed a joint committee for standardization in the information technology area, which is called ISO/IEC Joint Technical Committee 1 (abbreviated ISO/IEC JTC 1). Under JTC 1, there are currently 18 subcommittees (SC) and a large number of working groups (WG) for each SC. Two SCs are involved with computer networking: SC21, which is responsible for Open Systems Interconnection (OSI), and SC6 which develops the lower layer (transport layer and below) networking protocols.

The standardization process adopted by ISO/IEC JTC 1 is the same as that used by ISO. A standards proposal passes through five stages before becoming a standard, as shown in the following figure:

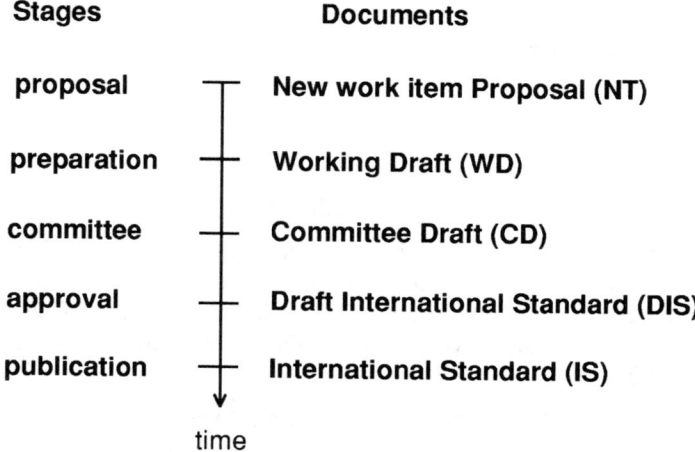

Figure 16 - ISO Standardization Process

Each new work item gets assigned a number. Standard documents are issued with this number, attached with the associated status.

The participants in the JTC 1 are national delegations appointed by the national ISO member. For example, ANSI (American National Standards Institution) is the ISO member for the United States; and BSI (British Standards Institute) is that for the United Kingdom.

Similarly, CCITT has wide collaboration with ISO/IEC on issues of data communications, even though CCITT's standardization process is somewhat different from that of ISO. For example, CCITT produces its standards in four year internals, called study periods[1]. At the beginning of each study period, the Plenary Assembly decides what work is to be done, summarized in "Questions". Study Groups (SG) are assigned to work on these questions. The SGs are subdivided into working groups. The standards produced are called "Recommendations".

Despite the differences between JTC 1 and CCITT, the two standards bodies work together when overlaps are identified. The working groups from both standardization bodies sometimes produce the same standard documents together. These documents would be given both an ISO/IEC number as well as a CCITT number.

The requirement levels of the ISO/IEC and CCITT standards in products are defined in functional profiles by the implementor's workshops. Three regional workshops are currently active:

---

[1] The study period system is being revised.

- Asia-Oceanian Workshop (AOW), in Asia;
- European Workshop on Open Systems (EWOS), in Europe;
- NIST OSI Implementors' Workshop (OIW), in North America.

A process is in place to give fully aligned functional profiles international standards status. These profiles are called ISPs, or International Standardized Profiles. The CMIP ISPs are listed in Appendix B.

2.4.1.2 References

As part of the same program to develop OSI network protocol standards, ISO/IEC JTC1 and CCITT are jointly developing the network management protocols. This effort, begun in the mid 1980s, has accelerated over the past few years. A large number of standard documents has been produced. By mid-1991, most of this series of documents (which include the definition of the management services, protocols, information model and management functions) reached either IS or DIS status. The actual managed object definitions (MIBs) for several OSI protocol layers are reaching IS or DIS status during the early part of 1992. A list of the relevant documents is included in Appendix B, with both the ISO/IEC and CCITT numbers, as well as their status. We give a brief summary of the important documents below, using only their ISO numbers for brevity.

ISO 7498, *The OSI Basic Reference Model*, is the architectural keystone to OSI standards, and 7498-4 is the *Management Framework* that provides a common basis for the coordinated development of management standards. This architecture is the basis for the *service definitions* and the *protocol* (ISO 9595 and ISO 9596), the *system management functions* (ISO 10164) and the *Structure of Management Information*, or *SMI* (ISO 10165). ISO 7498-4 also defines such basic terms as *managed object*, their *attributes* and *operations*. In addition, the document also defines the five major functional areas: fault, accounting, configuration, performance, and security.

ISO 9595 defines the *Common Management Information Services* in three categories: notification, operation, and association. It also defines the selection of managed objects. The CMIP protocol is defined in ISO 9596-1. ISO 9596-2, the *Protocol Implementation Conformance Statement Proforma*, provides a mechanism for the implementer of ISO 9596 to provide implementation information in a standard form. Together, these documents define the services and protocols that allow network management tools from different vendors to communicate with one another as peers.

ISO 10164 is a multi-part standard document that addresses the many different components of systems management. These components, in total, provide mechanisms for the monitoring, control, and coordination of resources within the OSI environment. ISO 10164 also includes OSI protocols for communicating information to those resources. The parts of this document, which are the systems management functions defined so far, are:

1. *Object Management*: defines managed objects as well as the creation and configuration of managed objects; defines the rules for creation, deletion, renaming, and listing of managed objects; and also defines how to delete and make attribute changes to objects.

2. *State Management*: identifies the state model for network management; permits two major state classification: administrative (busy, active, enabled, disabled); and operational (shutting down, unlocked, locked).

3. *Objects and Attributes for Representing Relationships*: provides a model for representing and managing relationships between managed objects; defines the relationships as direct, indirect, symmetric, and asymmetric.

4. *Alarm Reporting*: defines five generic alarm notification types (Communications, Quality of service, Processing, Equipment, and Environmental) and their parameters and semantics. In addition, an alarm record object is defined and 6 levels of severity indicated.

5. *Event Report*: defines the Event Report Management Model and a class of managed objects called the *Event Forwarding Discriminators*.

6. *Log Control*: defines a model for controlling event logs (record repositories).

7. *Security Alarm Reporting*: defines five types of security alarms (integrity, operational, physical, security service and time domain violations) and the notification formats used to report them.

8. *Security Audit Trail*: defines the event reports that should be in a log used for evaluating the security of an open system; the trails can be used to look for security attacks that are not detectable as they occur.

9. *Objects and Attributes for Access Control*: defines a model for controlling access to management information and operations.

10. *Accounting Meter*: defines a model for accounting for the usage of system resources and a mechanism for enforcing account limits.

11. *Workload Monitoring*: defines a model for monitoring the attributes of managed objects; defines managed object classes that can report events based on the values of counters and gauges that reflect the performance of a resource.

12. *Test Management*: deals with confidence and diagnostic test procedures; defines object classes used to control the tests.

13. *Summarization*: defines a model and object classes to summarize and apply statistical analysis to management information; provides for asynchronous reporting of summarized information.

ISO 10165 is a multi-part standard that describes the object-oriented approach to the modeling of management information. This corresponds to the information model in our terminology. The first three parts together are often referred to as the *Structure of*

Management Information (SMI):

1. Part one, *Management Information Model*, defines the information model of managed objects; gives the principals for (a) naming the managed objects and their attributes, (b) managed object classes and (c) the relationships into which they can enter. It also defines the Management Information Base (MIB).

2. Part two, *Definition of Management Information*, defines the managed object classes as specified by the GDMO template (Guidelines for the Definition of Managed Objects).

3. Part three (whose document number is 10165-4), *Guidelines for the Definition of Managed Objects*, provides guidance for other OSI standards to encourage consistency between managed object definitions and compatibility in OSI management.

ISO 10733 and ISO 10737 include the definitions of managed objects for the OSI network and transport layers. In other words, these documents contain the basic MIB for OSI lower layer protocols.

The Internet network management effort also considered the adoption of the ISO network management standard when it becomes stable (RFC1109). To this end, a couple of RFCs have been published. RFC1189, 1990 defines how CMIS and CMIP are to be used for the Internet; and RFC1214, 1991 defined the Internet MIB for management using CMIP. To date, SNMP has been much more widely implemented than CMIP in the market place, as can be judged by the volume of MIBs becoming standardized in the Internet community.

2.4.2 Protocol

The OSI *Common Management Information Protocol* (CMIP) is considerably more general than the SNMP. A distinction is made between the protocol (CMIP) from the *Common Management Information Service (CMIS)*. CMIS is an abstract procedural interface of a set of network management functions. CMIP is essentially the mapping of the CMIS into the OSI protocol suite. For our purposes, it is easier and quite adequate to review CMIS (ISO 9595) to get an overview.

The following table summarizes the CMIS services:

Service	Type
cancel-get	confirmed
event-report	confirmed/non-confirmed
get	confirmed
set	confirmed/non-confirmed
action	confirmed/non-confirmed
create	confirmed
delete	confirmed

Figure 17 - CMIP protocol messages

For network monitoring, the first three services are the most relevant. The *cancel-get* is an additional function in the optimization category. In case the user cancels a *get* operation, this function can be used to signal to the service provider (which may be remote) that no more effort should be expended on the previous *get* operation. The *get* and *event-report* functions are the two basic methods for network monitoring we discussed in Section 2.1.2. The Type of service indicates whether the request is followed by a response; if so, it is called *confirmed,* otherwise it is *non-confirmed.* The CMIS *event-report* function, which is also called a *notification,* can be either confirmed or non-confirmed, while most other management protocols require this function to be only non-confirmed.

2.4.3 Information model

The OSI management information model is significantly more general and elaborate than the Internet SNMP information model. This information model describes both a hierarchy of object types (in this case called object classes), and a hierarchy of object instances which is completely independent of the object type hierarchy. This model has a lot of similarities with the information model of the OSI *Directory Service* (ISO 9594).

2.4.3.1 Managed object classes

Each managed object belongs to an object class, called its *managed object class.* A managed object class has a globally registered object identifier and defines attributes, operations and notifications related to the managed objects in the class. In order to present the managed object definitions in a more structured and concise form, various ways to structure the object class hierarchy definition are included.

The simplest method is the use of *attribute group* definitions. A number of attributes that are commonly associated with many different managed object classes are defined separately. In the definition of a managed object class that contains all the attributes in the attribute group, only the attribute group need be referred.

A more prevailing technique is *class inheritance*. Managed object classes are defined as a hierarchy. The root object class is called *top*, which must contain attributes that apply to all object classes (which is a null set). The subclass of a managed object class inherits all the characteristics of its superclass, and includes additional definitions in its own definition. In this sense, the definition of a subclass of a class is also referred to the process of *specialization*. Let us consider some simple examples of inheritance. For example, Class X has attributes {A, B, C}; class Z is defined as a subclass of X and also has attribute {F}; so class Y has attributes {A, B, C, F}. For generality, *multiple inheritance* is also allowed. In the previous example, the class Z can also be subclass of Y which has attributes {D, E}; as a result, class Z would have attributes {A, B, C, D, E, F}. For managed object classes, the definition is more complicated since it includes operations and notifications in addition to attributes.

These tools are still not quite enough. The definition of attribute groups and the class hierarchy are fixed at the time the standard is specified. Often, depending on which options in the OSI protocol stack are built into a particular product, the definition of the managed object would be different. For example, OSI transport layer has several classes (5) that provide somewhat different transport services. A transport-layer managed object thus may have different definitions depending on which transport classes are implemented in a particular product. To cater to this level of dynamic grouping of object class definitions, the concept of *packages*, and in particular the concept of *conditional packages* are introduced.

A package defines a set of attributes, operations and notifications when a particular protocol option is implemented, somewhat similar to defining a subclass. The specialization in this case is related to different options related to a network protocol. The conditional package facility allows the definer to define managed object classes and delay the interpretation of the definition to the time when it is bound to a managed object in a particular product.

2.4.3.2 Managed object class template and other related templates

As in the case of the SNMP, the *Structure of Management Information* (SMI) documents for CMIP defined templates for defining management objects in (ISO 10165-4). We give some examples here to illustrate the templates and to explain some of the key concepts. For the complete definition of the templates, the reader should consult (ISO 10165-4).

The template for the definition of managed object class is:

```
<class-label>              MANAGED OBJECT CLASS
[DERIVED FROM             <class-label> [, <class-label>]*; ]
[CHARACTERIZED BY         <package-label> [, <package-label>]*; ]
[CONDITIONAL PACKAGES     <package-label> PRESENT IF condition
                          [. <package-label> PRESENT IF condition]*; ]
REGISTERED AS             object-identifier;
supporting productions
condition -> delimited-string
```

This template is based on very natural syntactical rules. For example, the capitalized phrases are keywords; the labels in <> are to be substituted by real label names; anything in [] is optional; the characters ";", space or end-of-line are used as delimiters; the character "*" is used to allow repetition, and so on.

The first line defines the name of the managed object class. The DERIVED FROM line defines the superclasses. Although it is in [], this part is really a mandatory part of the definition, except for the object class *top* which is not derived from any other class. Then the CHARACTERIZED BY and CONDITIONAL PACKAGES lines define the packages. Finally, the REGISTERED AS line defines the object identifier assigned to this managed object class. The rest of the lines at the end following "supporting productions" define any terms in definition that can be further expanded. In this case, "delimited-string" is a primitive convention for writing down a text string defined in (ISO 10165-4), so we know "condition" is simply a text string.

When another definition, for example a managed object class, or a package, is referenced, a label is used. The label is again expressed in terms of some conventions, but is ultimately reduced to one of two possible primitive ways of referencing:

- The name of a standard (in double-quotes) where the definition can be found, or
- The registered object identifier for the referred definition.

This is similar to the use of *descriptor* and *object identifier* as references in SNMP. We will see this in some real-world examples later.

Packages are defined using the following template:

```
<package-label> PACKAGE
[BEHAVIOUR         <behaviour-label> [, <behaviour-label>]*; ]
[ATTRIBUTES        <attribute-label> propertylist [<parameter-label>]*
                   [, <attribute-label> propertylist [<parameter-label>]*]*; ]
[ATTRIBUTE GROUP   <group-label> [<attribute-label<]*
```

ACCESS TO MONITOR INFORMATION

```
                           [, <group-label> [<attribute-label<]* ]*; ]
[ACTIONS        <action-label> [<parameter-label>]*
                [, <action-label> [<parameter-label>]*]*; ]
[NOTIFICATIONS  <notification-label> [<parameter-label>]*
                [, <notification-label> [<parameter-label>]*]*; ]
[REGISTERED AS object-identifier;

supporting productions
propertylist ->    [REPLACE-WITH-DEFAULT]
                   [DEFAULT VALUE     value-specifier]
                   [INITIAL VALUE     value-specifier]
                   [PERMITTED VALUES  type-reference]
                   [REQUIRED VALUES   type-reference]
                   [GET | REPLACE | GET-REPLACE]
                   [ADD | REMOVE | ADD-REMOVE]
value-specifier -> value-reference | DERIVATION RULE <behaviour-label>
```

The definition of packages differs from that of the managed object class in that the package definition refers to another set of definitions: BEHAVIOUR, ATTRIBUTE, ATTRIBUTE GROUP, ACTION, and NOTIFICATION; each of these has its own template for formal definition. Instead of presenting all these formally, we give a brief summary of what each definition includes.

1. BEHAVIOUR: gives an explanation of whatever is being defined in a text string; similar to the *definition* part of object type definition in SNMP.
2. ATTRIBUTE: defines the syntax, matching rules and possibly some error parameters associated with an attribute. This definition can also inherit from other attribute definitions.
3. ATTRIBUTE GROUP: defines a set of attributes as group members.
4. ACTION: defines the parameters, syntax, mode (confirmed or not) and gives a textual description of BEHAVIOUR actions.
5. NOTIFICATION: defines the parameters, syntax, and gives a behaviour description for notifications.

Let us now examine an example of a managed object definition from (ISO 10723).

virtualCall MANAGED OBJECT CLASS
DERIVED FROM "Rec. X.721 | ISO/IEC 10165-2 : 1992":top;
CHARACTERIZED BY vCMO-P PACKAGE
 BEHAVIOUR
  commonCreationDeletion-B,
  octetsSentReceivedCounter-B,
  virtualCallNaming-B;
 ATTRIBUTES
  virtualCallId GET,
  channel GET,
  packetSize GET,
  windowSize GET,
  ...;
 ATTRIBUTE GROUPS
  "Rec. X.723 | ISO/IEC 10165-5":counters
  ...;
 NOTIFICATIONS
  "Rec. X.721 | ISO/IEC 10165-2: 1992":objectCreation,
  "Rec. X.721 | ISO/IEC 10165-2: 1992":objectDeletion;
;;
REGISTERED AS {NLM.moi virtualCall (10)};

Although this is an example of a managed object class definition, the entire template of the vCMO-P package (from the line beginning with BEHAVIOUR until the line beginning with ;;) is also included in the definition. This is called *in-lining* as in the case of including a piece of macro in a program; this is permitted as long as it makes the definitions more readable. The key word GET after each attribute is part of the propertylist (see PACKAGE template definition) indicating that the GET operation can be applied to this attribute. Note that this example also indicates how other standards documents can be referenced by using "". The omissions of "..." are ours to make the example shorter.

This managed object class is to be registered as {NLM.moi virtualCall (10)}. In the same document, an ASN.1 module NLM is defined in which moi is defined as {joint-iso-ccitt network-layer (13) management (0) nLM (2) moi (3)}

So, the actual object identifier for the managed object class virtualCall is: 2.13.0.2.3.10, using the compact notation.

To complete the illustration, we now show one example each for the BEHAVIOUR, ATTRIBUTE, and NOTIFICATION templates:

   virtualCallNaming-B BEHAVIOUR

      DEFINED AS   A system shall ensure that all instances of MOs derived from the virtualCall MO which have a common x25PLE as their superior MO, shall have unique values for the virtualCallId attribute. This applies to both automatically generated names and those supplied by means of a CMIP create.;

The definition of BEHAVIOUR uses simply the key words DEFINE AS, followed by a text string. Note that BEHAVIOUR definitions are not registered by object identifiers.

   packetSize ATTRIBUTE

     WITH ATTRIBUTE SYNTAX NLM.PacketSize;

     MATCHES FOR EQUALITY, SUBSTRINGS;

     BEHAVIOUR interruptTime-B BEHAVIOUR

        DEFINED AS Value for Timer T26 (Interrupt Response Timer) in seconds;;

     REGISTERED AS {NLM.aoi interruptTime (82)};

This definition specifies the syntax to be NLM.PacketSize, where NLM is an ASN.1 module (defined in the same document) in which the syntax is defined as

   PacketSize ::= INTEGER(1...65535)

The matching rules EQUALITY and SUBSTRINGS are standard and do not require additional matching function specification. The BEHAVIOUR is again defined in-line. Finally, the registered object identifier prefix aoi is also defined in the NLM module, to be:

   {joint-iso-ccitt network-layer (13) management (0) nLM (2) aoi (7)}.

An example of NOTIFICATION is as follows:

objectCreation NOTIFICATION
   BEHAVIOUR   objectCreationBehaviour;
   WITH INFORMATION SYNTAX Notification-ASN1Module.CreateInfo
    AND ATTRIBUTE IDS
      sourceIndicator   sourceIndicator,
      additionalCreateInfo additionalCreateInfo;
   REGISTERED AS {Notification-ASN1Module.sni2Notification 6}

This definition refers to BEHAVIOUR and SYNTAX definitions elsewhere in the same document. The AND ATTRIBUTE IDS part specifies the correspondence of certain fields in the notification to attributes. Here, they happen to have the same labels. The object identifier prefix in this case is also defined in some other module where all the NOTIFICATION definitions are put together.

2.4.3.3 Object containment hierarchy

The managed objects instances are organized into a hierarchy. This hierarchy, however, must be distinguished from the object class hierarchy we described in the last two sections. The instance hierarchy implies that the managed objects (instances) are named hierarchically.

The instance hierarchy is constrained by rules, called *name bindings*. In simple terms, a name binding rule defines instances of object class X must be named as subordinate to instances of object class Y. In this sense, these rules for structuring management information is called the *containment hierarchy*.

Let us consider an example, again taken from (ISO 10723). The document specifies a containment hierarchy for the managed object instances in a networked system. A portion of this containment hierarchy is shown in the following figure.

Each box corresponds to a managed object (MO) class. We will not visit each one of them, but consider merely how to specify that instances of one MO class must be subordinate to instances of other MO class, or in other words, one MO class is contained by another.

ACCESS TO MONITOR INFORMATION 71

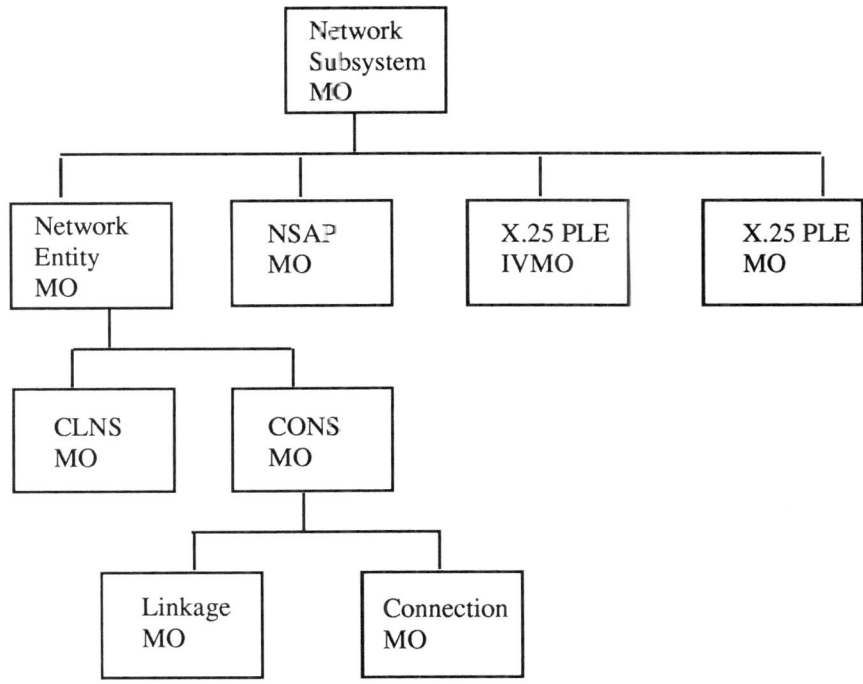

Figure 18 - Network layer containment hierarchy

The following definition defines the name binding between the Network Subsystem MO and Network Entity MO:

networkEntity-networkSubsystem NAME BINDING
    SUBORDINATE OBJECT CLASS networkEntity AND SUBCLASSES
    NAMED BY
        SUPERIOR OBJECT CLASS networkSubsystem AND SUBCLASSES
        WITH ATTRIBUTE
            "Rec. X.723 | ISO/IEC 10165-5":communicationsEntityId
    REGISTERED AS {NLM.nboi networkEntity-networkSubsystem (2)};

This definition follows the convention of the NAME BINDING template, the formal specification of which can be found in (ISO 10165-4). In this example, there are two components to the definition.

1. The line beginning with SUBORDINATE OBJECT CLASS identifies the subordinate MO class in the name binding. The key words AND SUBCLASSES says that all subclasses of the MO networkSubsystem also follows this rule.
2. The component beginning with NAMED BY gives two pieces of specifications:
   a. The superior MO class in the name binding. Again, the AND SUBCLASSES includes additional subclasses of networkSubsystem, if there is any, in this rule.
   b. The attribute in the subordinate MO class (in this case networkEntity) to be used for naming. This means that the name of an instance of networkEntity relative to an instance of networkSubsystem is always of the form:

      communicationsEntityId = <value>

      where <value> is some value of the attribute communicationsEntityId.

The relative name in 2(b) is called the *Relative Distinguished Name* (RDN) of a MO instance. Since each superior instance must also have an RDN, the concatenation of all RDNs until the global root of the MO instance hierarchy is reached is called the *Distinguished Name* of the MO instance. This definition of naming is directly imported from X.500 (ISO 9594).

In fact, the MO instance hierarchy is supposed to be grafted on to the global X.500 *Directory Information Tree* (DIT). For example, the X.500 Distinguished Name of a networked system may be:

country = US,
organization = ACME,
organizationUnit = SALES,
commonName = NODE_FOO.

The naming attribute for networkSubsystem relative to system is subsystemId (this is specified in a separate name binding). So the Distinguished Name for a particular instance of a Network Entry MO might be:

country = US,
organization = ACME,
organizationUnit = SALES,
commonName = NODE_FOO,
systemId = 1,
subsystemId = 2.

ACCESS TO MONITOR INFORMATION   73

The use of global Distinguished Names allows the managed objects to be referenced from anywhere in the world in a location independent way.

In CMIS, the identification of managed objects can be based on several forms of names, the Distinguished Name being one of the forms. This allows other ways of identifying a system than using an X.500 name.

2.5 IBM SNA MANAGEMENT AND NETVIEW

2.5.1 Background

IBM's networking products are defined by the System Network Architecture (SNA, see IBM, 1975). In SNA, the key networking components are the *Virtual Telecommunications Access Method (VTAM)* and the *Network Control Program (NCP)*. VTAM is the networking program that runs in the host (node), and NCP is the networking program in the network controllers used to off-load the hosts.

Descriptions of SNA's network management functions can be found in IBM, 1987 and IBM 1989. For SNA's network management, the architecture is defined in SNA Management Services; and the resulting product family is called NetView. In our terminology, NetView is a class of network management applications that reside on the hosts to help administrators handle various concrete management tasks, such as configuration, problem and change management, performance monitoring and tuning, accounting, and general operation of the network. For the subject of this book, our review will concentrate on those aspects related to change management, performance monitoring, and accounting. .

In NetView, all managed objects are connected to VTAM (mostly via NCP); thus VTAM is said to be the *focal point*, or *control point*, for management. The following figure shows a typical SNA environment. In this example, NetView is running on all three hosts, each of which is also running VTAM.

---

[1] SNA is continuously evolving. The emerging products of APPN and SystemView are not covered in this book.

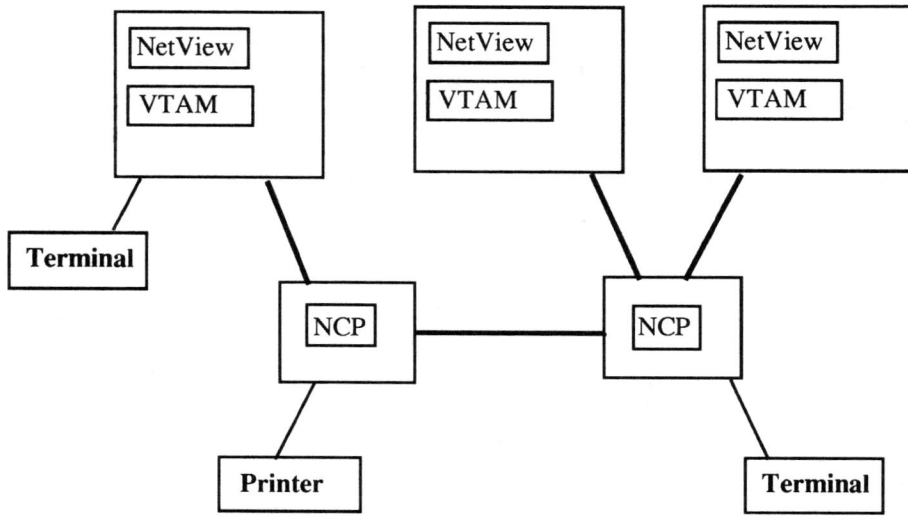

Figure 19 - Typical SNA configuration

NetView can monitor the network by the following means:

- Session AWareness data (SAW): VTAM maintains a log of all sessions involving the local host. Each session record contains information on the name of the session partner, data and timing information, session path through the network, amount of data transferred, response time measurement and other session parameters. Netview uses this information to show active and historical sessions.

- Receipt of VTAM messages: VTAM may generate messages to NetView based on its diagnosis of the network condition.

- Receipt of reports from the network components: All SNA network components can send management information asynchronously to VTAM and NetView to indicate network problems, configuration information, statistics and error summaries. The protocol used is the *Network Management Vector Transport* (NMVT)[1], to be reviewed in more detail later. This corresponds to the *event-driven* method of monitoring in our terminology.

- NetView network command capability: Netview has a rich command interface. These commands can be used to display status information, activate and de-activate

---

[1] In older products, REQMS (REQuest Maintenance Statistics) and RECFMS (RECord Formatted Maintenance Statistics) were also used. But these older protocols are subsumed by NMVT.

ACCESS TO MONITOR INFORMATION

network components, change configurations, run tests and measurements. When these commands involve remote components, the protocol used is also NMVT.

These mechanisms are summarized in the following figure:

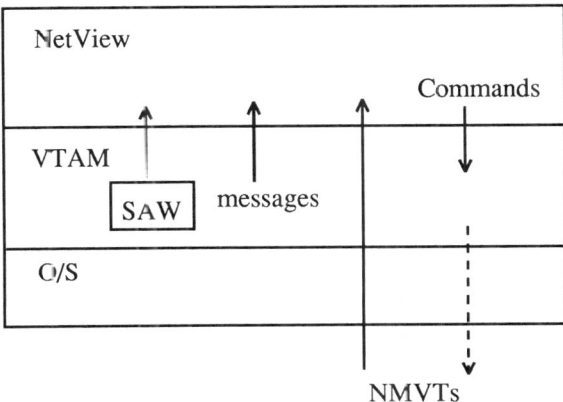

Figure 20 - **SNA management monitoring mechanisms**

Netview implements the following features to help the network administrator to monitor and manage a network.

- The NMVT messages are logged in NetView, so they can be reviewed to diagnose a problem.
- A filter can be applied to the NMVT messages so that only the ones that require urgent attention generate alarms.
- Command procedures can be used to program automated actions, based on given sequences of events in VTAM and NMVT messages.

In a multi-protocol environment, there are two ways that NetView can monitor and manage non-SNA devices and networks:

1. Build a gateway to make the non-SNA devices emulate an SNA device. This gateway, which is called a *service point*, sends (and receives) NMVT protocol messages on behalf of the non-SNA devices. For example, this is the method used to monitor PCs. The gateway (or service point) in this case is called NetView/PC. The configuration is shown in Figure 21:

2. Extend Netview to support selected protocols. For example, the support for SNMP and IP is done this way.

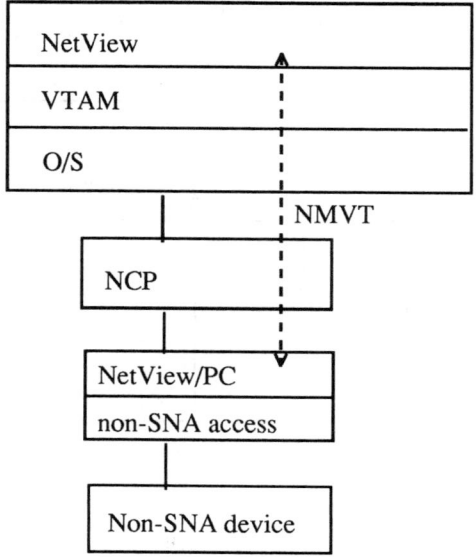

Figure 21 - NetView/PC as a management gateway

2.5.2 Protocol

The abstract model for SNA management is quite similar to what we outlined in Section 2.1.1, except that the terminologies are different. Each network addressable machine is called a *node*. In a *node,* there is always a *Physical Unit* (PU), which is essentially the same as what we called the monitoring agent. Each node may also have a *Control Point* (CP), which corresponds to the management agent in our terminology. A Control Point is capable of talking to multiple Physical Units, other CPs and interfaces with the network administrator (operator) who manages the network.

A Physical Unit is further modeled in terms of a set of *Local Management Services* (LMS) and a *Physical Unit Management Service* (PUMS) module. The PUMS actually implements the protocols for interacting with CPs on behalf of the LMSs. The corresponding protocol module on the CP side is called the *Control Point Management Service* (CPMS). The following figure illustrates a PU and its interactions:

ACCESS TO MONITOR INFORMATION 77

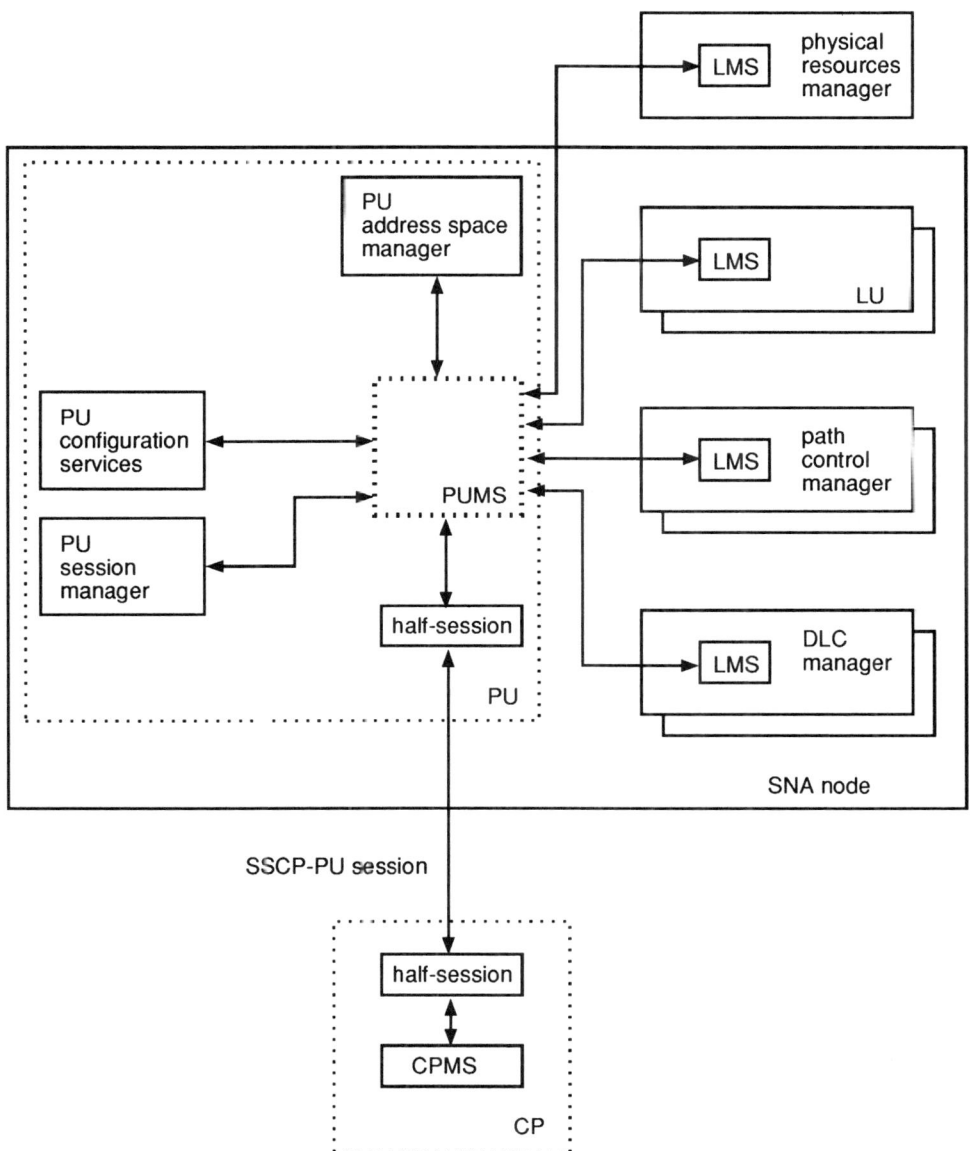

Figure 22 - PUMS protocol boundaries with other components[1]

[1] Reprinted by permission from *System Network Architecture - Format and Protocol Reference Manual: Management Services*, c 1987, by International Business Machines Corporation.

The protocol used by CP and PU is an application level protocol called the *Network Management Vector Transport* (NMVT). Each NMVT message is delivered in *Management Service Request-response Units (RU)*, which is a generic encoding for request/response messages. The first field of the RU contains a protocol type field that is used to identify NMVT. NMVT has a header for procedure ID and flags, followed by a management service major vector, which is the main body of the message.

protocol type	NMVT header	management service major vector

The major vector is consists of a list of subvectors:

length	key	subvector	subvector	...	subvector

where each subvector is a <length, key, data> triple.

The key for the major vector, a two-octet field, indicates the management function provided. For example, X'0000' indicates Alert, and X'0080' and X'8080' indicate Response-Time Monitoring. The key for the subvectors is a one-octet field. The architecture specifies that if the value of the key is from X'00' to X'7F' then the meaning of the key is independent of the major vector within which they are used; whereas subvectors with keys X'80' to X'FF' have meaning specific to the major vector within which they are used. The data field is a data structure that may contain subfields.

Both the polling and event-driven methods of access are supported. In SNA terminology, these two methods are called *flows*: the *unsolicited flow* and the *request/reply flow*.

In the case of unsolicited flow, a RU that carries the monitored data (here loosely[1] referred to as a data RU) is first sent from the PUMS to the CPMS, and then a response RU is sent back from the CPMS to the PUMS.

---

[1] RU, which stands for request-response units, can be either a request RU or a response RU. A data RU is simply a request RU that carries data.

ACCESS TO MONITOR INFORMATION

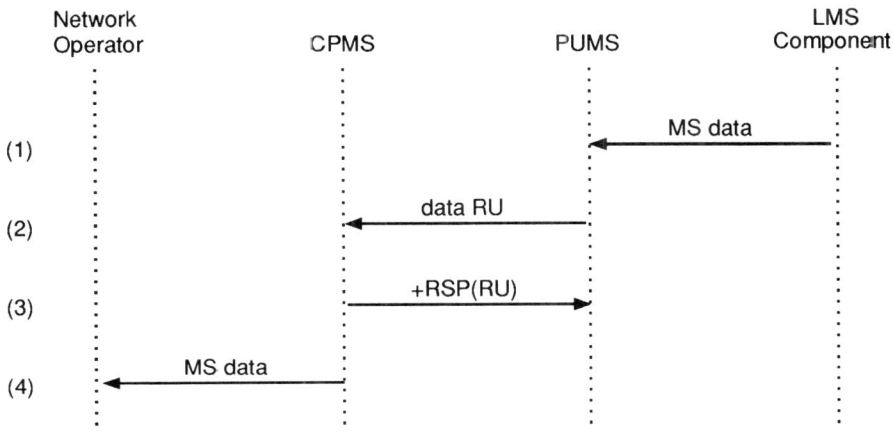

Figure 23 - The unsolicited flow[1]

The request/reply flow starts with a request RU from the CPMS, followed by a response RU from the PUMS; one or more data RU and response RU pairs may follow:

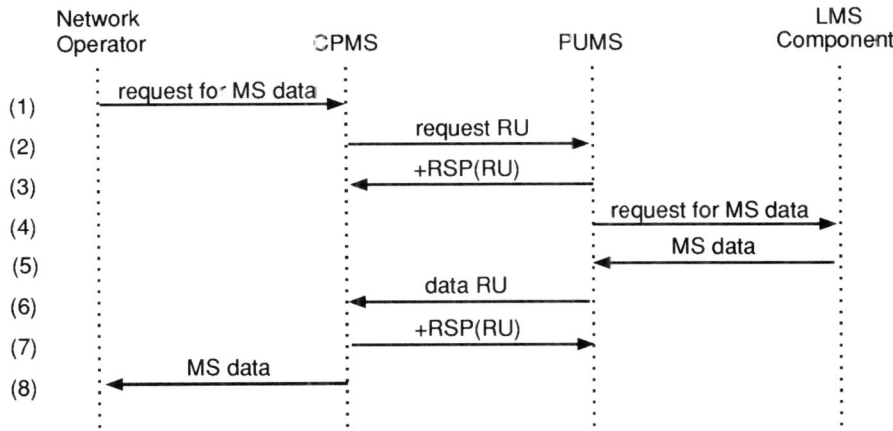

Figure 24 - The request/reply flow[1]

---

[1] Reprinted by permission from *System Network Architecture - Format and Protocol Reference Manual: Management Services*, c 1987, by International Business Machines Corporation.

80 CHAPTER 2

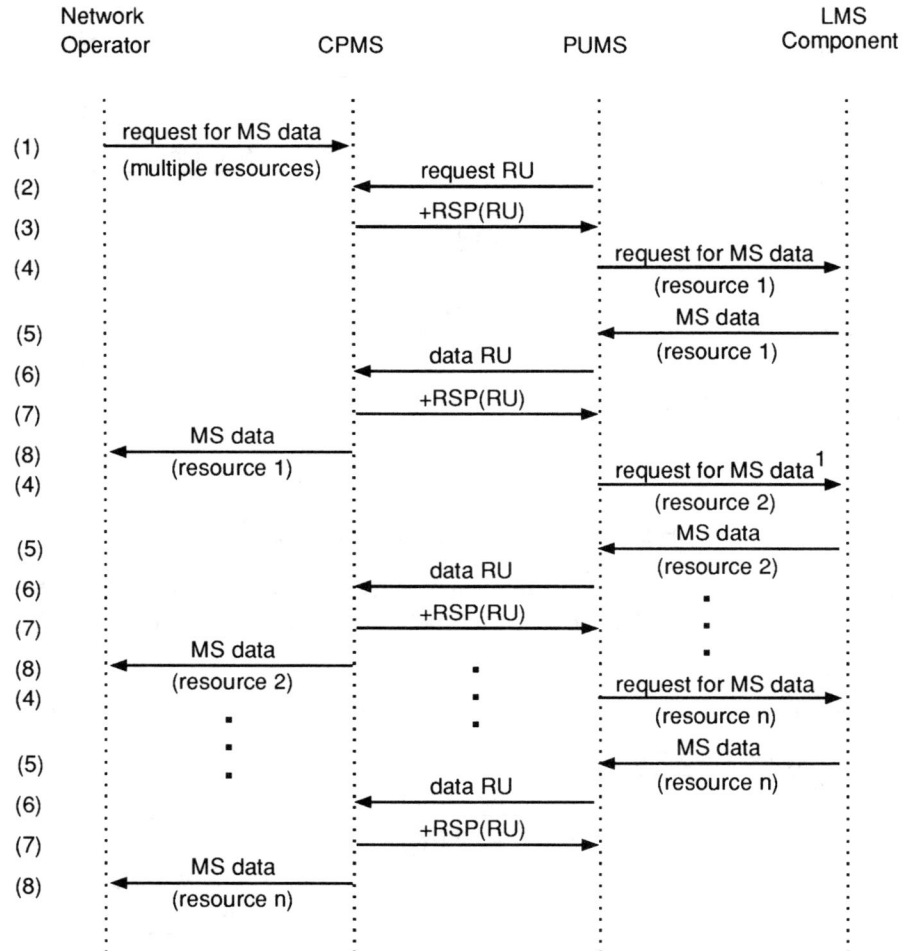

[1] The architecture allows requests to the LMS to be made before previous requests have been replied to and sent to CPMS.

Figure 25 - The request/reply flow (multiple resources)[1]

[1] Reprinted by permission from *System Network Architecture - Format and Protocol Reference Manual: Management Services*, c 1987, by International Business Machines Corporation.

2.5.3 Information model

With NMVT, there is no clean information model as in the cases of Internet's SNMP and ISO CMIP. The equivalent of the information model is reflected in what NMVT can carry in its protocol messages. The lack of an information model for the managed objects means that the permitted values for the protocol messages must be enumerated in lengthy manuals where the syntax and semantics of the information carried by the protocol are specified one by one.

The two major applications for NMVT are *Alert* and *Response Time Monitoring (RTM)*.

For Alert, a large number of alert subvectors (fields in an alert message) are specified. Each of these subvectors corresponds to some attribute of the alert, such as *when* and *where* it occurred, as indicated in the following table (IBM, 1987, page 8-10)..

X'00'	Text Message	O
X'01'	Date/Time	CP
X'03'	Hierarchy Name List	CP
X'04'	SNA Address List	CP
X'05'	Hierarchy/Resource List	CP
X'10'	Product Set ID	P(n)
X'31'	Self-Defining Text Msg	O
X'42'	Relative Time	CP
X'51'	LAN Link Connection	CP
X'52'	LCS Configuration Data	CP
X'8C'	SDLC Link Station Data	CP
X'91'	Basic Alert	O
X'92'	Generic Alert Data	P
X'93'	Probable Causes	P
X'94'	User Causes	CP
X'95'	Install Causes	CP
X'96'	Failure Causes	CP
X'97'	Cause Undetermined	CP
X'98'	Detailed Data	O
X'A0'	Detail Qualifier	O(n)

Key: P   = Present one time
      P(n) = Present one or more times
      CP   = Conditionally present one time
      O   = Optionally present one time
      O(n) = Optionally present one or more time

Figure 26 - NMVT Alert subvector types

The Basic Alert subvector and the Generic Alert Data subvector carry the actual alert information, identifying the alert type, cause of alert, component type, description code, user action code, text explanation and so on. The Generic Alert Data subvector is used for carrying most of the IBM defined alert types; whereas the Basic Alert subvector is a more primitive alert message that is used to carry more application-specific alert types. For illustration, the Basic Alert subvector (X'91') is shown here:

```
octet 1:      length
octet 2:      key = X'91'
octet 3:      flags
octet 4:      alert type
octet 5:      general cause code
octet 6-7:    specific component code
octet 8-9:    alert description code
octet 10-11:  user action code
octet 12-13:  detailed text reference code
octet 14:     retired
```

Figure 27 - Format of the Basic Alert subvector

The other major application of NMVT is response time monitoring (RTM), which is carried in a different type of message (major vector). For the RTM message, again a set of subvectors are defined:

```
X'01'   Date/Time           CP
X'04'   SNA Address List    CP
X'42'   Relative Time       CP
X'45'   Data Reset Flag     CP
X'7D'   Sense Data          CP
X'91'   RTM Status Reply    CP
X'93'   RTM Data            CP
```

Figure 28 - NMVT Response Time Monitoring subvector types

Note that some of these subvectors are actually the same as those allowed in the Alert major vector, whereas some are specific to RTM.

The actual response data is contained in the RTM Data subvector (IBM, 1987 page 8-86) which is shown in the following illustration:

octet 0:   Length, in binary, of this subvector
octet 1:   Key = X'93'
octet 2:   RTM measurement definition in effect:
                 e.g. X'02' = measured from the attention or action
                 key depression until the LU is ready to accept
                 input from its end user
octet 3:   Response time unit of measure:
                 e.g. X'00' = 100 milliseconds
octet 4-5:   Reserved
octet 6-7:   Retired
octet 8:   RTM data collection parameters:
                 bits 0-3, the number of response time measurement
                 boundaries returned;
                 bits 4-7, the number of boundary sets for which
                 valid data was collected
octet 9:   A set of response time measurement boundaries
octet (p+1)-q: The number of measured exchanges for each response
                 time interval
octet (q+1)-(q+2): Overflow: the number of exchanges durations
                 greater than the maximum boundary specified
octet (q+3)-(q+6): Total of all individual times for all exchanges
                 measured and reported by this record, including
                 overflow, in measurement units defined by octet 3
octet (q+7)-(q+8): Last measured exchange duration in the
                 measurement units defined by octet 3

Figure 29 - Format of an RTM Data subvector

Since the management information is directly defined in terms of protocol messages, the syntax and semantics of the various objects and their attributes are defined at multiple places. This lack of a more structured information model makes the specifications harder to read and manage.

2.6 DIGITAL'S EMA and DECmcc

2.6.1 Background

The Digital Network Architecture (DNA), and the networking product DECnet, is one of the earlier networking systems that became prominent in the industry. DNA is a peer-to-peer network architecture, emphasizing architectural simplicity and performance. The more recent version, DECnet/OSI (also known as Phase V, described in Martin & Leben, 1992; and DEC, 1987), has extended the architecture to support OSI standards while simultaneously supporting existing DNA applications. This new version of the architecture allows almost infinite scalability in terms of naming and addressing using OSI addressing conventions and a naming service, provides mechanisms for auto-configuration of objects and supports multiple-protocol networks.

With these new features, the complexity of the architecture has increased. Network management has become a particularly important functional requirement. Together with the development of DECnet/OSI, the original DNA network management was significantly extended as part of the *Enterprise Management Architecture (EMA,* described in Fehskens, 1989; DEC, 1989; and Sylor, 1988).

EMA is a very general model that is designed to supports network and system management in an enterprise-wide, heterogeneous, multi-protocol and distributed environment. Central to EMA is a consistent definition of globally accessible managed objects based on a model of *Entities* and *Attributes*. This modeling work on managed objects is culturally very similar to management objects in OSI network management standards. In addition, EMA also includes a very general model of a generic management application (called a *Director* in EMA). Both aspects are discussed in the following sections.

2.6.2 Protocol

Prior to Phase V, DECnet's network management protocol was the *Network Information Control and Exchange (NICE)* protocol.

The management protocol for DECnet/OSI is DNA CMIP. DNA CMIP is an evolution of NICE. Although the functions are basically the same, DNA CMIP is much more extensible and scalable for large networks. The following are the major difference between the two:

- *Treatment of other operations* - In NICE, each new operation requires a new kind of message, whereas in CMIP a general extension mechanism, the Action, is provided.

- *Naming* - NICE supported a limited number of Entities (8) and provides a rudimentary naming hierarchy based on the notion of "qualifying attributes". DNA CMIP supports hierarchical Entity names, and is essentially unlimited in the number of Entities it can deal with. DNA CMIP is also much more extensible in naming attributes, attribute groups and event reports. Some of these will be evident in the next subsection.

- *Encoding* - DNA CMIP uses ASN.1 while NICE used fixed fields and a private Type/Length/Value encoding of attributes and arguments.

Since DNA CMIP was developed while the ISO CMIP standard was still in development, the two are not exactly the same. When the ISO CMIP becomes a stable standard, DNA CMIP is expected to migrate to be compatible with the ISO CMIP.

DNA CMIP actually consists of two separate protocols, used for the two methods of access as described in Section 2.1.2

1. *Management Information Control Exchange (MICE)* - which is the protocol used for polling method of access
2. *Management Event Notification (MEN)* - which is the protocol used for the event-driven method of access.

These two protocols operate over separate connections, to keep things simple The triggering mechanisms for these two access methods are different. A MEN connection is established when a managed object wishes to report an event; whereas a MICE connection is established when a management application wishes to invoke an operation on the managed object To coordinate these two activities to share the same connection would introduce additional complexity. Using separate connections, the network resource allocation for these different types of activity is also left for the network itself to deal with.

A very good discussion of this material can be found in Sylor, 1991.

2.6.3 Information model

In EMA, the managed objects are synonymous with *Entities*; the monitoring agent is generically referred to as *Agent*, and the management application is called the *Director*.

2.6.3.1 Entities

For a Director to be able to communicate with an Agent regarding managed objects, the information about managed objects must be structured according to conventions. A central element of the EMA *Entity Model* (Sylor, 1988) is its hierarchical and structured approach for defining such information.

The EMA Entity Model supports a framework for defining classes or types of Entities according to the properties they share. This framework is consistent with the ISO/OSI Structure of Management Information (SMI). Entity classes are given names to identify them and are defined by common properties. These properties are assigned to one of the following subsets: *attributes*, *attribute groups*, *directives*, and *events*.

Attributes consist of atomic pieces of specific data that provide the management information about Entities, for example, STATUS, BYTES RECEIVED and NUMBER OF BUFFERS. An attribute group consists of a set of related attributes, such as counters and characteristics (operating parameters defined by management). Directives consist of requests that a Director can send to the Agent of the Entity. Directives are supported through commands such as SHOW, SET, ADD, REMOVE, CREATE, ENABLE, DISABLE and TEST. Events consist of unsolicited information that an Entity's Agent can send to a Director to indicate state transitions or configuration values. For example, a new node broadcasts an event message when it comes on line.

Entity classes form a hierarchy. Classes that belong to other classes in a hierarchical relationship are called *Subordinate Entity Classes*. For example, an Entity class, NODE, might contain a Subordinate Entity Class called LINKS.

In the world of Entity instances, an important concept is that of a *Global Entity*. A Global Entity has a unique global name. All the Entities that are of classes subordinate to that of the Global Entities are named relative to these Global Entities, thus also acquiring global names. The most important Global Entities in DECnet/OSI are of class NODE; all the other Entities are defined relative to node Entities.

A *node* is a computer system. The bounds of that system are left vague. For example, a single processor system, a multi-processor system and a system with or without disks can all be considered nodes. The important aspect is that a node has a name (and also a unique identifier in case the name changes over time), an address and an Agent that allows it and its sub-Entities to be managed.

2.6.3.2 Agents and Directors

The *Agent* is the management software collocated (or communicates) with managed objects, whereas the *Director* is the management application software.

In EMA, the Director is modeled (Shurtleff & Strutt, 1990) to include a set of the following modules:

1. Access Modules (AM): Each access module provides the mechanism for the transfer of management information pertinent to a particular class of managed objects. For example, one AM might be for DECnet devices, another for voice/data switches, and yet another for Internet objects.

2. Function Module (FM): Each function module is configured to provide a particular *value-added* function. For example, when it is desirable to generate some statistics based on accessed information about managed objects, a particular function module may be design to perform that function; the alarm capability, which also filters on observed information about managed objects, may be done in a separate function module.

3. Presentation Module (PM): These modules provide the user interfaces to the user.

The Agent, like the Director, also supports multiple access modules for network management in a multi-protocol environment.

In the DECnet/OSI products, two general kinds of Directors are provided. The first kind of Director is a simple one, tailored to expose the directive and event primitives associated with the DECnet/OSI Entities. This kind of Director is universally available (on every node). In terms of the above model, this kind of Director has only the most primitive function module, and the presentation module (user interface) is a command line language called the *Network Command Language (NCL)*. For this reason, these Directors are referred to as NCL Directors. They replace the Digital *Network Control Program (NCP)* that was used on older DECnet nodes.

The second kind of Director is a generalized one that is configurable and extensible. In terms of the model, this kind of Director has sophisticated and/or multiple functional modules. The presentation module can either be the same NCL language, or a window-based graphical interface. These Directors are installed on machines accessed primarily by network administrators. Digital's network management products, under that general family name DECmcc, provide a variety of directors.

NCL was designed to be English-like, and extensible. Similar to most command line languages, the syntax consists of a verb, the name of an Entity (or Entities if the name is wild-carded), a list (possibly empty) of arguments, and a list of qualifiers to the command (possibly empty). For extensibility, the Entity definitions are loaded from a dictionary. As new EMA Entities are defined, or older ones extended, new versions of the NCL dictionary can be provided that allow the Entities to be managed without having to reimplement the Directors.

3

The Design of Network Monitors

3.1 MONITORING AGENTS

While the applications and implementations of network monitoring agents may vary significantly, there are a few broad functions that are common to nearly all such mechanisms. These common functions include the following:

1. Sensing - Making direct contact with the communications environment and acquiring information from it.
2. Filtering - Removing extraneous information from the input stream and retaining only selected data.
3. Collecting - Storing the filtered data either temporarily or permanently (or until such time as it is needed by a management application).
4. Reporting - Providing stored data to a management application as required.

Some monitoring agents may provide certain of these functions at a minimal level. For example, a real-time data analyzer may report information directly to the display screen, with no real intermediate storage media. This is a degenerate case, however, and it is more common for a monitor to include each of the above functions, regardless of its internal design

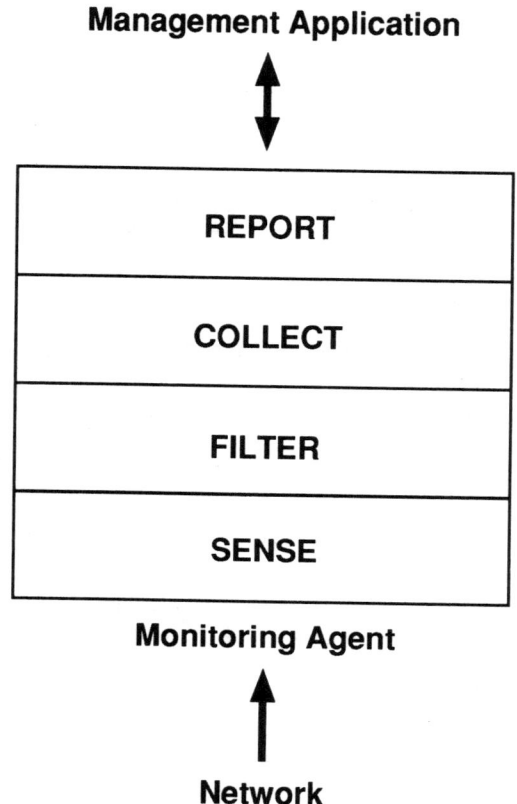

Figure 30 - A monitoring agent

3.2 INTEGRATED VS EXTERNAL MONITORS

There are two orthogonal ways of characterizing network monitoring agents:
1. according to the layer (as in the OSI reference model) the agent is monitoring, or
2. according to whether the agent is integrated with or external to the component or resource being monitored.

Both of these classifications have an effect on the way the monitor is likely to be designed and implemented. Because of this influence on design choices, we will examine the nature of these categorizations more closely.

3.2.1 Integrated monitoring agents

Integrated monitoring agents can be part of either a particular network application, or the networking software itself. In the latter case, the networking software could include some layered network service, such as: a Remote Procedure Call (RPC) communications service; the networking software in the base operating system, such as network device drivers; or part of a network component, such as software or firmware running in a front-end concentrator. As an example, it is common to keep event counters in each network layer. The software that maintains these counters is a form of monitoring agent. In this example, at the end of performing a given function, or perhaps when some other event occurs, one or more counters are updated. These counters can then be read by management applications to record the frequency of occurrence of such events.

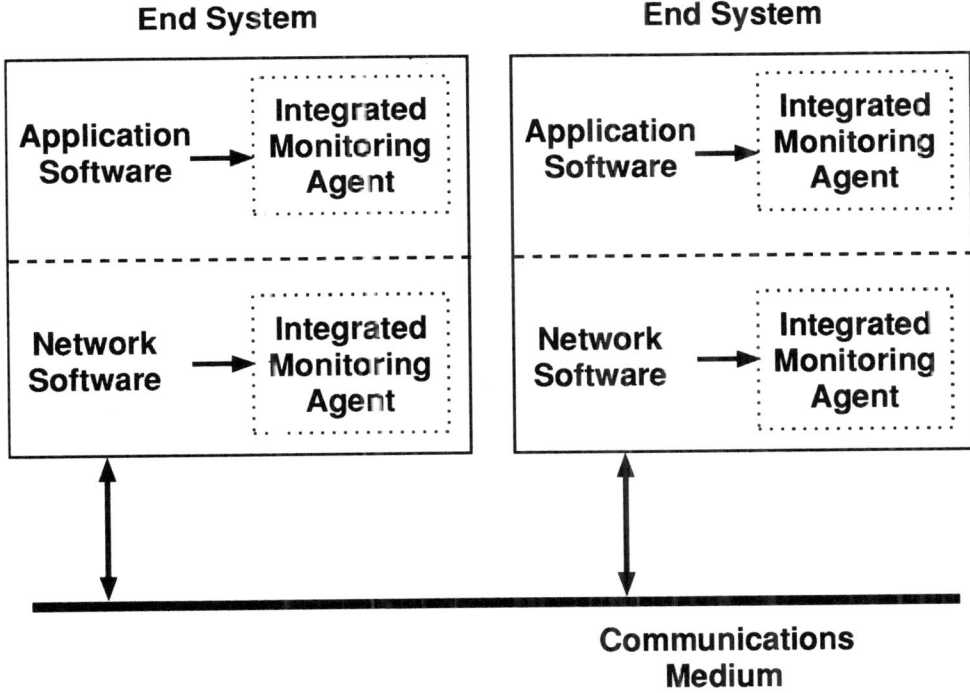

Figure 31 - Integrated monitoring agents

There are several advantages to this approach to monitoring. These include the following:

1. A rudimentary agent is generally required to provide a remote diagnostic capability, and this can often be easily extended to perform more comprehensive monitoring functions.
2. In the case where the monitoring agent is integrated into a specific application, it can be tailored to the needs of that application, rather than performing more generic functions.
3. Since the monitoring agent is integral to the function being monitored, and frequently has access to the same resources, it can be a very accurate source of information on that function.
4. The monitoring is "built-in", and may therefore have certain advantages in terms of cost and administration.

On the other hand, there are also a few disadvantages to this approach:

1. Since the monitoring agent is running on the same platform as the network service and the applications, the monitoring can have a negative impact on the overall performance of the application.
2. The cost of collecting the output of the monitoring agents can be significant, perhaps outweighing the value of the information to the management application. Furthermore, the delays inherent in the collection process may make some of the monitor data obsolete before it can be utilized.
3. Depending on what body of software the monitoring agent is integrated into, it may have to be reimplemented many times. For example, if the monitoring agent is part of the application software, a new agent may have to be implemented in every network application. If it's integrated into the operating system at some level, a new agent may have to be implemented for each operating system, etc.
4. Similarly, it is possible that each implementation of a given monitoring function may provide a different reporting format, making the task of developing management applications much more difficult and costly. This problem can be avoided to some extent through the use of standard reporting formats. Some significant effort must go into the creation of such standards.
5. Network monitoring may take a relatively low priority in the overall requirements on the application and/or operating system, and may therefore not be allocated adequate development resources.

3.2.2 External monitoring agents

External monitoring agents are implemented in some component external to the software that delivers the actual network service. These agents monitor by "eavesdropping" on the information being transmitted through the network. Because of this, they can capture only shared states that can be inferred from the network protocols, and cannot monitor the internal states of a software component. But since they are passive and easily adaptable, they are very popular in Local Area Network environments. In a LAN, all local End Systems share the same medium, so one monitoring agent can capture all available management information in one place.

External monitoring agents don't have to be attached to LANs. They could also be inserted in a point-to-point communications link, attached to a bus in a computer system, or spliced into the connection between the system and the network.

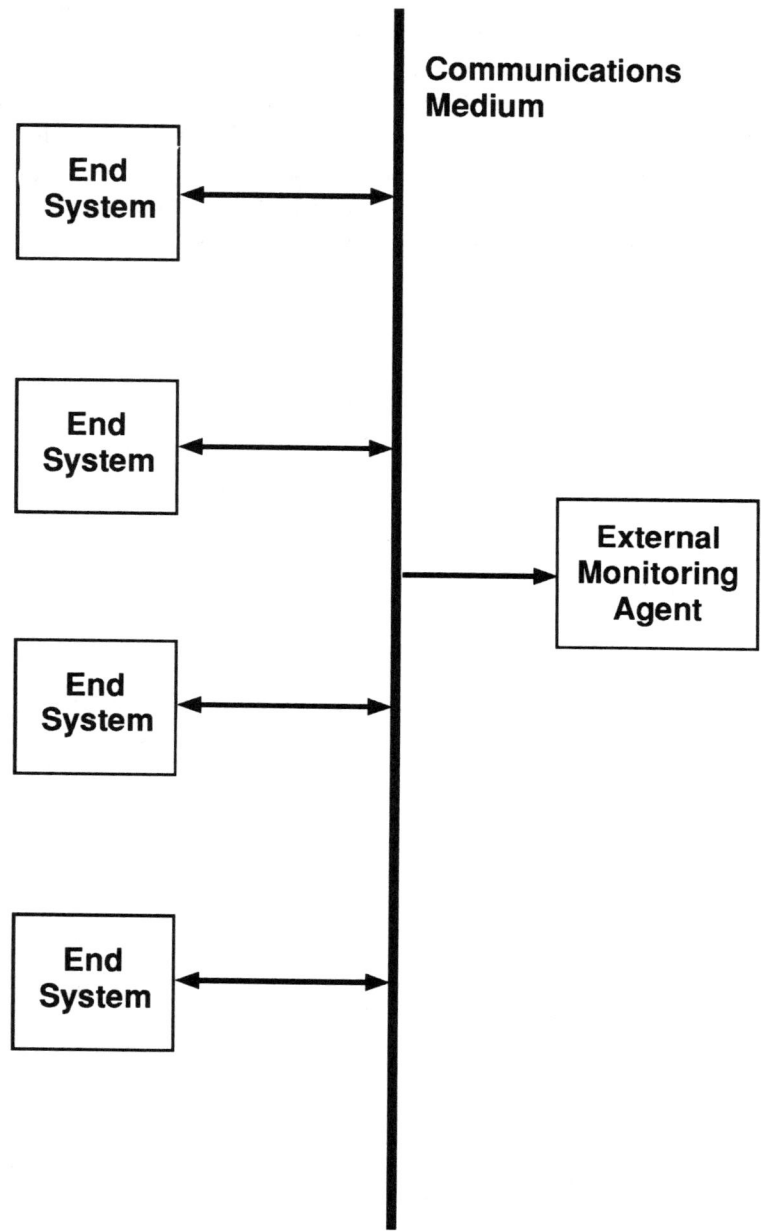

Figure 32 - External monitoring agents

Like integrated monitoring agents, there are advantages and disadvantages to this approach to network monitoring. Here are a few of the major advantages to external monitoring agents:

1. Because the monitoring agent is external, it can be implemented in dedicated hardware, and doesn't have to compete for resources with the network service and application. This reduces the likelihood of monitoring causing a degradation in network performance, and creates the opportunity to use specialized hardware and software to provide performance levels for monitoring that would not be possible in an integrated design.
2. Greater economies can be realized, both from the standpoint of development resources as well implementation cost, since a single monitoring agent may be able to provide information for a wide variety of operating systems and applications.
3. Being an independent component, the monitoring agent can more easily be modified and extended, and failures in the monitoring agent are less likely to result in denial of network services.

Some of the disadvantages of external monitoring agents are as follows:

1. Because they are "eavesdropping" on the network, and represent a separate security domain, they are a potential source of security threat in terms of privacy of information on the network, or even tampering. To some extent these security risks can be eliminated through proper design, but again, there is some cost associated with such measures.
2. The information they collect cannot be guaranteed to be a precise representation of the states of the monitored components, but only an approximation. Certain applications may not find this acceptable, for example, for the billing of customers for network usage.
3. Because they are gathering data for a large number of End Systems, they must have a very high performance capacity. This can potentially increase the cost of engineering and manufacturing them beyond a useful limit.

3.2.3 Technological evolution

To some extent, the evolution of technology has affected the decision as to when to use integrated versus external monitoring agents. External monitoring agents, in particular, have changed significantly due to a number of factors. Principal among these are:

1. the bandwidth of network communications media
2. shared access to the medium
3. CPU processor speeds

4. the cost of computer memory

3.2.3.1 Network bandwidth

In the early days of computer networking, most physical connections were made via point-to-point links, using modems and dial-up telephone circuits. The bandwidth of these links was typically around 300 bits per second. Over time, these speeds increased to 1200, 2400, 9600 and 19,200 bits per second as the reliability of the network components was improved. Today there are standards for digital communications over public and private telephone circuits for terminal access with data rates as high as 64 Kilobits per second, and for computer-to-computer communications at rates in excess of 10 Megabits per second. The cost of these higher speed technologies, however, may put them out of reach of the average network user. This factor has been addressed by Local Area Network technologies, which lower the cost of access through the used of a shared medium.

LAN technologies began to be commercially deployed on a large scale in the early 1980's. These networks generally provide bandwidth on the order of 10 Megabits per second. One example of this technology is Ethernet (Metcalfe & Boggs, 1976; DEC, Intel & Xerox, 1980). Although this bandwidth is shared among all the user of the LAN, it is often accessible to any single user for short periods of time due to the bursty nature of network usage. As the decade progressed further advances were made, resulting in another order of magnitude increase in bandwidth to more than 100 Megabits per second. Networks of this nature are beginning to find their way into active use.

These increases in data rates have had a tremendous impact on the nature of external monitoring agents, because there are correspondingly large increases in the amount of information a monitor must be able to process.

3.2.3.2 Shared medium

In networks built from point-to-point links, external monitoring had little to offer in the way of cost benefits. Since any given agent could monitor the interactions between only two End Systems, the cost of monitoring all interactions in a network could be significant. For this reason, external monitoring agents were used primarily for diagnostic purposes, being deployed only as needed for specific trouble-shooting activities.

Most network monitoring for WANs consists of integrated monitoring agents that trigger event logging or alarms. These agents can typically be accessed through simple command interfaces that allow states to be set and recorded. In some cases, the states can be read by remote management applications that may record them in a common database or use them to update real-time displays, as described in Chapter 2.

With the advent of LANs, external monitoring agents have become much more practical and cost-effective.

3.2.3.3 Processor speed and memory cost

Fortunately, as the technology of network components has evolved, and placed greater demands on the capabilities of monitoring agents, the technology with which the agents themselves are implemented has also evolved.

When dedicated network monitors were first developed, they were typically based on early microprocessors, with CPU speeds on the order of .1 million instructions per second (MIPs). Most of these processors were also limited to 4-bit data paths, and the program development tools were very crude. Over the period of a decade or so, from about 1970 to 1980, microprocessors improved significantly. 8-bit and 16-bit processors came to be widely employed, with speeds up to 1 MIP. This evolution was driven largely by the personal computing industry, and indeed many network monitors have since been implemented on personal computer hardware.

In the following decade, speeds increased another order of magnitude or more. This time driven by the workstation market, 32-bit and 64-bit Reduced Instruction Set Computer (RISC) processors have been developed that can provide a powerful base for a network monitoring agent.

Along the same lines, memory costs have gone down, and packaging has become more and more compact. It would have been unusual in the early 1970's to have a network monitor with more than 4 Kilobytes of memory. This grew to around 64 Kilobytes by the end of the decade, and it is now not uncommon to have low-priced systems with more than 1 Megabyte of memory.

Other aspects of the technology have had comparable impact on network monitor designs and capabilities. Storage devices have become smaller and faster, with greater and greater capacity and access speeds. Display technology has evolved from primitive character cell devices to bit-mapped graphics displays. Windows, icons, pointing devices and other facilities are now readily available, even in low-end systems. Power supplies and other components have gotten smaller, resulting in systems that are much more portable. And program development tools have improved, making it easier to create sophisticated monitoring applications.

	1970's	1980's	1990's
Processor Speed	.1 Mips	1 Mips	10 Mips
Memory Size	4-16 K	64-512 K	> 1 Meg
User Interface	16x40 character cell	24x80 character cell	bit-mapped graphics
Development Tools	Assembly language, device emulators	Compilers, debuggers	CASE tools
Storage	Paper or cartridge tape	Removable disk	Hard disk and/or network access

Figure 33 - **Evolution of network monitoring technology**

These changes have helped to offset the increasing demands being placed on the network monitors, and have made possible a whole new generation of external monitoring agents and applications. There is also little doubt that ongoing improvements will be made in nearly all aspects of the technology over the next decade, and this will continue to shape the requirements on and capabilities of external monitoring agents. We will examine some of the future trends more closely in Chapter 5.

3.2.4 State-of-the-art external monitoring agents

Due to the limitations on the available technology, as well as cost, early external monitoring agents had very limited functionality. They were typically based on custom hardware and firmware. This required a significant engineering investment to produce even the simplest monitors. They were dedicated system, with fixed functions for performing a specific application.

Today, most network monitors are based on standard components, including personal computers and workstations. They often use existing operating systems as a software base, making possible much more sophisticated applications with much less engineering investment. They are often user programmable, and extensible to meet the needs of a wide range of applications. And finally, they are increasingly becoming integrated into a larger scheme of network and system management, with network interfaces that allow other management applications to control their function and collect monitored data.

3.2.5 Summary

We have explained how integrated and external monitoring agents differ, and described some of the advantages and disadvantages to these distinct approaches. In conclusion, it should be understood that both methods have useful applications, and are in fact quite complementary. It may be preferable to employ integrated monitoring agents to collect certain information, for example, to meet requirements for accuracy, security, ease of use, etc. At the same time, external monitoring may be a more effective choice for collecting other information about the network because it is more cost-effective, less likely to degrade network performance, etc. The decision as to which of these methods should be employed for any given monitoring function must be made on a case by case basis, considering all of the trade-offs inherent to each method.

3.3 WHAT LAYER TO MONITOR?

Up to now, we have been broadly characterizing network monitors as being either integrated or external monitoring agents. But it is important to understand that within these categories there is a wide range of functions for a monitor. One thing that distinguishes a particular monitoring agent is the layer of the network on which it operates.

As described in Chapter 1, network communications is implemented by a sophisticated body of software, residing in End and Intermediate Systems. This software is designed in "layers", each having its own peer protocol, as well as its own states that require monitoring and management. A monitoring agent is typically designed to operate on only one (or possibly a few) of the network layers. For integrated monitors, this depends on how the Management Information Base (MIB) is defined. For external monitors, it is more a matter of performance and product packaging. Without going into detail of all of the applications, which will be described more fully in Chapter 4, we will give some examples of the different requirements on monitoring in the different network layers. This will be helpful in better understanding the case studies of monitor designs that follow.

1. Data Link Layer - The data link layer is responsible for the actual movement of data from one point in the network to the next. It is typically the lowest layer in the networking software, and is very closely related to the actual physical medium. In this layer, monitoring is often used to detect software and hardware errors, which result in corruption or loss of data. Very often problems in higher layers of the network can be detected and isolated by monitoring at the data link layer, since all of the data must pass through this layer.

2. Network Layer - The network layer is responsible for managing individual circuits

in the sub-network to provide end-to-end connectivity to the transport layer. It is the function of the network layer in a connection-oriented architecture to route packets over various circuits to their common destination, transparently to the layers above. One example of monitoring in this layer is reporting when circuits are "up" (available) or "down" (unavailable). This information can be used by the network manager to avoid congestion or loss of connectivity.

3. Transport Layer - The transport layer guarantees the reliable delivery of messages within a connection. Monitoring at this layer can be useful to record the overall level of activity in the network, because it is a common entry point into the network for all applications. For example, it is common in today's networks for many transport protocols to be supported, such as OSI Transport, TCP/IP, DECnet NSP, etc. Transport level monitoring can aid in configuration management and capacity planning by informing the network manager of the relative level of utilization for each transport protocol.

4. Session Layer - The session layer provides extensions to the transport layer, such as establishing the identity of users and applications, and making transport connection failures transparent to the application layers. Monitored data from the session layer can be used to characterize the overall workload on the network by application and/or user. This can be helpful in load balancing and accounting applications.

5. Application Layer - The application layer, and the actual network applications themselves, are other potential candidates for monitoring. For example, an application level monitor might be used to detect the failure of a server process in a client/server application. By notifying the network manager of this failure some recovery action could be taken before the application user even becomes aware that network operations have been interrupted.

It is important to observe that, in many cases, the information collected by the monitoring agent is the same regardless of the layer being monitored. However, depending on the application, the agent might filter the information very differently. For example, it is common for monitors of any of the above layers to collect information on the amount of data transferred on the network. How this is filtered and reported may vary significantly. An application level monitor performing some accounting function might report the exact number of bits transferred by a specific application. On the other hand, a lower level agent, such as a transport level monitor is more likely to aggregate this information across all applications and report it in summary form. This is as much a function of the limitations on the monitoring technology for a given layer as it is on the management requirements for that layer.

3.4 CASE STUDIES AND EXAMPLES

We will now examine some examples of real network monitoring agents to get a better understanding of their design characteristics. It should be noted that the design of monitors varies significantly, and it is impossible to capture all of the design considerations in a few examples. However, we have tried to choose examples which are representative of the technology as a whole, as well as providing a wide range of functionality which should give some feeling for the diversity of monitor designs.

For each of the cases we present, we will consider a number of factors that influence the design of the monitoring agent. These include:

1. The general functionality, or the application for which the monitor is specifically intended.
2. The major architectural and implementation tradeoffs to be considered for a monitoring agent of this nature.
3. The performance characteristics resulting from the design decisions.
4. A comparison of the cost of implementation and use for the given design versus other approaches to obtaining the same information.
5. A few scenarios describing the actual use of the monitor in network management applications.

3.4.1 A datalink monitor

Datalink monitors were one of the first types of external monitoring agents to be developed. They came into use in the very early days of network communications, before LAN technology was available. At this time, networks consisted primarily of point-to-point links, and the only way to monitor communications externally was to insert something into the physical path between two points in the network. As mentioned previously, this approach to monitoring is expensive, since it requires a monitoring agent for every network link. For this reason, datalink monitors have been used most often as diagnostic troubleshooting tools, which could be deployed on an 'as needed" basis rather than being permanently installed to collect monitor information.

Due to the physical characteristics of most point-to-point communications media, it is not really possible to listen passively to data flowing on the link as it is with some LAN media. Datalink monitors are, therefore, often inserted into the link as an actual intermediary. This can be done at a location where a junction of some sort would normally occur, or special junctions can be provided in the media to permit the insertion of a monitor.

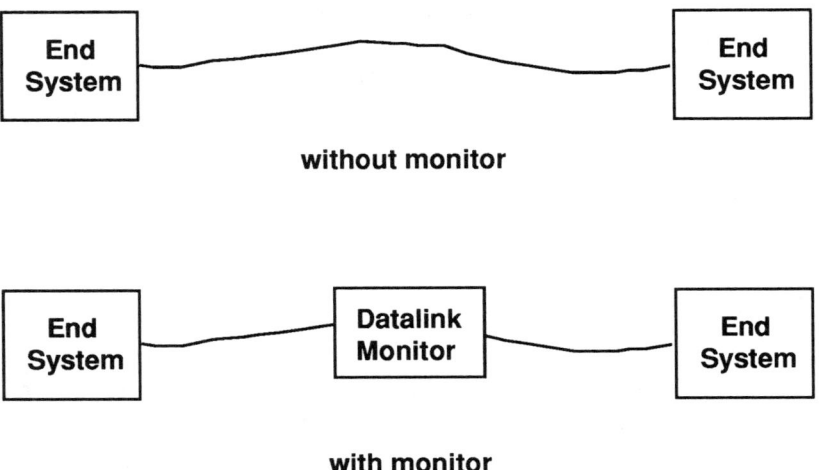

Figure 34 - Installation of a datalink monitor

In order to avoid interference with the normal traffic on the link, it is important that the monitor appear to be completely transparent. That is, it must be able to receive, process and forward data at line speeds, and it must under no circumstances alter the network data or add data on the link.

It should be mentioned that point-to-point links can provide various forms of traffic flow, including *simplex* (data flows in only one direction on the link), *half-duplex* (data flows in both directions on the link, but not at the same time) and *full duplex* (data flows in both directions at the same time). Some datalink monitors can accommodate half-duplex and full duplex transmission, but some can monitor traffic on the link in only one direction at a time, even if the link itself is full duplex. For simplicity, we will restrict our design discussion to a datalink monitor with a simplex traffic flow capability.

3.4.1.1 Design overview

Although datalink monitors vary significantly in the level of functionality they provide, the basic design considerations are fairly consistent. Because it is inserted into the physical medium, the datalink monitor must be able to perform the following functions:

1. Receive data from the link.
2. Process the data.

3. Transmit data on the link.

A typical monitor will have at least three internal buffers to facilitate this sequence. First of all, it has an input buffer to accept data from the link. Ideally, this should be large enough to allow data to be input without requiring any flow control messages between the monitor and the transmitter. Secondly, the monitor will typically have an internal buffer for storing data while it is being examined or stored. Filtering will often be applied between the receive buffer and the internal buffer to reduce the amount of data that must be processed. However, in the simplest case, all of the received data will be moved directly to the internal buffer, which might actually be a display buffer that permits the data to be examined visually. Finally, the data must be moved from the receive buffer to a transmit buffer, so that it can be forwarded immediately on the link to the intended recipient.

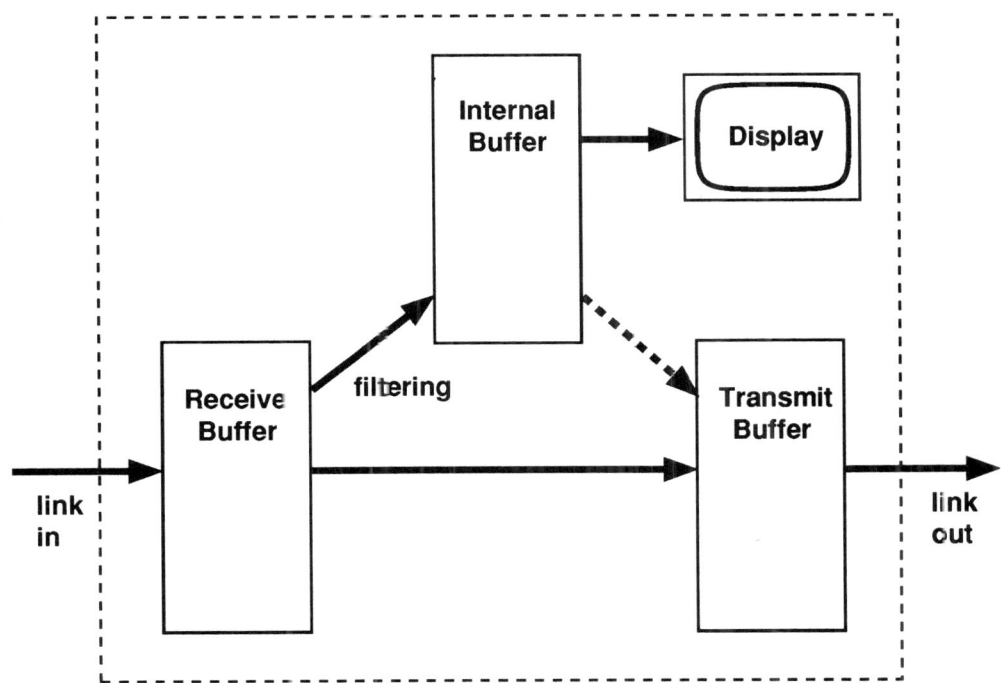

Figure 35 - Datalink monitor design

The steps as described are not necessarily entirely sequential. Often more than one processor is employed to perform multiple steps in parallel. For example, to maintain a higher speed of operation it is possible to be filtering the data and copying it into the internal buffer at the same time it is being copied into the output buffer. Also, some portion of the data, such as a message segment, might be processed internally before the entire message is received by the monitor. This would help the monitor meet the real-time requirements imposed by the network traffic rates. However, the degree to which this form of optimization is employed is limited to some extent by the nature of the functions performed by the monitor. If it is not entirely passive, for example, it may not be possible to achieve a high degree of parallelism among the processing steps.

3.4.1.2 Modes of operation

The simplest datalink monitors may be capable of only one function: displaying data on the screen in real-time as fast as it is received. More sophisticated monitors, however, provide a number of operational modes that can be more helpful in detecting and analyzing network problems.

One common feature is a buffering, or "screen freeze" mode of operation. This permits data in the display to be held for some period for closer examination, while the monitor continues to receive and forward data on the network in the background.

Some monitors may provide multiple buffers into which data can be captured. They permit buffers to be compared, so two messages can be checked to see if certain fields in their protocol headers are the same. This can be extended to make the monitor more automated by permitting buffers to be captured based on some *trigger* function, such as a specific sequence of bits or bytes of data. This is very useful for troubleshooting intermittent problems. The trigger function can be based on some user-defined input, or it can be based on previously captured data.

Another useful diagnostic aid is the ability to use the monitor to insert data into the communications stream. In this mode, it is actually performing more than a monitoring function, but it is a natural extension to the buffering capabilities previously described. For instance, a message can be captured, and then forwarded to a different destination, simply by modifying the destination address field in the message header. This can sometimes be combined with a trigger function, so that a particular message is forwarded automatically when some other message is received.

This leads into full programmability of the monitor, permitting the operator to create applications that can scan the input stream searching for specific patterns or field values, modify field values or create new message formats, and generate data on the network to simulate the behavior of other network components. Modern datalink monitors have all of these capabilities, and are still one of the most useful diagnostic tools for management of lower-level networking functions.

3.4.1.3 Display formats

Again, as technology has evolved, the user interface of datalink monitors has

THE DESIGN OF NETWORK MONITORS 105

continued to improve. Early monitors consisted of a small display, perhaps limited to only a few lines, with a small number of characters of data per line. They had only a few buttons for command input, with very few modes and options. Over time, displays have become larger, and datalink monitors developed keypads, keyboards, and other means of inputting commands. It is now common to be able to display the monitored data in a variety of formats: hex, octal, binary, ASCII, EBCDIC, etc. Some monitors have built-in knowledge of protocol message formats, and can display messages with fields and their values demarcated. Split-screen formats may be used to permit multiple buffers to be examined and compared simultaneously.

3.4.1.4 Sample reports

```
THIS IS A TYPICAL DISPLAY OF DATA N AND CONTROL CHAR
ACTERS COMBINED ON THE SCREEN. N FOR EXAMPLE: NNH NOTE
THAT CONTROL CHARACTERS ARE EMBEDDED DIRECTLY IN T
HE TEXT. SOMETIMES THE CONTROL CHARACTERS MIGHT BE
HIGHLIGHTED, LIKE THIS: NAVE TO MAKE THEM STAND OU
T. ALTERNATIVELY, THE DATA MIGHT BE HIGHLIGHTED. T
HE ENTIRE DISPLAY MIGHT BE CONVERTED TO SOME OTHER
FORMAT, SUCH AS BINARY 00100100 11011011 01010111 10
11100, HEX 0E AB 30 3D FE 14 2D, OCTAL, AND SO ON.
```

```
FOR A HALF-DUPLEX OR FULL DUPLEX MONITOR, IT IS PO
SSIBLE THAT THE SCREEN MIGHT BE SPLIT TO PERMIT SI
MULTANEOUS EXAMINATION OF THE DATA FLOWING BOTH DI
RECTIONS ON THE LINK. THE SPLIT-SCREEN MIGHT ALSO
BE USED TO PERMIT A SEGMENT OF DATA TO BE CAPTURED
AND EXAMINED WHILE REAL-TIME DATA CONTINUES TO BE
DISPLAYED ON THE SCREEN, OR TO PERMIT TWO DATA SEG
MENTS TO BE COMPARED VISUALLY.
```

Figure 36 - Split-screen monitor display trace

3.4.2 An event logging monitor

A network can be viewed as a very large real-time system, implemented over an extended geographic area, and can be represented as a complex state machine. Changes in state are continuously occurring at each logical layer of the network, in each of its components. Most of these state changes are routine, and in many cases of little interest, except during development of the components themselves. Once the network is functioning correctly they can usually be ignored. However, the more significant state transitions are an indicator of the "health" of the network, and can provide a network administrator early warning of potential problems. Armed with this knowledge, remedial action can often be taken, before a fault severely impacts normal operation of the network.

Event logging monitors are designed to collect reports from the various network components on significant changes in state, and make this information available to the network administrator. Many event logging monitors actually comprise a combination of monitoring agent, management agent and management application. An event logging monitor typically uses the network itself as a means of collecting information, although it may use fairly low-level protocols to do so. It is desirable that the event logging monitor have as few dependencies as possible on the correct behavior of other network components, so that failures in these components will not affect the ability to collect event traces.

3.4.2.1 Event capacity

As with other network monitors, the most challenging part of the design of an event logging monitor is being able to handle large amounts of data in real-time. In modern networks, consisting of many thousands of End Systems, each representing a number of managed objects, it is quite possible for millions of events to be generated over a period of a second or less. Because no one monitor could handle all of these events, other approaches are taken.

For example, in many environments the management of the network is decentralized, by the dividing the network up into smaller management domains. In this case, there may be no need for event reports to cross from one domain into another, and therefore the number of events which must be handled within a given domain can be bounded.

Another approach is to employ a hierarchical scheme of distributed event logging monitors. Low-level events can be reported to a "local" monitor, which can filter events for components in its area, and only forward events of a particular severity up the hierarchy. In this way, all events can be captured at some level, but it is still possible for a centralize management function to respond to critical failures anywhere in the network.

Yet another optimization involves the use of event *histories* to avoid repeatedly reporting the same event. Also, in some protocols, an event is reported only when a certain threshold is exceeded, and will be reported again only if the state falls significantly below the threshold, and then rises again. These designs can get very sophisticated, all with the intended goal of reducing the number of events that need to be reported on the network.

3.4.2.2 Design overview

Other than these considerations, the actual design of an event logging monitor is quite simple. Each managed object is configured to report state transitions of a particular nature (which is specific to that object type) via its monitoring agent. The monitoring agent is configured with the address of a management agent, or agents. When an event occurs, a message reporting the event is sent directly to the management agent, which is listening for such messages. The management agent logs the message immediately, and returns to the listening mode, waiting for more event reports. Meanwhile, management applications can take action on the event as required.

Event logging monitors typically have the ability to display data in real-time, such as on a video monitor, or to log event traces to a disk or tape media as a permanent record. Real-time displays have the benefit of immediately notifying administrative personnel of changes in the state of the network. Log files are useful for historical analysis, or when a broader view of changing events is required. It should be noted that events don't really occur in isolation, but as a response to other events. Sometimes the cause of an event can only be determined by replaying some sequence of events which reproduces a specific set of conditions in the network.

3.4.2.3 Timestamping events

This raises another concern regarding the design of event logging monitors, which has to do with the accuracy of time, and the synchronization of time across network components. The timestamp for an event can be generated either by the monitoring agent reporting the event, or by the management agent recording the event. In some ways, the former is preferable, because the management agent cannot know the exact time that an event occurred, only the time that it was reported. On the other hand, some low-level network components may not have access to an accurate clock. Even if clocks are accessible, there is no guarantee in many networks that the clocks are synchronized to any common time standard. Thus, it is possible that even though an event in some component occurs before an event in another component, if the clocks are skewed, the first event may appear in the event trace output to have occurred later. The management agent can at least properly sequence the arrival of event reports.

The ideal in terms of event logging monitor design is probably to have both the time of occurrence of the event as measured at the component, as well as the time of arrival of the event report as measured by the management agent, be recorded.

3.4.2.4 Sample reports

```
Critical  Node4   Node Unreachable  91-6-15-10:6:13  BOSTON
Major     Node4   Node Unreachable  91-6-15-10:6:13  BOSTON
          Node17  Starting          91-6-15-10:6:15  LONDON
          Node6   Routine Shutdown  91-6-15-10:6:15  NEW YORK
          Link2   Diagnostic        91-6-15-10:6:16  TOKYO
Critical  Node4   Node Unreachable  91-6-15-10:6:17  BOSTON
Major     Node4   Node Unreachable  91-6-15-10:6:17  BOSTON
          Node17  In Service        91-6-15-10:6:20  LONDON
          Link5   Reconfiguring     91-6-15-10:6:20  BERLIN
          Node8   Routine Shutdown  91-6-15-10:6:21  PARIS
Critical  Node4   Node Unreachable  91-6-15-10:6:17  BOSTON
          Node11  Starting          91-6-15-10:6:15  PARIS
          Link2   Diagnostic        91-6-15-10:6:16  TOKYO
```

Figure 37 - Event logging trace output

This display reports the typical output of a real-time event logging monitor, a sequence of timestamped trace records. It displays events reported by a number of remote components in the network, giving some indication whether the events are "routine", or might require some kind of response to correct a fault condition. In the latter case, in indication of the severity of the fault is given to alert administrative personnel as to the urgency of taking corrective action.

3.4.3 A LAN traffic monitor

Modern Local Area Networks have created multi-access networks which allow traffic for many connections to flow over the same physical medium. As the amount of traffic on the media has increased, and the nature of the traffic become more diverse, the need to accurately monitor the network has grown. There is no longer a situation such as existed in the past with dedicated links, in which systems could make use of the network

THE DESIGN OF NETWORK MONITORS

resources more or less autonomously. A LAN is usually a shared resource, and like other public utilities, it is important to measure and regulate its use.

Because LANs represent a relatively inexpensive form of networking, whose purpose is generally to encourage the widespread exchange of information over the network, LAN monitoring is not typically done to account for network usage. It is more likely to satisfy the need for fault isolation and repair, configuration management, and other maintenance-oriented applications. Due to the design of many LAN technologies, it is sometimes possible for a single network user to inadvertently render the network temporarily unusable by others. LAN monitors can help to identify the causes of such outages as well as help to prevent them from occurring in the future. For this reason they have become an integral tool in the workshop of the LAN administrator.

There are numerous LAN monitors reported in the literature, such as those described in Soha, 1987; Network General, 1986; and Excelan, 1986.

3.4.3.1 Design overview

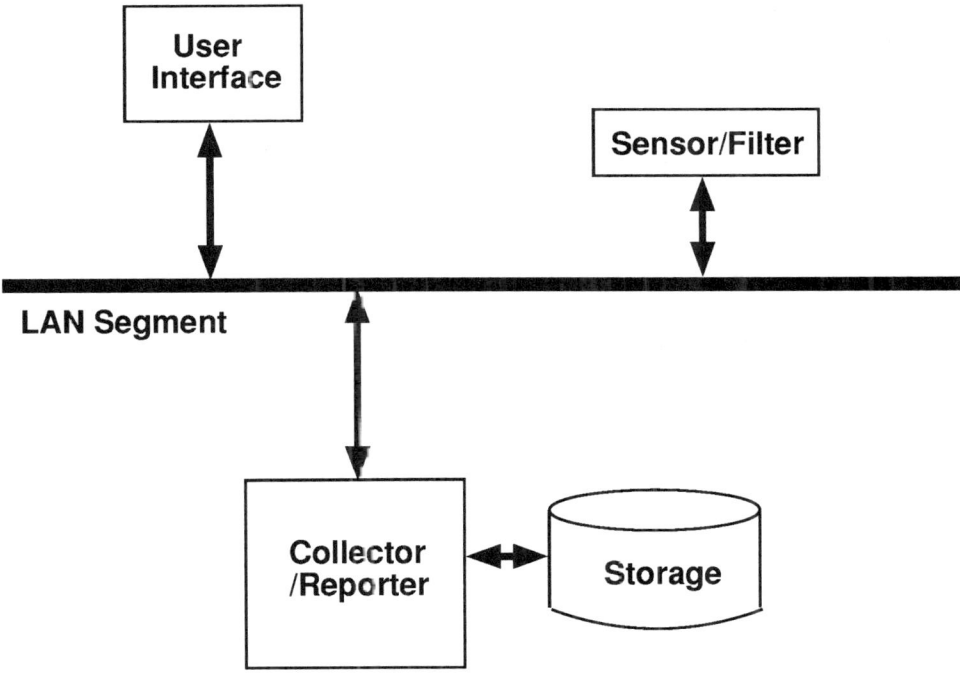

Figure 38 - LAN traffic monitor design

In this particular design, the monitoring function itself is distributed using the network. The component *Sensor/Filter* is a microprocessor-based device with a LAN interface that listens on the LAN in "promiscuous" mode. In this mode it can read all frames on the LAN regardless of their intended destinations, without interfering with their normal delivery. This device also contains special hardware in the form of a 48-bit content-addressable memory, which permits it to do extremely high-speed matching on LAN addresses. When it reads a frame from the LAN it does a lookup on the source and destination addresses in the packet header to see if it has already identified the End Systems participating in this particular communications. If it has not, it adds these new addresses to its internal table.

All new frames that have been received and identified are used to update counters that are kept in the device memory. At periodic intervals (or when the internal memory has been filled), the *Sensor/Filter* transmits all of its stored data to the *Collector/Reporter*. This is a much larger system that includes disk storage, to which the monitor data can be written. Since the disk is much larger than the internal memory of the *Sensor/Filter*, the data can accumulate there and be stored for much longer recording intervals. Also, the data from multiple *Sensor/Filter* devices can be stored by a single *Collector/Report*. This lowers the overall cost of the system, as well as permitting higher performance to be achieved by distributing the compute-intensive sensing and filtering functions among a number of *Sensor/Filter* devices. The *Collector/Reporter* has the ability to merge data from a number of sources into a single database.

As required, a *User Interface* system can be used to invoke the *Collector/Reporter* and perform queries on the database of monitor information. Several sample reports resulting from such queries are provided. An example of a protocol that allows this form of access for SNMP can be found in Waldbusser, 1991b.

The main advantage of this distributed monitor design is to allow systems of appropriate cost, size, power, etc., to be used for specific functions. This improves performance and lowers the total cost, making this type of monitoring feasible for many applications in which a dedicated system that had to perform all of the functions would not suffice.

3.4.3.2 Sample reports

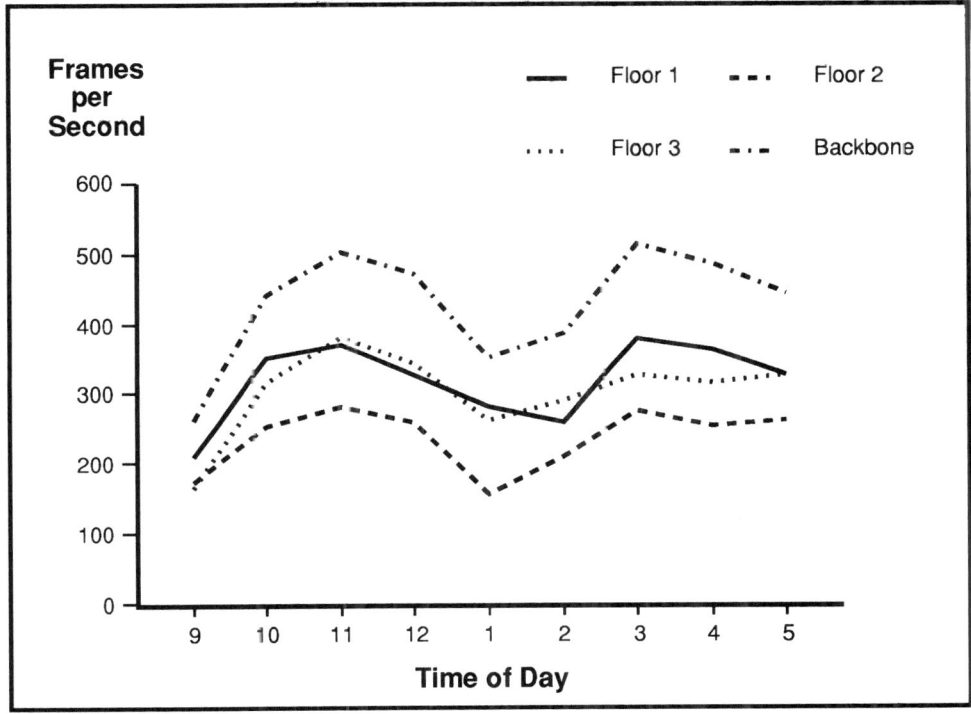

Figure 39 - LAN utilization by segment

This display reports the total utilization on each segment of a LAN configuration over the course of a single work day. In this case, the LAN consists of three segments (one per floor in a building), connected by a backbone segment. The floors are separated from the backbone by bridges, which isolate the traffic local to the segment from the backbone. The information in this report could be very helpful in planning the configuration of the network, such as where to install new End Systems, or where to place repeaters or bridges. For example, in this particular installation there is a significant amount of traffic over the building backbone. A more careful analysis of the source and destination of the traffic on the backbone might indicate that End Systems could be relocated onto the same segment to reduce the load on the backbone.

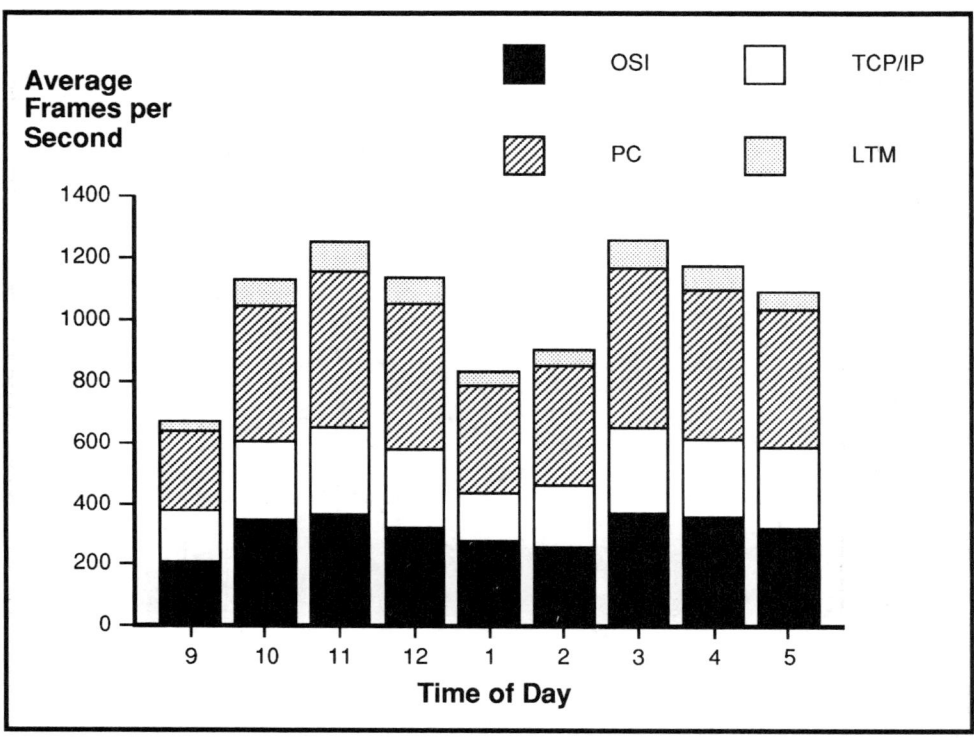

Figure 40 - LAN utilization by protocol type

This display reports the amount of traffic being generated on the LAN for each protocol type over the course of a single workday. On this LAN, four protocol types are in use: OSI, TCP/IP, a PC networking protocol, and the protocol used by the LAN Traffic Monitor itself for reporting. The data is reported at hourly intervals, providing an average count (over the preceding hour) in frames per second for each protocol type. In this case, it can be seen that the proportion of network traffic of each protocol type is fairly uniform over the course of the day. It can also be seen that the traffic falls off significantly during the lunch hour, and that this decrease is more noticeable for TCP/IP than for the other protocol types.

Information of this nature can be used effectively in network configuration planning. In this example, the load on the network could be reduced significantly by providing a separate LAN for PC traffic. It would be difficult to anticipate the results of such a configuration change without the benefit of the monitor data.

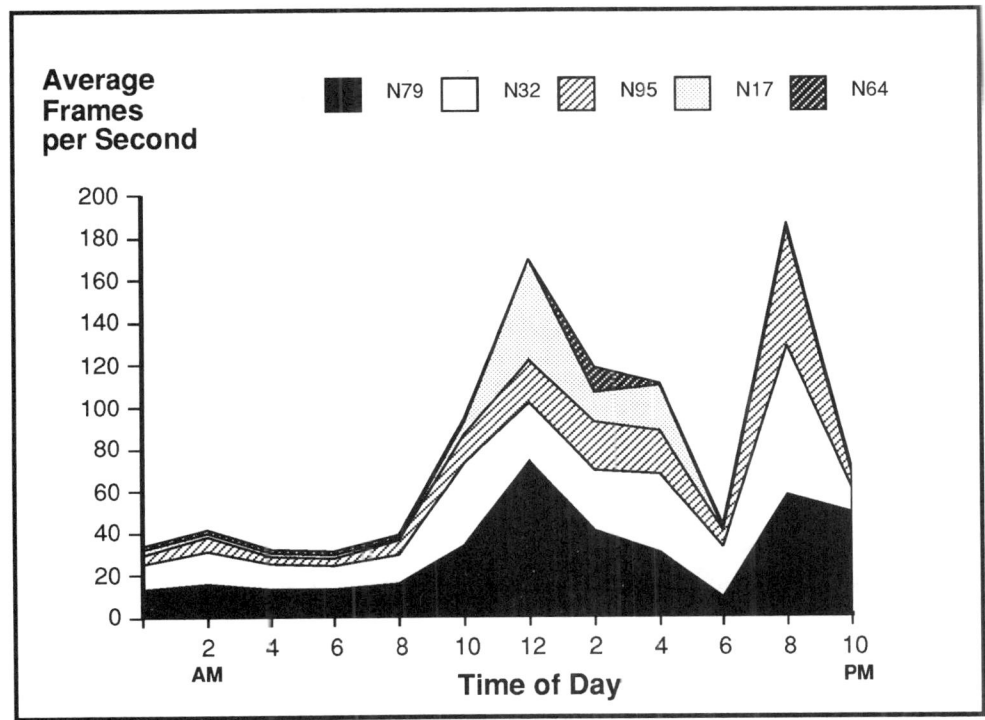

Figure 41 - Top five sources

This display reports the top five sources of data on a LAN segment. It reveals which End Systems are generating the most traffic. A complementary report could provide information on the top destinations of network traffic. This information on network loading and traffic patterns is helpful in configuration and capacity planning. The relative loading over the course of the day is also of some interest, because it can be used to identify periods of lighter resource utilization, which could be used in planning job execution. For example, in this particular case there is a peak load coming from a few systems around 10:00 P.M. that is probably the result of some batch operation, such as a network file backup. It can also be seen that there is very little network utilization during the period from midnight to 8:00 A.M. By moving some of the file backup operations back a few hours, the traffic load would be better balanced and the peak load would be reduced.

3.4.4 A network workload monitor

This section describes a sophisticated system (Sudama & Chiu, 1990) designed to monitor application workloads in a mixed LAN/WAN environment. Managing such environments effectively requires understanding the nature of the distributed activities and accounting for them according to the users and applications that initiated them. This information is often readily available in networks based on connection-oriented protocols, if one has the ability to monitor the network at this level.

A connection is the means by which two processes communicate with each other. Some network architectures also provide higher-level associations between communicating processes, such as sessions and application-level associations in OSI. To the extent that the application-specific information in the connection control messages is formalized (such as is the case when a session layer exists) it is also possible to capture information about the applications using the connections.

For management purposes, the following aspects of a connection are typically of interest:

1. the application, or purpose of the connection,
2. the user who started it;,
3. the geography of the connection (initiator and target addresses and any path information),
4. the duration of the connection, and
5. the activity statistics (number of packets, acks, in each direction).

In a circuit-switched world, it is relatively easy for a telephone system to keep track of telephone connections since connections are directly layered on to circuits in the infrastructure. In a packet-switched network, the packets that correspond to a connection are interleaved with other packets. Thus the monitor must process each packet and attribute its contribution to the right connection.

The design of a monitor capable of capturing network connections in real time can be quite challenging. The major difficulty is to be able to handle the tremendously bursty network traffic on a LAN. Not only must all packets be read into the monitor system, but the protocol information contained in each packet must be interpreted so that they can be identified, classified, and attributed meaningfully. In addition, various accounting records (connection records and others) must be updated, some displayed and some logged when requested.

3.4.4.1 Design overview

As described in the previous section, the goal of the monitor is to capture all network connections. Each connection involves two parties, an *initiator* and a *target*[1]. By promiscuously listening to all packets (or at least, the packet headers) on a LAN segment, it is possible to capture all connections initiated from and targeted to that segment.

Assuming there were enough memory and processing power, one could imagine that the monitor maintains a record for every connection that ever occurs. As each packet comes by, the monitor processes the packet and updates the record of the connection to which the packet belongs.

In reality, there is not likely to be enough processing power using a single processor, and there is not enough memory to keep all of the connection records over any useful period of time. Also, the total processing is composed of separate operations with different urgency. For example, receiving a packet from the wire normally has the highest urgency; the storage of connection records onto non-volatile storage has relatively lower urgency. It is most helpful to group the processing of these different types of operations into different tasks.

The specific tasks in the monitor design are illustrated in Figure 42.

---

[1] We use the terms *initiator* node and *target* node to indicate the two nodes involved in a particular connection. It is important to distinguish these from the terms commonly used in communications, *source* and *destination*, which apply on a per-message basis, and not for an entire connection.

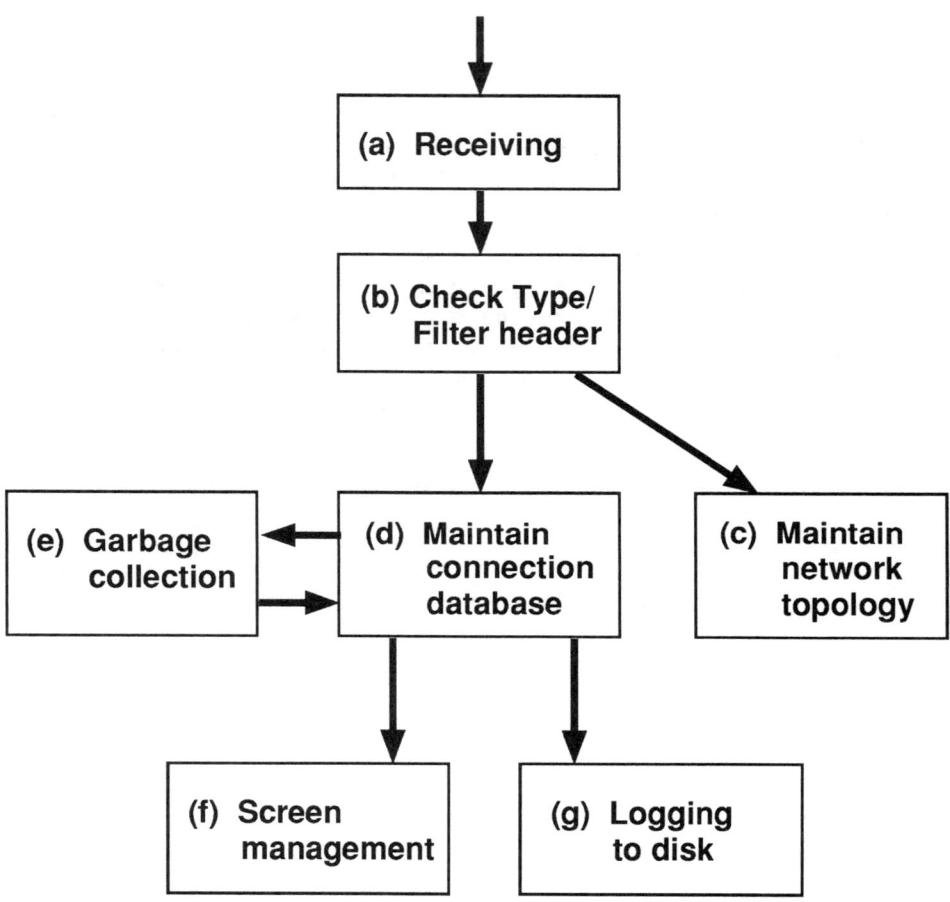

Figure 42 - Tasks performed by a workload monitor

The most challenging part of the design is to identify these tasks, map them onto off-the-shelf processors, and schedule them to minimize the loss of information.

The use of multiple processors can help achieve real-time performance through pipelining. The network adapter listens to the Ethernet in promiscuous mode. A micro-programmable adapter is used to execute tasks (a) "Receiving" and (b) "Check Type/Filter header". The adapter is programmed to pick up only the packet headers containing the actual network protocol information, ignoring any user data that is included in the packets. It also filters out packets of the wrong protocol types. The packet headers are then put into a ring buffer for the device driver running on the main processor. All the rest of the tasks (c through g) are executed on the main processor as one user-level process.

As far as performance is concerned, the capacity of the monitor is limited by the speed at which the processor can perform tasks (c), (d) and (e).

Scheduling the remaining tasks to run on one processor requires care. In this design, actually, no dynamic information is displayed (i.e. task (f), "Screen Management" is null). Any network control packet is passed to task (c), "Maintain network topology". The connection control messages are all passed to task (d), "Maintain connection database", which is the heart of the whole system. Task (d)'s flow is as follows:

1. identify the connection this packet belongs to; if none, create one by using an empty connection record from the free queue.
2. process the packet and update the affected connection record.
3. if from this packet the connection is known to be terminating, then submit a handle of this connection to an output queue for task (g), "Logging to disk".

After task (g), "Logging to disk", finishes writing out the connection record to disk, it places the record in a queue for task (e), "Garbage collection". It is the job of the garbage-collector to keep cleaning up previously used connection records and recirculate them to the free queue. The division of these operations into separate tasks is motivated by the fact that output and garbage-collection take a relatively large amount of processing time compared to processing the packets. The internal scheduling gives packet processing higher priority to avoid losing any packets during a burst arrival.

3.4.4.2 Connection record identification

Generally speaking, the monitor processor is mostly utilized by task (d) "Maintain connection database". Other than the protocol decoding part, the most critical operation in the tight loop is to identify and locate the appropriate connection record.

The key that uniquely identifies the connection to which a packet belongs (unique over a reasonable interval) is the combination of the initiator's address and the connection identifier that it assigns.

connection key = <initiator address, connection identifier>

Whenever a new connection is identified by the monitor, a record of events for that connection is created in the dynamic memory. In most cases, this happens when the first Connect Initiate message for the connection occurs. However, in some cases it occurs at some time after the Connect Initiate message has been sent, either because the event occurred before the monitoring was started, or because the Connect Initiate message was missed by the monitor for some reason. Records of such connections are specially marked and are handled differently in the statistical reports, as will be described later.

At the time the connection record is created, the connection key is written into the record header. For all packets that are observed by the monitor, two keys are computed: one consisting of the source address and the source connection identifier, the other consisting of the destination address and the destination connection identifier. Both of these keys are compared against all of the stored connection keys. When a match is found, it indicates not only the connection with which the packet is associated, but also the direction of the packet, that is, whether it was transmitted by the initiator node or the target node.

Since the space of possible connection keys is much larger than the typical number of active connection records in the monitor, a hashing function is used to locate connection records. The selection of the hashing function is a trade-off between the search time and the available dynamic memory space in the monitor. When a collision occurs on a lookup, it is necessary to search down the list of connections associated with that index. Processing the list is much more time consuming than simply indexing into the table, so the larger the table is, the more efficient the search will be.

3.4.4.3 Connection states and termination

Another important aspect of recording and classifying connection events is the ability to recognize the states through which a connection transitions. It is not possible, however, for the monitor to infer the actual states of the nodes involved in a connection simply by observing the messages which are exchanged. For example, a message might have been sent from one node which never reached the other node due to some problem with the network. Since the packet would be observed by the monitor it would have to assume that it reached its destination, when in fact this was not the case. The actual state of the destination node and the state that would be inferred by the monitor would therefore differ.

Furthermore, the total number of states that a connection could be in would be the Cartesian product of all of the states that the initiator node could possibly be in and all of the states that the target node could possibly be in. Even if it were possible to infer all of these states, it is a level of detail that is not generally useful. Instead, the monitor uses its own set of connection states, which correspond to the following:

1. CONNECT_RECEIVED : A Connect Initiate message with a connection key that is not currently active is observed by the monitor.

2. RUNNING : A Connect Confirm message for a connection that was previously in the CONNECT_RECEIVED state has been observed by the monitor.

3. DISCONNECT_INITIATE : A Disconnect Initiate message for a connection that was previously in the RUNNING state has been observed by the monitor.

4. CLOSED : A Disconnect Confirm message for a connection that was previously in the DISCONNECT_INITIATE state has been observed by the monitor.

5. DISCONNECT_REJECT : A Disconnect Initiate message for a connection that was

previously in the CONNECT_RECEIVED state has been observed by the monitor.

6. REJECTED : A Disconnect Confirm message for a connection that was previously in the DISCONNECT_REJECT state has been observed by the monitor.

To account for connections that either started before the monitoring began, or were still open when the monitoring ended, another variable is maintained for each connection that indicates one of the following conditions:

1. NOT_TERMINATED : The connections had not terminated by the time the monitoring ended.

2. NOT_STARTED : The Connect Initiate message for the connections was never observed by the monitor, and is presumed to have been sent before the monitoring began.

3. COMPLETED : A Connect Initiate message for the connection was observed, and it terminated properly by the time the monitoring ended.

For doing statistical analysis for network applications only the data for COMPLETED connections is used (although the data for all connections is recorded in the output of the monitor). One effect of this that should be noted is that any connections which last for a long time relative to the length of time that monitoring is done may not be contained within the recording period and will therefore be ignored in our reports. This effect can be minimized by running the monitor for longer periods.

3.4.4.4 Connection locality

Other than monitoring the network layer activities, the task (c) "Maintain network topology" also maintains a local node database to let task (d) "Maintain connection database" separate the connections into these categories:

1. INITIATOR_LOCAL : The initiator node for the connection is on the same extended LAN as the monitor, but the target node is not.

2. TARGET_LOCAL : The target node for the connection is on the same extended LAN as the monitor, but the initiator node is not.

3. BOTH_LOCAL : Both the initiator node and the target node for the connection are on the same extended LAN as the monitor.

4. NEITHER_LOCAL : Neither the initiator node nor the target node for the connection is on the same extended LAN as the monitor. This situation is also referred to as "route through".

This information helps in understanding the locality of use for various network applications. When connection records are collected at multiple sites in a wide area network, this locality attribute is also helpful in avoiding double-counting of the remote connections.

3.4.4.5 Connection duration

Simply counting the number of bytes or packets transmitted between nodes does not provide an adequate means of characterizing application use. It is desirable to know how long it takes to start each connection, how long the connections last, and how long it takes to terminate them. This is accomplished by recording the times of specific events as observed by the monitor. These timed events include the following:

> *Connect Initiate message*
> *Connect Acknowledge message*
> *Retransmitted Connect Initiate message*
> *Connect Confirm message*
> *Disconnect Initiate message*
> *Disconnect Confirm message*
> *Connection termination*

This set is quite generic for any protocol based on a three-way handshake to establish connections.

The accuracy of the times recorded for these events is limited by the design of the monitor system. Logically speaking, packets are timestamped as they leave task (b) "Check Type/Filter header", so some imprecision is introduced here. More importantly, the clock which is used to generate the timestamps has a resolution of only 10 milliseconds, so there is an unavoidable quantization error. It should also be emphasized that these times represent the times that the events are observed by the monitor, not the times that the events occurred at either of the connection nodes. This difference might be considerable in the case where one or more of the nodes is remote, making it more likely that significant network delays will be introduced.

However, with all of these things taken into account, the event times still provide a reasonably accurate representation of connection characteristics, simply because there is generally a comparatively large amount of time between connection events.

Given the event times, it is possible to generate the following characteristics for each connection:

1. STARTUP_TIME : For completed connections, the time from the first Connect Initiate message to the time of the first Connect Confirm message.

2. REJECT_TIME : For rejected connections, the time from the first Connect Initiate message to the time of the first Disconnect Confirm message.

3. CONNECTION_DURATION : For completed connections, the time from the first Connect Initiate message to the time of the first Disconnect Confirm message.

4. TEARDOWN_TIME : For completed connections, the time from the first Disconnect Initiate message to the time of the first Disconnect Confirm message.

3.4.4.6 Connection activity

For each connection a count is kept by the monitor of the total number of data packets and data bytes transmitted in each direction. This provides a measure of the overall connection activity, as well as giving the average size of packets in use during the connection.

3.4.4.7 Performance

We have described a generic model for implementing a monitor of this nature. We can also consider the actual performance of a real implementation based on this model. In this case, the monitor is designed to record all traffic on an Ethernet LAN segment. Since the Ethernet has a bandwidth of 10 Megabits per second, or slightly in excess of 1 Megabyte per second, this places an upper bound on the amount of traffic that the monitor might encounter. For this analysis, we can assume a minimum packet size of 64 bytes, since that is the smallest packet that can contain any useful amount of protocol information. 8000 such packets per second would consume approximately 40% of the full Ethernet bandwidth. In practice, it is unusual for an Ethernet to be loaded in excess of 40% of capacity at peak load, and to have an average loading in excess of around 20%.

The basic performance goal is simply to keep up with this packet rate, without missing any packets. This means that each task must be given sufficient processing power to prevent its becoming the bottleneck of the monitoring system. In this sense, it is more important to strike an overall balance in the way the monitoring system handles packets, connections, display and logging as a whole. Monitors based on the design described in this section have been implemented using state-of-the-art hardware technology that can achieve an average processing rate of 4000 packets per second.

3.4.4.8 Sample reports

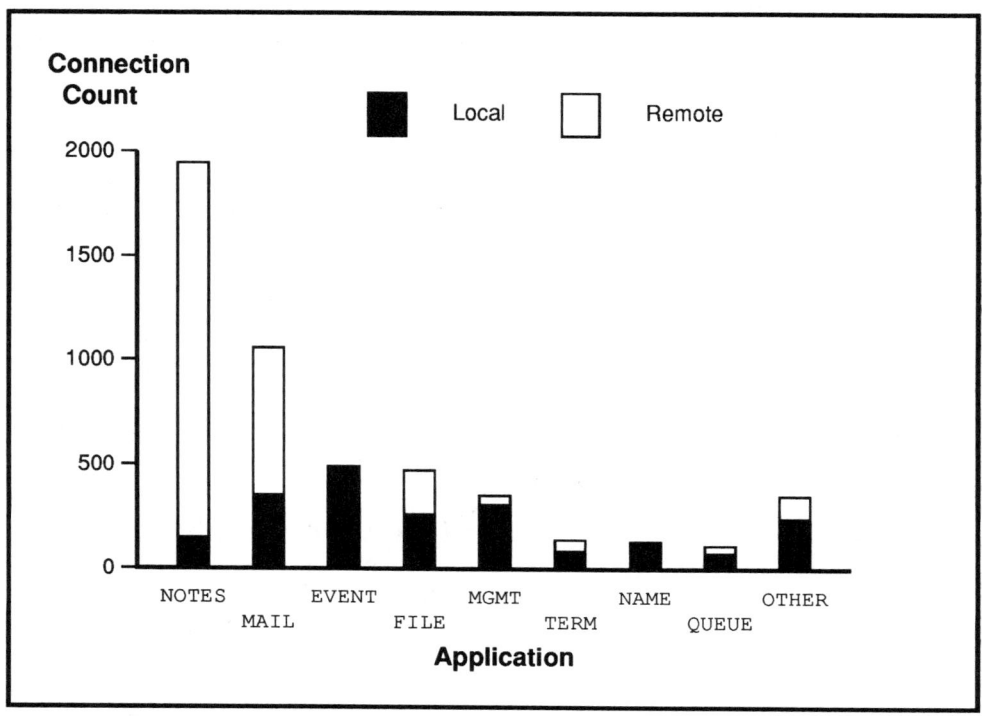

Figure 43 - Total network connections by application

This display reports the total number of connections for each of the top network applications over a given monitoring interval. This information could be very useful for configuration planning, or for some accounting applications. For example, network capacity can more be predicted more accurately based on application usage, if the load put on the network by particular applications is well understood. It is easier to determine the potential load generated by a single application than for the network in general. Data on application loading, combined with actual monitored information on application usage, can be an effective predictor of total network utilization.

In addition, this report indicates for each application the percentage of traffic in the local network, versus traffic going out to remote sites. Again, this information can be very helpful in planning for expansion of the network.

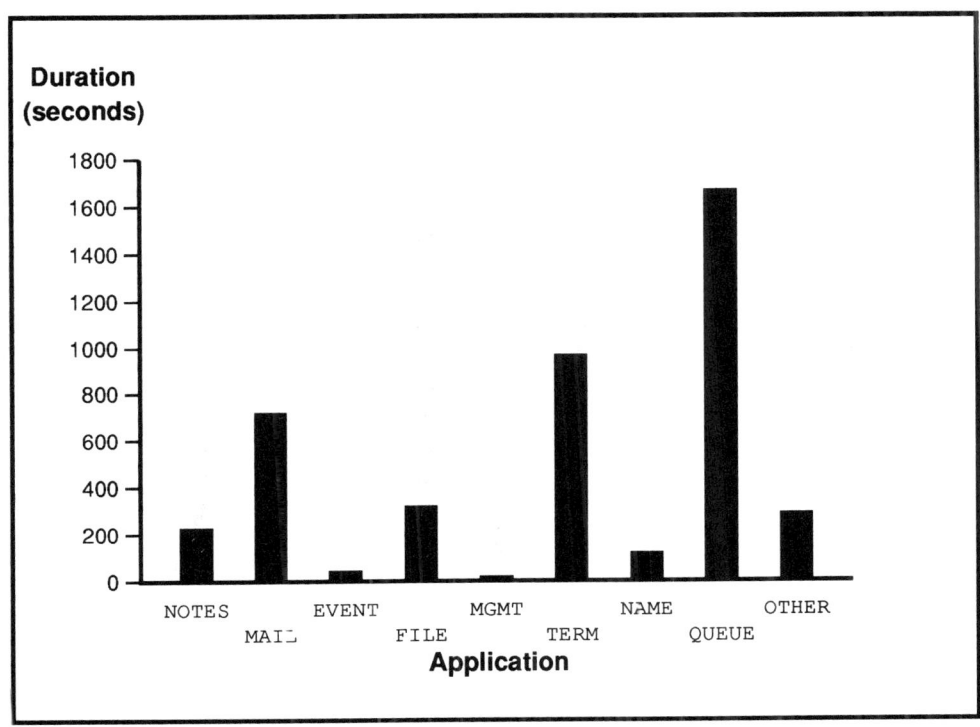

Figure 44 - Average connection duration by application

This display reports the average duration of connections for each of the top network applications over a given monitoring interval. This information can also be used in capacity planning for high availability. Applications with connections of short duration are less likely to be impacted by occasional loss of connectivity in the network.

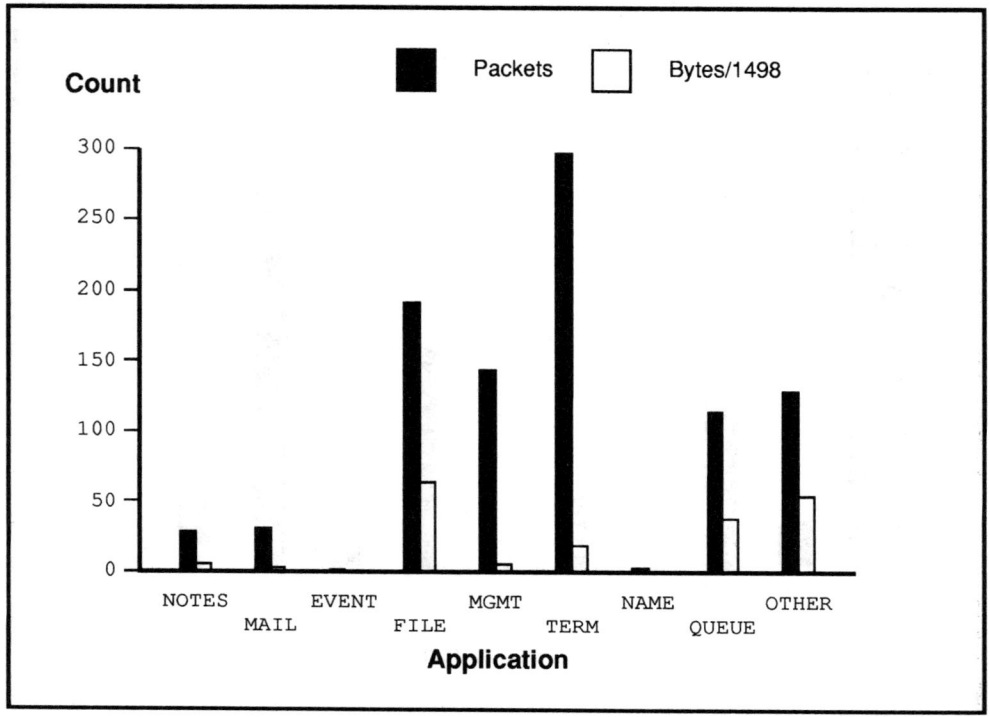

Figure 45 - Average data transfer by application

This display reports the average amount of data transferred by each of the top network applications over a given monitoring interval. It also reports the average number of bytes in a packet for each application. This is an indicator of how efficiently the network is being used by each application, since there is a fixed overhead associated with packet transmission. This information could potentially be used in a redesign of the applications to make their protocols more efficient.

THE DESIGN OF NETWORK MONITORS 125

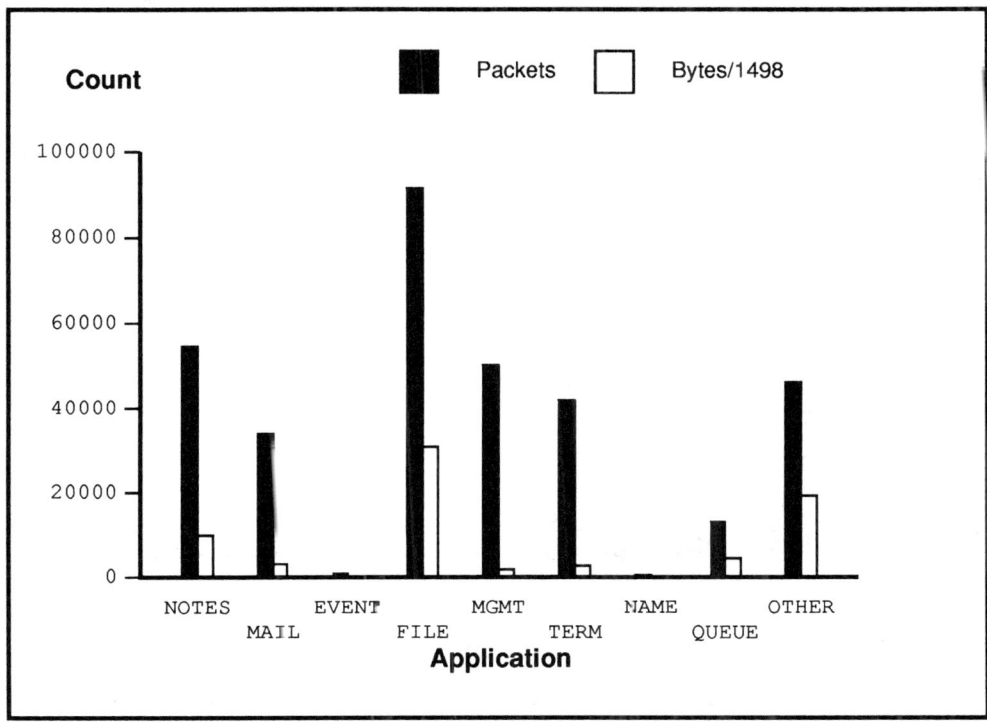

Figure 46 - Total data transfer by application

This display reports the total amount of data transferred by each of the top network applications over a given monitoring interval. This information could be utilized by accounting applications to charge for network usage.

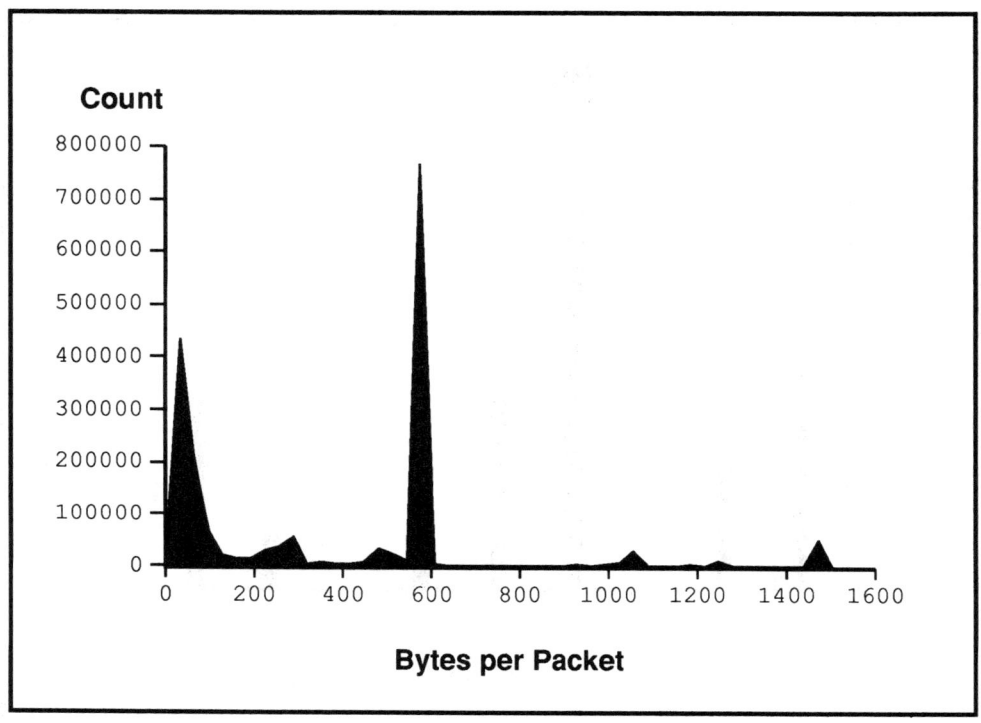

Figure 47 - Network packet size distribution

This display reports the count of packets of all sizes (in bytes) over a given monitoring interval. This is again a good indicator of how efficiently the network is being utilized. In this particular environment, for example, it can be seen that the peaks are for packets of under 100 bytes, and for packets of around 500-600 bytes. Since this is a LAN network with a maximum packet size of 1498 bytes of user data, these packets are relatively small. This means that the network is not being used as efficiently as it could be. This could be a function of the fundamental nature of the network applications, or it could be a function of the application design.

For example, a remote terminal application will typically generate relatively small messages. This is due to the fact that a message will be transmitted on every line termination (on input), to insure acceptable interactive performance. The application could possibly be changed to provide local screen-oriented editing, so that a full screen buffer of data could be sent in a single message.

4

Applications of Network Monitoring

4.1 INTRODUCTION

Network monitoring is a base technology on which a wide variety of management applications can be built. We have already mentioned several of these applications in our previous examples of monitor designs. In this chapter, we will describe some of the more common applications in greater detail.

Among the principle uses of modern computers are data processing and information sharing. From a management standpoint, monitoring is one of the main sources of data regarding the state of the network and its components. As we have discussed, management of networks consists largely of collecting monitor information, analyzing it, and using the resulting knowledge to apply controls to the network to modify its state. This simple model functions at many levels of abstraction, however, and for each level there are different management applications to support this feedback process.

The applications of network monitoring that are described in this chapter fall into the following categories, in terms of the level at which they affect the network:

1. Protocol analysis and tools for debugging distributed software affect the networking software itself, and network applications. Monitoring is used in this context during the design and testing of software to improve the overall quality of service provided by the network.

2. Fault and configuration management affect the physical components of the network, and the network topology. These applications of monitoring affect the operational aspects of the network, and are typically part of the broader network management infrastructure.

3. The use of monitoring for security and accounting purposes has a direct, and often visible, effect on all network users. These applications are approaching end-user services, and will often be tailored to specific customer requirements.

4.2 FRAMEWORKS FOR MANAGEMENT APPLICATIONS

Before getting into the details of the monitoring applications themselves, it should be noted that there are at least two distinctly different environments in which those applications can be developed. Traditionally, most network monitoring applications have been of a "stand-alone" nature. In many cases, they are implemented on specialized hardware, or on dedicated platforms intended specifically for the purpose of running monitoring applications. Even when implemented as more generic applications on a general-purpose operating system, monitoring applications have often been point products with a relative restricted and sophisticated user audience.

Over the past few years, a number of "standard" management frameworks have emerged which are likely to have an impact on future trends in monitoring applications. These frameworks consist of complete network management systems, which provide an environment in which many different management applications can coexist. The principle features of most of these common management frameworks include:

1. A uniform user interface to all applications - This insures a consistent look and feel to the applications, regardless of their functionality, and facilitates the process of learning to use new applications.

2. A common database, and shared object definitions - All management applications can store data in a common repository, and can share information through this mechanism.

3. A consistent communications paradigm - Having a single way of communicating among applications permits them to share control, and allows new applications to be built easily from existing ones.

4. A full set of system services, such as time management, queuing, environment variables, etc. In other words, these frameworks have become operating systems themselves, from the standpoint of the application programmer.

The most important point to be made about management frameworks is that they can permit applications to share information and control almost transparently. For example, a monitoring application could generate output that could be processed directly by a separate configuration management application, or an application which filters events and generates alarms. A single monitoring application could feed information to a number of other applications. Any of these other applications, in turn, could be fed information by a number of applications that were monitoring different aspects of the network.

There is no doubt that stand-alone monitoring applications will continue to be developed for specific purposes. But it is likely that more and more future applications will take advantage of the convenience and flexibility of the broader management frameworks.

4.3 PROTOCOL ANALYSIS AND DESIGN

The development of computer networking software is typically an iterative process. The protocols are designed and implemented based on the projected requirements of the network applications. After the implementation, the software undergoes tests and analysis to see how it performs in a simulated or real-life environment. This evaluation can be used to modify the protocol design and implementation, or make adjustments to the parameters to improve the performance and efficiency of the original design. Network monitoring is an invaluable tool for such design analysis (Bertsekas & Gallager, 1987; and Schwartz, 1987).

In the following, we give several examples of design issues, and then review some network monitoring case studies that have been widely cited in the protocol design literature.

4.3.1 Examples of protocol design and implementation issues

Reliable delivery of packets from one system to another is typically guaranteed by acknowledgment packets sent from the target system back to the initiating system. The initiator buffers the packet it sends out until it receives the acknowledgment, so that if the acknowledgment is not received within an expected (timeout) period, the packet can be resent. To achieve pipelining, the initiator is usually allowed to send multiple packets before waiting for any acknowledgment. The number of simultaneous outstanding packets allowed is called a *window*. Since each acknowledgment packet takes some bandwidth and processing overhead, a sophisticated protocol allows the target system to delay returning the acknowledgment momentarily so that one acknowledgment packet can acknowledge the receipt of several packets; and if the target system also has a data packet to send to the originator, then the acknowledgment packet can be *piggybacked* on the normal data packet traveling on the return path. The implementation of the above design requires a good knowledge of application level behavior. For example:

1. What timeout value should the originating system use before it decides to resend an unacknowledged packet?
2. What delay should the target system use to minimize the number of acknowledgment packets?
3. What should be the window size, the number of simultaneous unacknowledged packets?

In sophisticated protocols, these parameters are often designed to adapt to the dynamic behavior of the application and the network. For example, in case (1), the intelligent answer for when to timeout would depend on the expected time for a packet to successfully reach the target and an acknowledgment to come back, which is called the *round-trip delay*. It is possible to estimate the expected round-trip delay based on previous round-trips, which is typically built into the software. The actual algorithm for estimating the round-trip delay, and the selection of initial values for the timeout interval, would benefit greatly from a knowledge of how the network is configured and how the network applications behave.

In case (2), an intelligent choice would depend on the likelihood of additional packet arrivals (in either direction). If it is unlikely that there is any opportunity for acknowledging multiple packets or piggybacking on a data packet on the return path, then it is more beneficial to send the acknowledgment right away. In deciding whether to use delayed acknowledgment, and how much to delay, one would benefit from an insight into the pattern of packet exchanges for a typical connection.

In case (3), the window size is often adjusted continuously, depending on the dynamic condition of the buffering space available at the two communicating systems. The potential for pipelining in the network path also need to be taken into consideration. This function is called *flow control* or *pacing*, in networking terminology. The design of the flow control algorithm, and the selection of the initial window size, require a lot of knowledge of application and network behavior.

Another fundamental design issue has to do with preventing and recovering from congestion. A computer network consists of many shared resources. During normal usage, only a small percentage of users would use the network simultaneously at any given moment. This normal usage pattern determines the capacity of the network[1]. When a large number of users happen to use the network simultaneously, triggered by some external event, the network experiences congestion. Severe congestion can sometimes completely paralyze a network, just like a gridlock of automobile traffic during rush hour. The algorithms for preventing as well as recovering from congestion are all based on slowing down the demand for the critical resources. A *congestion avoidance* scheme prevents congestion by continuously monitoring the network and slowing down the demand as soon as the network resources begin to experience congestion. A *congestion control* scheme recovers from congestion by removing the load and restarting everything very slowly. The effectiveness and efficiency of these algorithms depends on the behavior of the applications and the configuration of the network. Usually, these algorithms are designed by modeling the application behavior and using it to simulate the effectiveness of the algorithm under various common network configurations.

Another area of algorithmic design that generated years of research and debate is the protocols for multi-access media. In a sense, this is a special case of the congestion problem with the exception that the shared resource, the transmission medium, must be used by only one End System at a time. The more widely deployed versions of these protocols, CSMA/CD (Carrier Sense Multi-Access with Collision Detection, also known as Ethernet, which was later standardized as IEEE 802.3), Token Bus (IEEE 802.4) and Token Ring (IEEE 802.5) solve the resource sharing problem differently, yielding different levels of performance (delay), capacity (throughput), fairness and robustness, at different load levels. There are many more variations than those implemented in these standardized protocols, each emphasizing certain requirements above others. The motivations for these different designs, and the true basis for comparing them, are all derived from an understanding of how to optimize the overall

---

[1] How this is done is discussed in a separate section on performance and configuration management.

performance of the network applications.

4.3.2 Review of protocol performance studies

4.3.2.1 A case study of LAN traffic

Shoch & Hupp, 1980 is one of the earliest and most widely quoted studies of LAN workload characteristics. The results were based on monitoring an Ethernet LAN, then a state-of-the-art technology. The paper reported monitoring results from both a real-life environment as well as *controlled* experiments. The method of measurement used was a monitoring station that passively listened to all packets traveling on the LAN. This represents an early version of the passive LAN monitors.

The measurements based on real-life environments considered the following aspects:

- Utilization: Very light utilization levels were observed. On a daily basis, the utilization was between 0.6% to 0.8%. But for shorter intervals, utilization levels could be considerably higher: as much as 3.6% over the busiest hour; 17% over the busiest minute; and 37% in the busiest second. Utilization levels of this nature were the norm in the early days of LAN deployment. Over the next ten years, as the traditional time-sharing system paradigm was gradually surpassed by the distributed systems paradigms with the availability of terminal servers, file servers, remote windowing servers and remote printing, LAN traffic volume has seen significant increases.

- Packet length: This is one of the most interesting results given in this paper. The knowledge of packet length distribution is one of the key parameters in modeling the Ethernet to predict its capacity and delay characteristics. The packet length distribution was usually assumed to be *exponentially* distributed as shown in Figure 48. This distribution is most convenient for analytical modeling and analysis. The results from measuring the real-life environment showed a bimodal distribution, also shown in Figure 48. This led to more detailed simulation studies of the Ethernet (Metcalfe & Boggs, 1976).

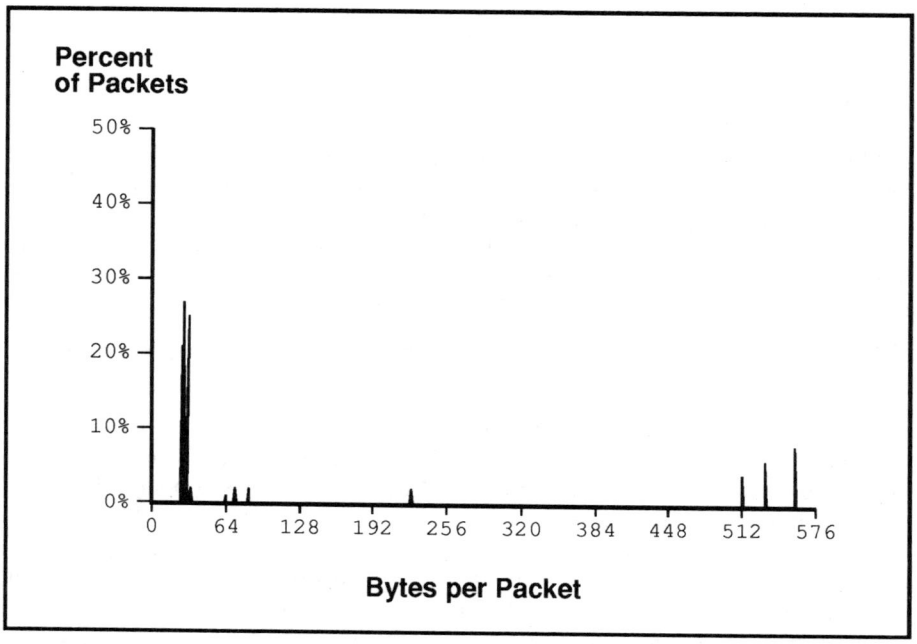

Figure 48 - Distribution of packet lengths

- Traffic patterns: Two observations were made here. First, it was observed that approximately 72% of the traffic was between systems connected by the same Ethernet, and the rest was between a system on the Ethernet and some other system connected with the Ethernet through a WAN. This observation turns out to be a very good rule of thumb. Many subsequent performance studies of LAN environments also found the LAN/WAN traffic division to be roughly an 80/20 or 70/30 split. The second observation was that most of the traffic involved one of the few servers on the LAN. This observation also withstood the test of time - it is still the traffic pattern on LANs today (Chiu & Sudama, 1987; Paxson 1991; and Caceres, *et al* 1991).

- Inter-packet arrival times: This is another important parameter for the performance models. For the convenience of analytical models, the distribution of inter-packet arrival times was also often assumed to be exponentially distributed. This study showed the actual distribution, which was close to, but different than, an exponential distribution, and explained the behavior. Another performance study that we will review later goes into much more detail on this topic (Jain & Routhier, 1986).

- Latency and Collisions: These observations were made from a single sender, rather than by using a monitor as the other tests. Again due to low traffic volume, collisions were extremely rare; and there was usually zero latency. Nevertheless, these are two very important metrics. At the time, these could only be studied by relying on controlled (or artificial) experiments.

The observations from the controlled experiments were mainly relating to the issues of stability and the theoretical maximum capacity of the Ethernet. Ethernet relies on a distributed back-off algorithm to arbitrate the use of the shared transmission medium. Inherent in the algorithm is some wasted bandwidth due to collisions and randomized back-off. The crucial questions were whether under extremely adverse loading, the wasted bandwidth would be so high that effectively no useful traffic is serviced (this is the stability question); and assuming the algorithm is stable, what is the percentage of the network bandwidth consumed by useful traffic (this is the maximum capacity question). There is also the concrete question of how to bound the delays seen by a sending system in heavy load situations.

The simple-minded analytical models (Metcalfe & Boggs, 1976) predicted that the Ethernet was stable and could achieve a maximum capacity of approximately 40% of the original bandwidth (limited by the transmission speed which is 10 megabits per second). This analysis, however, was based on the exponential distributions and an assumption that there are an infinite number of systems sharing the Ethernet. The measured results from this paper indicated that the true maximum capacity was very much dependent on how many stations are simultaneously sharing the use of the Ethernet, and the packet lengths. The measured maximum capacity was summarized by the following table.

| | Packet lengths | | | | |
Number of systems	512	128	64	6	4
5	97%	95%	94%	72%	
10	97%	91%	89%	68%	58%
32	97%	90%	83%	64%	56%
64	97%	92%	85%	61%	54%

4.3.2.2 Packet trains - a model of network traffic based on measurement

Jain & Routhier, 1986 reported the results of extensive measurements of network traffic, and studied the temporal arrival behavior of network packets. The conclusion was that network packets tend to arrive in a sequence, like a multiple-wagon train. The authors then described the various characteristics of the train model based on the measurement data.

In many modeling studies of computer network or network components, the packet arrival process is assumed to be *Poisson*. This means that the time between two arrivals are random (following an exponential probability distribution), and the time between the arrival of one pair of packets is independent of the time between another pair of arrivals. In reality, it has long been realized that packets arrivals tend to be more bursty. Therefore, the *Poisson* model is often extended to allow a number (possibly random) of packets to arrive at each arrival instance. Both of these variations of *the Poisson* model require additional parameters (for the probability distributions) to be used in a modeling study.

The study by Jain and Shawn achieved two purposes. First, it demonstrated how the *Poisson* models deviate from real-world measurements, and proposed an alternative model that more closely reflects what was observed. This does not necessarily negate the usefulness of the *Poisson* models, since the new model is not as amenable to abstract analysis as the *Poisson* models. A second contribution, however, is that the study provided insight into what the parameters of the train model are, which can also be used to determine what parameter to use for the corresponding *Poisson* model as approximation to the train model.

The paper pointed out the following applications of the train model:

1. Protocol modeling,
2. Predicting the likelihood of the next packet destined for the same target,
3. Determining the number of buffers in routers/gateways/bridges,
4. Determining when to stop a temporary circuit (also known as a *dynamic circuit*), and
5. Determine whether reservation switching is suitable.

4.3.2.3 Measurement of network application behavior

Chiu & Sudama (1988) published a study of applications and network protocol behavior based on monitoring the DEC corporate network. More recently, Paxson, (1991), and Caceres, *et al* (1991) also reported results of similar kind of study based on measurement and monitoring on the Internet backbone. A common thread is that these papers characterize how network applications utilize the underlying network infrastructure.

There had always been a crude characterization of network application into two broad categories: terminal traffic and file transfer traffic. Terminal traffic is interactive, with a human user. It is characterized by relatively long sessions with many requests and responses, and the flow from the human end typically consists of small packets. File transfer traffic, on the other hand, is characterized by a long sequence of back-to-back packets, the size of the sequence being dependent on the size of the file. These more comprehensive studies of the whole suite of network applications give a much clearer view of what the design center for a network ought to be.

The following figures show the mixture of applications in each of the three case studies:

APPLICATIONS OF NETWORK MONITORING   135

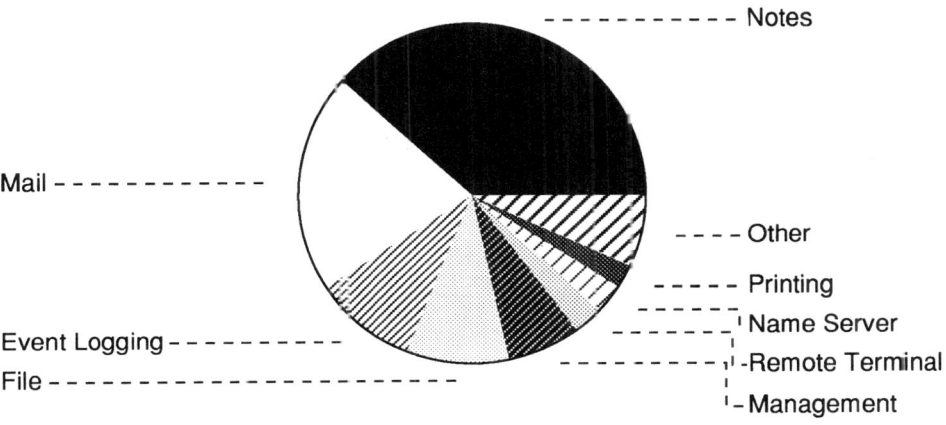

136 CHAPTER 4

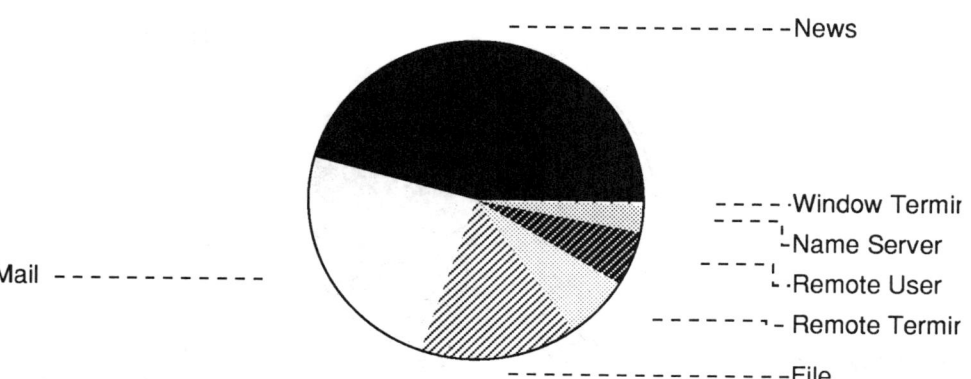

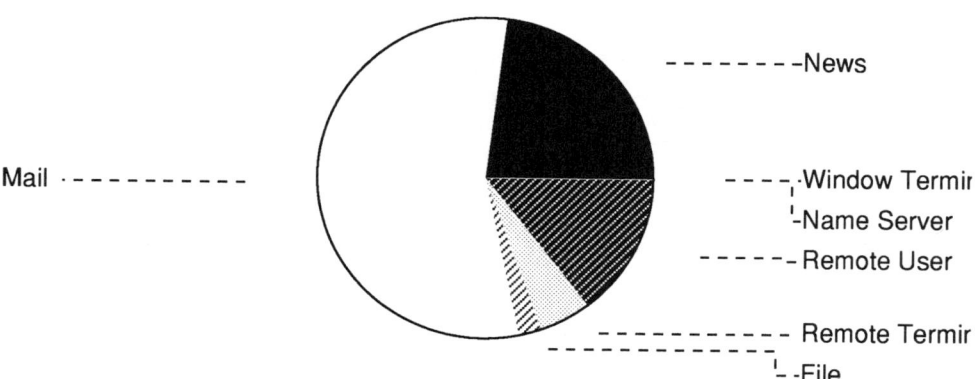

Although the studies were done in different environments and at different times, there are a lot of similarities in the mixture of network application types. The data from Chiu & Sudama, 1988 included all network applications originating on or destined to the LAN, so it comprised both LAN and WAN sessions. The other two studies observed only WAN sessions, so certain LAN applications, such as shared-printing, were not analyzed in these studies.

The way these applications use network resources was considered by the different authors using similar metrics. The following aspects were typically captured:

- (Relative) frequency of sessions/connections invoked by a given application type.
- Amount of data transferred in each direction, in terms of the number of packets and number of bytes
- Duration of the sessions/connections
- Locality of the sessions/connections

In Paxson, 1991 and Caceres *et al*, 1991 the measured data for each category was used to derive statistical properties (average, standard deviation and a "best fit" probability distribution).

The conclusion of these papers can be summarized in the following two categories:

1. Such measurement data and application characterization can be used for protocol design, implementation and optimization. Chiu & Sudama, 1988 indicated how their measurements were used to assess how various protocol features (such as delayed acknowledgment, piggybacked acknowledgment, on/off flow control and congestion control) performed in real LAN and WAN environments. Caceres, *et al*, 1991 indicated that the study of application mix is very useful for the problem of multiplexing application datagram traffic over wide-area virtual circuits. This problem is especially relevant with the advent of high-speed Asynchronous Transfer Mode (ATM) networks. In such networks, the traditional datagram traffic (which was characterized in these measurement studies) needs to be mapped into ATM virtual circuits in a way that provides adequate performance, as well as maintaining high bandwidth utilization. A good traffic model would be useful for designing this mapping.

2. Such network monitoring and analysis techniques can be used for network management, design and capacity planning. In Paxson, 1991, the author described two separate measurements, one in November of 1990 and one in March of 1991. Based on the change in the observed data, the author was able to predict certain trends and characterize the growth in resource and capacity requirements. Chiu & Sudama, 1988 also indicated the use of session monitoring on a continuous basis to do accounting and capacity planning.

4.4 TESTING AND DEBUGGING DISTRIBUTED SOFTWARE

At this time, there are relatively few software applications for networks, compared to the vast number of non-networked computer applications. One of the main reasons for this is that developing distributed applications is much more difficult than normal application development. The network presents many complexities that are unfamiliar to most programmers, and many of the existing software implementation tools are inadequate to deal with them effectively. Some of these complexities are:

1. Independent failure of components - In a non-distributed environment, components are likely to fail together. For example, if a program calls a subroutine, and the system fails during execution of the subroutine, both the caller and the subroutine will stop executing. In a distributed environment, however, it is possible that the system on which the subroutine is executing might fail, but the system on which the calling program is executing might continue to operate. In this case, if the calling program can detect the failure of the other system, it might be able to recover from this failure and try to execute the subroutine again on a different system. The programmer must be conscious of the different semantics of failure in cases such as this, and plan for them accordingly.

2. Lack of shared address space or data storage - It is common in software to take advantage of features such as global variables and shared files to facilitate communications within an application. Many of these traditional methods simply won't work, or will work differently, in the case of distributed software. For example, there is no shared memory between systems on a network, so any state information that needs to be shared must be communicated explicitly over the network.

3. Signaling, or interrupt handling - These facilities, which are typically provided by the operating system, must be extended to function over the network. Again, to achieve equivalent functionality in an application it may be necessary to include such features in the application protocol.

4. Crossing security domains - Non-distributed applications generally operate in a security context that is managed by a single operating system, and therefore have a relatively uniform environment to contend with. Programmers can often take these services for granted, and can largely ignore security considerations within their applications. Distributed applications, by their nature, cross security domains, and this raises a number of issues which often must be dealt with directly in the applications. Features such as authentication, authorization and encryption must be added to applications to provide a level of security equivalent the non-distributed application.

5. Concurrency - For the most part, non-distributed applications are serial in nature. That is, there is little benefit to designing concurrency into the application, unless it is to take advantage of some performance improvements possible in a

multi-processor system. In this case, automated tools (such as special compilers) are usually required to take advantage of the the fine-grained nature of the parallelism. Distributed applications, on the other hand, can often use the multiplicity of systems in a network to great advantage, executing many operations concurrently to improve performance and reduce execution time. This level of concurrency is much more likely to be directly under the control of the application developer, and is an important part of effective design for distribution.

6. Time synchronization - Since non-distributed applications run on a single system, they have to contend with only a single concept of time, which is maintained by the system. Events can therefore be easily ordered with respect to this common clock. Distributed applications, on the other hand, have to accommodate that fact that different systems will have different concepts of time, since there is no easy way for them to coordinate their clocks. Several protocols have emerged which permit some level of clock synchronization among systems on a network, but there are practical limitations on how highly this can be achieved. Application developers must be cognizant of the degree to which they depend on synchronization among system clocks, the level of synchronization available in target networks, and the consequences of losing synchronization on the application and the data it manages.

7. Differences in datatype representation - Over time a number of different representations of data have been developed, for reasons both practical and arbitrary. For example, there are "big endian" and "little endian" integers, ASCII, EBCDIC (and now multibyte) characters, various representations of floating point numbers, etc. As long as one was operating on a single system, or among systems from a vendor or vendors who shared the same data representations, this presented no problem. But as more and more systems are taking advantage of network communications, and network environments become increasingly heterogeneous with respect to equipment from multiple vendors, the differences in data representation have become a major obstacle to information sharing.

Fortunately, new service are being defined such as Remote Procedure Call (RPC), and other presentation level translation services, which can automate the conversion of data from one format to another. However, to the extent that these services are not available, or are not entirely transparent, the application developer must be aware of and possibly perform these conversions.

8. Non-distributed tools - Further complicating the job of the distributed application developer is the fact that most existing software tools were not designed for distributed operation. This includes editors, compilers, linkers, debuggers, source management and build management facilities, etc. Not only are many of the tools not distributed, but the user interface and behavior are likely to vary significantly from one network platform to another. All of this must be accommodated by the application developer, who may have to use different tools on different platforms to perform the same job.

4.4.1 Distributed vs. non-distributed testing

In many respects, the design, development, testing and deployment of distributed applications is an evolving science. Testing and debugging, in particular, are areas in which new techniques and tools are constantly emerging. This trend is likely to continue at least through the next decade, as more and more distributed applications are introduced.

Most of the current methods for testing and debugging distributed applications are based on those used for non-distributed software. The tools vary depending on the stage of development of the software. For example, during the implementation stage, it is common to use compilers for syntax checking, software debuggers for unit testing of code, source code analyzers and runtime path tracing tools to aid in performance optimizations, etc. During the integration and system testing phases it is likely that more automated test systems, such as regression test suites, would be used. Locating and correcting faults in deployed software might depend more on application-generated error messages and system memory dumps.

To some extent, these existing tools can be adapted for use in distributed application development. Compilers may be enhanced to automate the creation of code involved with communications, such as Remote Procedure Call (RPC) compilers, which make many aspects of distribution transparent to the programmer. Multi-window user environments with remote access capabilities make it fairly easy to run multiple instances of traditional debuggers on the same display, providing some coordinated control over the various distributed software components. Automated software test systems can be extended to support the execution of tests on multiple systems in the network. At some point, however, new tools have to be developed to replace the old.

4.4.2 Integrated vs. external monitors for debugging

Both integrated and external monitors have a place in debugging distributed software, but often for different purposes. Because external monitors have limited access to application and system state information, their main use is in testing and debugging protocols. Their ability to trap, analyze and compare, and even generate messages on the network, as described in a previous chapter, makes them ideal for detecting problems in message formats, sequencing and timing that might otherwise be very difficult to detect. Of special utility is the fact that they can often monitor the activity of multiple systems, whereas integrated monitors are, by definition, limited to examining the activities visible on a single End System.

As an example, consider a scenario in which a defect in some application program causes it to go into a state in which it generates an extraordinarily large number of messages on the network. This state transition is caused by some particular sequence of messages the application receives from other End Systems. In turn, the messages generated by this instance of the application causes other instances to enter the same state. The result is a flood of messages on the network, bringing normal operations almost to a standstill. This situation is referred to as a network "storm".

In a case like this it is difficult to even detect the onset of the storm, much less determine its cause, without an external monitor. If properly configured, the external monitor can capture all messages leading up to the beginning of the storm, identify the application instance responsible for initiating it, and help in identifying the specific sequence of events that triggered the debacle. This analysis would be very difficult to carry out otherwise.

Integrated monitors, on the other hand, are often more suited to software debugging activities, and can be more easily tailored to specific application requirements. Because they can potentially have access to system and application state information that is not visible on the network, they may be able to isolate problems that could not be solved with external monitoring. For example, as we mentioned earlier, external monitors have only a second-hand view of timing information. They can detect when certain events appeared on the network, but not when they actually originated or terminated on some End System. An integrated monitor might have access to the system clock, and be able to detect events directly at their point of origination or termination. They can therefore capture and much more accurate representation of the timing and sequencing of events.

There are numerous other examples of state that may be accessible to an integrated monitor that could be useful in debugging software. In addition, the control and output of an integrated monitor is possibly more consistent with other tools familiar to the application developer. In general, their ability to more closely monitor events and coordinate with other activities on the system provide integrated monitors with advantages over external monitors for many types of problem solving.

4.4.3 Logging event traces

One of the most common applications of network monitors in debugging is for logging *event traces*. An event trace is a sequence of records, each containing information about a specific event detected by the monitor. This information might include things such as the nature of the event, the time at which it was detected, the source and destination of the activity, and so on. These records are typically written to some form of permanent storage, such as a disk or tape. From there, they can subsequently be read back, processed and analyzed at a convenient time. They can also be processed repeatedly to perform different types of analyses.

Event traces are useful because it is often difficult or impossible to report and analyze events as they occur in real-time. In an application of any significance, so many events are generated in such a short time that special tools are required to filter and process the results. Due to the complexity of these tools, they take much longer to execute than the time period of the events themselves. They can only function, therefore, against input from a previously logged event trace.

4.4.4 Merging event traces

As we have mentioned, one of the limitations on the use of integrated monitors for testing and debugging is that they are constrained to monitoring events on a single End System. To some extent, this limitation can be overcome through the use of event traces. If event traces are captured by integrated monitors on a number of End Systems, they can later be collected and merged into a single trace. This single record of events then provides a unified view of events as they occurred throughout the network.

The main difficulty to be overcome in merging event traces in this manner is resolving the sequencing of events on different systems. Each system will record the time of local events based on its own clock. But in many networks, there is no coordination of these local clocks, and therefore there is an inconsistent definition of time across the network. This makes it impossible to properly determine the order in which events occurred on different systems, since the time value recorded is system-relative.

One solution to this problem is the use of a distributed time service, which keeps the clocks on various systems in close synchronization. If all systems share a common definition of time, then the times recorded in individual event traces can be relied on to properly sequence events when merging the traces. It should be observed, however, that most time distribution protocols cannot guarantee complete consistency of all system clocks. The degree inaccuracy in the time synchronization must be taken into consideration, because it limits the ability to order events reliably. For example, suppose time is synchronized across systems to within 50 milliseconds. The times logged by the monitors can be used when merging event traces, as long as no two events occur within 50 milliseconds of one another. If the recorded times for any two events places them less than 50 milliseconds apart, they cannot be ordered reliably.

4.4.5 Use of event traces in simulation and testing

There are applications for the event traces logged by network monitors other than fault detection and problem solving. Event traces can also be very useful as input to simulation and testing systems.

Due to the distributed nature of state in a communications network, and the complexity of network components, it is very difficult to simulate the behavior of networks of any significant size. What makes this even more challenging is the fairly random nature of events in most network environments. Good simulations require good source data, and one of the best sources is the record of events as logged by monitors in real network configurations.

These traces are also very useful for testing of specific network components and configurations. Previously recorded event traces can be played back in a network test configuration to generate real loads that would otherwise have to be artificially contrived. This helps manufacturers of network components, as well as planners and installers of networks, determine the performance characteristics of particular configurations. It can also help to determine the boundary conditions for effective use of the network by "stress testing" it beyond the point that would be likely to occur in normal use.

4.4.6 Related papers

The following papers discuss various aspects of debugging distributed applications:

>Tokuda et al. (1988)
>Bei (1985)
>Bhatt and Ramanujan (1987)
>Maxion (1986)
>McDaniel (1977)
>Miller et al. (1984)
>Miller and Yang (1987)
>Schiffenbauer (1981)
>Lamport (1978)
>Lampson and Redell (1980)
>Jaffe (1979)
>Svobodova et al. (1979)
>GarciaMolina et al. (1981)
>Stankovic (1980)
>Bates (1989)
>Miller (1985a)
>Baiardi et al. (1983)
>Bates and Wileden (1983)
>Macrander (1984)
>Miller (1985b)

4.5 FAULT AND CONFIGURATION MANAGEMENT

4.5.1 Fault management

Fundamental to fault management is the ability to detect network faults. In Chapter 3, we have already shown the design of an event-logging management application that can be used to keep track of various events. The events that indicate faults in critical components are often referred to as *alarms*. When network faults are detected, a network administrator must have access to various event logs. There are usually separate functions to indicate alarms. The task of isolating and correcting faults is invariably a very difficult task; a well-designed fault management application helps to make this task easier.

Fault management also includes monitoring of the network to prevent faults from occurring. This *pro-active* function is based on monitoring key components in the network to see if they are moving into *danger zones*. Danger zones are defined by setting thresholds on the attributes and states of managed objects. The monitoring can be done either by both polling or event reporting. The following table gives examples of some definitions of thresholds on generic components.

Object type	*Attribute/Event*	*Threshold*	*Explanation*
Node	number of sessions	100	application-dependent used to indicate node is busy
Node's line	utilization	70%	possible congestion
Router	state	non-operating	must be down or re-init
Bridge's line	collision rate	10%	possible LAN congestion

Figure 49 - Defining thresholds for fault prevention

4.5.2 Configuration management

There is a large set of management applications that fall into the category of *configuration management*. These include tools that help network administrators keep track of an *inventory* of what nodes are being managed, what communications hardware and software these nodes are using, their licenses, their locations, and how they are connected to the network. Some of these information management functions are generic database operations required in many resource management tasks, and do not need support from network monitoring. Other aspects do rely on monitoring of the network. For example, some network applications provide a facility to detect the location of devices on a LAN. Also, a lot of the information in the inventory database can be derived automatically by using network management protocols.

Configuration management goes hand-in-hand with fault management. Faulty conditions are often caused by misconfiguration. To isolate and correct faulty situations it is often essential to have accurate and up-to-date configuration information.

4.6 PERFORMANCE AND CAPACITY MANAGEMENT

4.6.1 Network utilization and performance monitoring

One of the tasks of managing a network is planning for its growth. As more and more computers are connected into networks, and networking services and applications become an increasingly popular paradigm for computing, it is important to ensure that the network has sufficient capacity to support the growing usage. To be able to monitor the network, and keep the data on network usage, is very helpful in performing this task.

For the simple objective of managing the capacity, only network layer traffic volume needs to be monitored. An external LAN traffic monitor can be used to monitor LAN bandwidth utilization on an instantaneous basis. Many LAN traffic monitors can also be configured to record such utilization data for historical analysis. In a WAN, it is more common for a network management application to use the management protocol (as described in Chapter 2) to monitor and record the usage levels. One network application could gather all such information from the routing and switching devices in the network periodically, at times when the network traffic volume is low (for example, at night). In a large network this application may be distributed to collect data at multiple locations.

In a network where it is possible to control how different applications and users use the network (for example, by giving priority to certain applications and users) monitoring network usage by application and user becomes very useful. This was touched upon when we described various monitors that could monitor application and user specific network traffic.

In addition to monitoring the utilization, it is sometimes useful to monitor the response time, to determine when the user requirements for performance have been met. This gives the administrator an idea of how fully the network capacity is being utilized. It can, however, be a poor metric for determining the performance actually delivered to the user. At the same bandwidth utilization, the user performance can range from very poor, if the traffic is very bursty, to very satisfactory, if the traffic is evenly distributed over time.

To illustrate, consider a simple example of N sources sharing the same link in a WAN. Each source has the same unit of data to send through this link. If the data units from all sources arrive at the router at the same time (assuming the router can queue them up for transmission on the link one by one), then the delays seen by the sources over this link are 1, 2, ... N, depending on the order of arrival at the router, with an average delay of $(N+1)/2$. Now consider a different scenario in which each arrival of a data unit at the router happens only after the previous arrival has already finished using the shared link. In this case, the delay for each transmission is simply one (the transmission time). Notice that in these two examples the utilization of the link is the same. This shows that the difference in the burstiness of arrival can produce very different response time characteristics, even at the same utilization level.

4.6.2 Examples of capacity planning

When a multi-access LAN is over-utilized, it is common to divide the LAN into two LANs, and connect them together using a *bridge*, or a WAN (by using a router). This reduces the traffic on each of the two LANs because the traffic local to each LAN is not seen on the other LAN.

For example, there are a set of nodes on a single LAN that generate bandwidth utilization U. Now we divide the nodes into two groups A and B. The traffic among the nodes in group A contributes U_A to the utilization. The traffic among the nodes in group B contributes U_B. The traffic between groups A and B contributes U_{AB}. By definition, the total utilization $U = U_A + U_B + U_{AB}$. When the nodes in groups A and B are separated into two LANs, the utilization seen on the LAN for group A is $U_A + U_{AB}$, and that seen on the LAN for group B is $U_B + U_{AB}$. Typically, the goal for choosing which nodes to put in each group is to minimize U_{AB}, and roughly balance U_A and U_B. This produces reasonably well-balanced traffic on the resultant LANs, and each will have close to half the utilization of the original LAN.

When there are multiple multi-access LANs being managed, the allocation of nodes to LANs can be done by a *cluster* analysis to minimize the utilization on each LAN. The resultant LANs can be connected either using bridges (Hawe, *et al*, 1984) or via a WAN. In order to perform such a cluster analysis, it is necessary to monitor the average traffic between each pair of nodes. The equivalent of this cluster analysis can also be approximated if the administrator has a good idea of the traffic patterns based on the organizational relationships and other configuration information.

It is difficult to design WAN networks in this fashion, based on traffic data. The concept of finding the clusters as described above is still applicable, and will result in a spanning tree of nodes. The design of such a network has the additional goal of maximizing the availability of communication paths between any pair of nodes, even when isolated routers or links are down. This can be formulated as a mathematical programming optimization problem to be solved by sophisticated design tools.

Given an existing WAN, planning for growth can also be done incrementally, by adding capacity to over-utilized resources, and making other incremental and localized changes. While such upgrades based on local analysis may not necessarily yield global optimality of the network, it is simpler and much more manageable, and usually quite adequate.

4.7 SECURITY

4.7.1 Security in monitor information

In many respects the *management* of computer networks is at odds with the *security* of the communications they provide. Network monitoring as a management concept is no exception to this. By definition, monitoring implies some intrusion into the privacy of information on the network, and the main questions are, to what extent is this information revealed through the output of the monitor, and how is access to that information controlled? These two issues must be considered together in determining how secure a given method of monitoring really is.

For example, a data analyzer that is capable of displaying the actual contents of the user data portion of messages is potentially a serious security threat. But if it is kept physically secure from use by any unauthorized personnel, its purpose may be justified. On the other hand, the output of a monitor that shows only link traffic summaries, and provides no means of accessing user data, may be considered safe enough in many cases to be posted publicly.

Another issue that must be considered in many monitoring applications is the feasibility of tampering with the output of the monitor itself. In some methods of monitoring such tampering may be more viable than in other methods, in which the mechanisms used in the monitoring process are less prone to sabotage. With certain access methods, the output can be protected using modern distributed systems security services, such as authentication and access controls.

4.7.2 The use of monitors in security applications

Recently there have been many developments in the area of network security. Modern distributed systems include security services that provide the means to:

1. Authenticate principals - A principal is some entity in a network that might be the source or destination of an information interchange. Principals can include both human users of the network, as well as components, such as software applications, that might act as agents for human users. The purpose of an authentication service is to permit the identity of a given principal to be determined reliably. In simple terms, it lets you know exactly who you are talking to. This is very important in networking, in which identities are often intangible, and easily impersonated. Authentication services rely on some form of information which can be known only to the principal with the correct identity, such as a password. There are various schemes for managing this secret information, including storing it in a central repository, and maintaining it on some media carried on the user's person. Regardless of how these secrets are managed, authentication services are intended to provide a guarantee that information won't be provided via the network to someone other than the party for whom it is intended.

2. Authorize access - Authorization services are equally important to protect resources available through the network, as well as the network resources themselves. Through authorization, access to resources can be restricted to only selected principals. Given that the identity of a principal is already known through authentication, there may be some qualification on what information and what resources they are permitted to access. There are various forms of authentication services as well, such as *capability-based* services, in which the authorization information is assigned to and held by the user, and *access control lists*, in which the information is associated with the resource itself. In either case, the purpose is to insure that parties do only what they have been permitted to do, by whatever authority manages the resources accessible on the network.

3. Insure privacy - Privacy of information exchanged on the network can be protected through the use of data encryption services. This further protects the users of the network from attacks such as eavesdropping and piracy. Although methods of encrypting network data have been around for some time, there is a significant cost in terms of performance. For this reason, only selected data (if any) is encrypted in most environments. However, this cost is likely to come down rapidly, and as it does, more and more data will be encrypted prior to transmission.

Monitoring also has its place in a complete security infrastructure. One of the characteristics of many security systems is that, once compromised, it may be very difficult to protect anything from an intruder. This is much like a home security system, for example. Once inside the house, a thief has access not only to the resources in the home itself, but often to information, such as charge account numbers, that extend the scope of the "break-in". Monitoring can help to maintain the integrity of the security system to prevent such intrusions, or at least to detect and report their occurrence as early as possible.

One example of the use of monitoring in security is a monitoring agent that can scan the configuration of an End System (or other network component), to detect any non-conformance with some security policy that might potentially lead to a violation of network security. This is analogous to a home monitor that might warn you that the door was left unlocked when you turn the lights out at night. The monitor doesn't determine security policy. This is set by some central administration, or possibly by the local system manager. At periodic intervals, the monitor simply checks the system configuration against the policy it has been provided, and reports any irregularities. This might be in the form of accounts, files or network applications with improper access controls defined, passwords that are too easily guessable, or need to be changed for other reasons, and so on. These non-conformances will usually be reported immediately to the policy administrator (or some other authority) so that corrective action can be taken to avoid the possibility of a security violation occurring.

Another example of the use of monitoring in maintaining a secure network environment is a monitor that is programmed to report certain abnormal activities. We have described previously how an external monitor on a LAN has access to any information communicated on the network. It is relatively easy, therefore, for a monitor to examine specific fields in network messages and check for conditions that might violate security policy.

A very likely application of such a monitor would be in identifying the source of a known security violation. This could be done either through an audit trail, based on data recorded by the monitor over some time period, or it could be done in real-time, in the form of an alarm. For example, suppose an intruder was known to have gained access to some system on the network, and through that access compromised some number of passwords in use on the network. Notifying all of the users and assigning new passwords might take some time, during which the network resources would be vulnerable. More importantly, it would be difficult to differentiate a valid use of one of the compromised passwords from an invalid one.

In this case, the network monitor might be programmed to identify any use on the network of one of the compromised passwords, and determine if the source of that usage was legitimate. Any illegal usage could be reported immediately to some authority, along with information on the source of the message that might aid in locating and capturing the intruder.

4.8 ACCOUNTING

Accounting for the usage of network and system resources is a broad application area with widely varying requirements. One area in which needs may differ significantly is in the accuracy of accounting data. The degree to which completeness and correctness of data are required affects the nature of the network monitoring technology that can be employed in support of any accounting application.

At one extreme, accounting may be of a very general nature, and may be tolerant of some inaccuracies in the source data. For example, internal corporate accounting may be used to help manage budgets, and determine what proportion of the cost of some shared resource should be allotted to each department. In cases such as this it is not of great importance to precisely measure every detail of resource utilization. This information is actually irrelevant, and would be lost anyway due to "rounding off" of the figures in the budget-balancing process.

At the other extreme, there are user-oriented utilities, similar in nature to the telephone company, the electric company, etc., that have a need for very precise billing. A telephone customer would be quite dissatisfied to be billed for services provided to someone else. Likewise, some computer applications need to carefully account for every detail of resource utilization, and cannot tolerate inaccuracies.

In between these two extremes is a continuum of requirements on accounting accuracy, all of which have implications on the underlying monitoring systems used to collect the source data. We will give examples here of only the two extreme requirements, and how they might be met using network monitoring technologies described earlier in the book. It should not be difficult to extrapolate from these examples to conceive a variety of uses of network monitoring in accounting applications.

4.8.1 Using a LAN monitor for departmental accounting

As we have explained, the high volume of traffic that needs to be processed makes it difficult and/or expensive to design LAN monitors that never lose monitor information by missing network messages. So even though they may have access to all information exchanged on some segment of a network, they are unsuitable for some accounting applications. However, there is a class of usages in which this level of reliability is perfectly acceptable.

Consider the type of internal accounting that is often done by large organizations, such as corporations, universities, etc. In these cases it is difficult (if not impossible), as well as unnecessary to account precisely for the use of resources that might be shared across departments within the organization. A copy machine, for example, might be charged to and administered by one department. But there is often nothing that prevents someone from another department from walking down the hall and using it to make a few copies. If this uncharged use becomes excessive, however, the management of the organization would like to know, so they can reassign the cost and administration of the resource to the organization that is getting the most use out of it (or buy another copier).

The same thing applies to network resources, and to the shared resources on systems that are connected to the network. Cost accounting procedures within the organization may require that some coarse level of accounting be maintained, so that the main sources of resource utilization can be identified and "charged" appropriately. In many cases, a LAN monitor might be ideally suited to this task, because of the ease and relatively low cost of collecting this data.

4.8.2 Using an integrated monitor for cost accounting

There are other network usages in which it is important to account precisely for every connection, every message transmitted, and possibly for every byte of data. This is analogous to the long-distance telephone network, and the way end-user billing is typically done. No one would be satisfied with a telephone accounting system that charged them for some percentage of time on the public utility which they didn't really use, simply because facilities for monitoring the network were imprecise.

For this level of accuracy in accounting data, integrated monitors are generally more suitable. Not only are they less likely to miss data, they can time events more precisely. They also have access to state information that may be useful in accounting, and which is hidden from an external monitor, as we have described.

In some cases, the event logs generated by a monitor built into a common network service, such as a session layer monitor, might be adequate for accounting for resource utilization on a system. In other cases, it might be necessary to have special monitors designed specifically to meet the requirements of a unique application and the resources it manages.

4.9 RESOURCE MANAGEMENT

The increasing popularity of networking has led to more and more computer resources being available through communications channels. Shared access to resources, such compute cycles, files, databases, printers, specialized hardware and applications, has led to a need to manage the use of these resources more effectively. This is a convenience to the user, in terms of being able to easily locate the required resources. It is also a necessity to network administrators, who are concerned about managing the cost of network usage. We will provide a brief description of some of the management services currently in practice, as well as those in development, as a background for describing the use of network monitoring in such systems.

Various terms have been applied to services of this nature, with slightly different connotations. All of the following have been used in one context or another.

4.9.1 Load balancing

Load balancing is a term most often used to refer specifically to distributing the workload of a given application or applications among a set of available End Systems, such that optimal performance is achieved overall. In many cases there is an implication that the only resource of interest is compute cycles. Load balancing can be examined from two perspectives:

1. the individual client application, which needs to choose from among a set of available servers, and
2. the "collective" clients of a given service.

In the former case, what the client needs to know is simply which servers are available, and what capabilities they have to perform the required task. For example, if Server A and Server B are both available, but Server A is on a machine that is twice as fast as Server B, or if more tasks are already executing on Server B on behalf of other clients, Server A would be the preferred choice for a new client task.

From the standpoint of "collective" clients, they form a pool of users of the available resources. Some clients in the pool may have higher priority than others from a collective standpoint, or there may be other factors that would enter into decisions on resource allocation. For example, Client A might have a slightly lower priority than Client B, but it might have a task to perform that requires only a few seconds, whereas Client B might tie up an available server for up to an hour. Given this information, an "intelligent" load balancing agent might choose to have the task for Client A performed first, so Client A could proceed with other things while Client B's task was executing.

This example shows that the simplistic, client-centric view of load balancing is not necessarily going to provide optimal use of available resources from a more global perspective. Simple approaches to load balancing also frequently fail to take into account the fact that there are many uses of resources in an application other than compute cycles.

4.9.2 Resource brokering

The term *Resource brokering* has been used to refer to a broader set of application resources than simply balancing CPU loading among multiple server systems. Resource brokering systems recognize that there are a wide variety of resources which might affect which server a client would select for any given application. For example, an application which uses large amounts of memory might make memory size a consideration in selecting a server. Likewise, an application which requires the use of temporary files on disk might make disk capacity a consideration. Other applications, such as a print distribution service, might have even more specific requirements, such as whether a color graphics printer is available on a given print server, or one capable of two-sided printing. Resource brokering services focus on allowing applications with diverse and specialized requirements to locate the resources they need.

4.9.3 Resource management

Resource management is a higher-level term that is typically used to span the full scope of services required for proper management of shared resources, encompassing both load balancing and resource brokering. A typical resource management service consists of three major components:

1. The shared resources themselves, which in this case have well-defined attributes and methods.

2. A management information base, in which resource attributes and methods are stored.

3. A resource manager, through which prospective clients can obtain information about resources stored in the management information base.

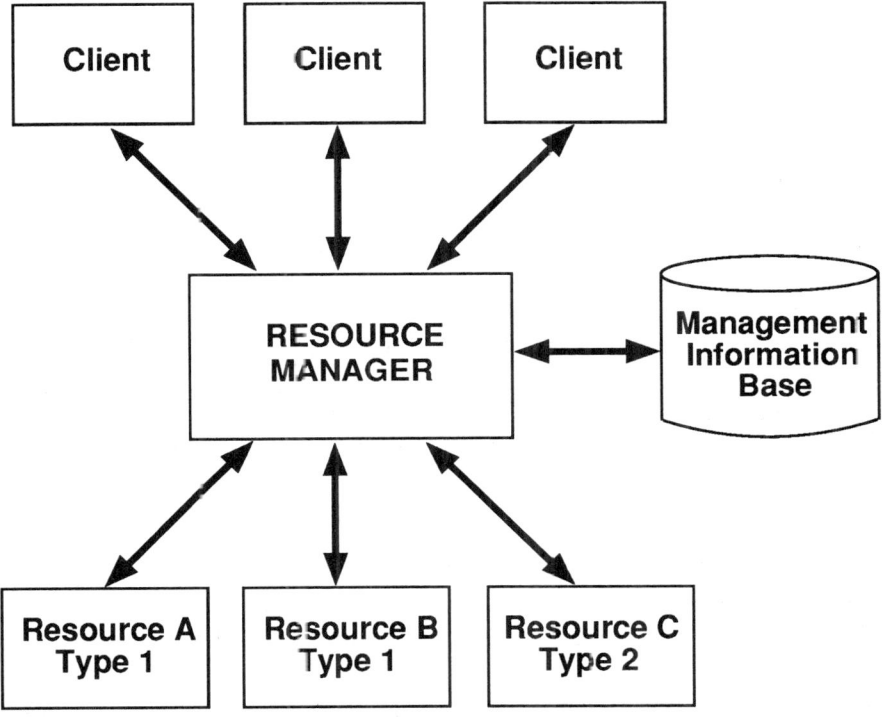

Figure 50 - A resource management service

These are just some of the characteristics that a comprehensive resource management service might have:

1. Type inheritance and containment - a means of defining the attributes of resources using object-oriented methods, in which a resource (object) can be defined by inheriting the attributes of some other object.

2. Dynamic addition of new resources to system - the ability to create new resource objects, add them to the system and have them be immediately available to potential clients.

3. Notification of resource availability - the ability of a client to request notification of availability of a required resource from the management service.

4. Query-based lookup - the ability to look up resources based on potentially complex combinations of their attribute values.

5. Timestamps and timeout values - the ability to date information on resource availability and provide that information to prospective clients for use in resource selection.

4.9.4 Static vs. dynamic attributes

One of the most difficult aspects of managing shared resources is dealing with the wide range of attribute types. One characteristic of resource attributes that has a major influence on the design of resource management services is the frequency with which they change state. Some attributes of resources are very static, and change rarely, if at all. For example, the physical location of a large printer is not likely to change very often, simply because it is difficult to move. Other attributes may change with an extremely high frequency. The number of available compute cycles on a given processor, for example, could vary significantly over a period of just a few milliseconds.

It should be fairly obvious that it is much more difficult to collect timely and useful information about the attributes of resources that change with a high frequency. Not only is there more data to process - by the time an answer is obtained it is very likely to be of no use to the client, because the data on which it is based is already obsolete! Resource management services for resources of this nature are generally very limited in scale, because the useful lifetime of database entries is very short. Resources must be able to report their state with a high frequency, and clients must be able to acquire information quickly and use it almost immediately. This results in a lot of traffic being generated on the network, which may not be acceptable in many shared networking environments.

One way to avoid these problems is to change the nature of the information being monitored for a particular resource. This is sometimes referred to as "raising the semantic level" of the information contained in each update. For example, if an update contains the information, "This is my state at this instant in time," the effective lifetime of the database entry for that resource is very short, and frequent updates are required. On the other hand, if the update contains, "This is the average of my state over the past minute," the lifetime of the entry is much longer, and the frequency of updates is much lower. Unfortunately, if the task to be performed is of very short duration, this average may not be useful.

It should be seen from this example that, for any given resource, there is a tradeoff to be made between the granularity of the state changes recorded in the resource management database and the granularity of the operations that can be performed on that resource. It is this need for balancing the two on a case by case basis that makes it difficult to design a general-purpose resource management service.

4.9.5 The use of monitors in resource management

We have described how resource management services utilize a database of information about the attributes of resources to allow clients to select among the available resources. The updates to the resource management database are a form of monitor information, which can be supplied by the resource itself, or by some monitor designed specifically for this purpose. The considerations as to whether this function should be integrated into the resource itself, or provided as a common service for a variety of resource types, are much the same as those described in Chapter 3 on integrated vs. external network monitors.

4.9.6 Summary

It should be noted that, although comprehensive resource management services provide a higher level of functionality than load balancing or resource brokering services, there is an associated cost. The overhead of maintaining large databases, providing for dynamic registration of new resource types, permitting complex queries to be made, and so on, all have a potential impact on performance. For resources with very dynamic attributes, simpler management mechanisms employed on a smaller scale may be more appropriate for effective brokering.

Effective resource management relies heavily on the integration of network and system management, a subject we will touch on in the next chapter. The techniques we will describe for "intelligent" monitoring can also be applied to the area of resource management.

5

Summary and Future Directions

5.1 SUMMARY

As we have seen, there are a wide variety of computer network architectures, component technologies and configurations in current use. As networks grow in scale and complexity, monitoring has become more and more of a necessity to keep the networks, and the systems attached to them, fully operational. Monitors provide information on the state of the system that is essential to many management applications. They are the "nervous system" of the network itself.

Just as a nervous system monitors the various functions of the body and sends impulses to the brain for evaluation, network monitors record events in the network as they happen, and supply that information to management applications. We have described a variety of ways in which monitor information can be made available to applications. Whether they are polled directly, log events to a listener on demand, or routinely update a shared management information base, the function of monitors is essentially the same: to observe and record state information on the network and its components.

The combination of increasingly heterogeneous networks, along with a greater and greater dependency on them, has led to a desire to standardize the ways in which networks are managed. Ideally, any given management application should be able to control components from different vendors, even in networks based on mixed architectures. This level of interoperability is very difficult to achieve without some form of standardization. This applies even more strongly to network monitors, which are both a supplier of information to and a consumer of information from other management applications. It is essential to the development of general-purpose monitoring services that the protocols and information formats used in network management applications be standardized.

There are many issues that come into play in the design of a network monitoring system. The two broad categories under which monitor designs can be classified are *integrated* and *external* monitors. But within these categories there is is tremendous design flexibility, limited only by the state-of-the-art in the technologies on which monitors are based. As these implementation technologies have evolved, the capabilities and applications of network monitors have continued to expand. We can only conclude that in the future monitors will become cheaper, faster and capable of processing much greater volumes of information than ever before. This will be essential to meet the needs of high-speed networks of increasing scale, but it will also present new possibilities for applications of monitor information.

We have described some of the more common applications of network monitors. There is no doubt a much larger list, limited only by the ingenuity of the user in adapting monitors to solving specific problems in network management. Many of the applications that are common today probably could not have been conceived of by users of network monitors a decade ago. The coming decade will almost surely see significant new applications develop for this fundamental technology. While we cannot anticipate all of these possibilities, we can examine some of the trends that are likely to influence this development.

5.2 FUTURE DIRECTIONS

5.2.1 Directions in network technology

As we indicated in Chapter 3, network monitoring technology has tracked the evolution of networks themselves. While we can't predict the future, there are some clear trends in computer networking that are very likely to continue, at least through the next decade. We can consider the effect of those developments on network monitors.

5.2.1.1 Scale

Not too many years ago, computer networking was a relatively immature technology, and only the highly skilled would venture to install and maintain their own networks. These early networks were relatively small, in terms of the number of End Systems, and management tools were still fairly primitive. In this environment, monitoring played a limited role, being used mainly as a debugging aid in isolating the causes of network failures. The dependency on monitors was not insignificant, even at that time, as outages were common, and difficult to troubleshoot.

As networking technologies have become more sophisticated, they have also become more robust, and perhaps to some extent the use of monitors for performing low-level diagnostics has diminished. However, the need for monitors has increased overall, as new applications have been found for monitor information. Many businesses have come to depend on computer networks, literally for their life. As the networks get larger and larger, the management of them becomes more and more complex, and the need for information about the state of the networked systems increases proportionally. Network management in general is rapidly becoming a task that cannot be performed without the aid of automated tools, and these tools are largely driven by information generated by network monitors.

We have shown how networks have grown in size over the past few decades, from small configurations of just a few End Systems to very large configurations of tens of thousands of End Systems, with numerous Intermediate Systems and complex interconnections. The coming decade is likely to see networks growing to the hundreds of thousands, and possibly millions of End Systems. Advances in the technology are also making it easier and easier to merge isolated networks into larger ones, and political and economic changes throughout the world are likely to make such merges more and more common. And finally, if some of the international standards succeed in their goals, we may eventually have all the world's computer systems joined by a single global network.

It is inconceivable to install and maintain networks of this scale without highly automated management tools, driven by the data provided by network monitors. Thus, network monitors will play an increasingly important role in the information systems that will have a direct affect practically every aspect of our lives.

5.2.1.2 Heterogeneity

This complexity of computer networks is further driven by the increasing mix of systems from multiple vendors in the same network. Many organizations have networks that consist not only of different network architectures, but of systems with different hardware architectures and datatype representations. This is frequently not the result of network planning, but due to lack of it. Different sub-groups within an organization may make different purchasing decisions in isolation, and then discover the need to connect things at a higher level. In other cases, a corporation with an internal networking standard might join another corporation, through merger or acquisition, with a very different internal standard. This has led, over time, to the point that it is very uncommon for a network of any size *not* to be fundamentally heterogeneous.

Heterogeneity in networks has a significant impact on monitoring. Many monitors are designed to work operate on a limited set of protocols belonging to a single architecture. This leads to having multiple monitors that perform basically the same function when more than one architecture is in use on the network. Monitors are increasingly being designed to accommodate more than one architecture, to reduce cost and simplify network administration. It is likely this trend will continue, until sometime in the distant future that standardization reaches a point where all network implementations conform to some common set of protocols.

Heterogeneity in datatype representations also has in impact on network monitoring. To the extent that network monitors can be considered distributed applications, they suffer from the same problems other network applications have to deal with. Integer, floating point and character representations differ from one hardware architecture to another, making it difficult to share data across systems. Again, monitors can be designed to accommodate this to some extent. In some cases, communications services such as Remote Procedure Call (RPC) may be available, which can perform transformations on the data as it is being transmitted to hide these dissimilarities. Monitors using such access methods can benefit from these services. But as in the case of network architectures, the best solution long-term is common standards for representing monitor information. The OSI management framework, and the definitions of object data described in Chapter 2, are the solutions most likely to influence monitor designs over time.

5.2.1.3 Bandwidth

The decade of the 1980's presented dramatic changes in the nature of computer networks. This was mostly driven by the commercialization of Local Area Network technologies. As we entered the decade, most computer networks operated at relatively low speeds - 10 K bits per second was considered to be fast. By the end of the decade, many networks were running at speeds of 10 M bits per second, and some as high as 100 M bits per second. This increase of 4 orders of magnitude in network bandwidth is rather astounding, and it has had an impact on the whole way that computers are used. We have gone from an environment of large, central time-sharing systems, to one of distributed desktop computers, with remote access to shared resource via the network.

Network monitoring technology has not yet fully caught up with these developments. While there are monitors that are capable of functioning at the speeds of modern networks, the infrastructure to gather the monitor information, and the applications to process it, are still being developed.

It is our expectation that the coming decade will see some leveling off of the upwards curve of communications bandwidth. While there will no doubt be new developments in the technology, and networks in general will continue to be upgraded to the state-of-the-art, the kind of explosive growth in bandwidth seen over the past decade is unlikely to continue. The emphasis in network monitoring, therefore, will shift from the raw technology requirements to the focus on the end-user requirements for monitor information.

5.2.1.4 Network security

In Chapter 3, we discussed the design tradeoffs between integrated monitors and external monitors. For many applications, there are some clear advantages to using external monitors. External monitors, however, rely on the ability to "eavesdrop" on the network as needed to collect their raw data. In the past, it has been easy for anyone who could access the network media physically to listen to all of the traffic on the network. In fact, this capability was absolutely essential to being able to detect faults in the network and application software. Most commercial network monitors available today, which for the most part are external monitors, depend on this ability to tap into the network at will.

Unfortunately, this same ability which has made monitoring so easy has also opened up channels of illegitimate access to information transmitted on the network, which many users unknowingly assume to be "private". Increasingly, mechanisms are being developed to prevent unauthorized access to this information.

Network security is a growing technology, which already includes services such as

SUMMARY AND FUTURE DIRECTIONS 161

authentication, authorization and data encryption. All of these services have an impact on network monitoring, because they are all basically intended to prevent anyone but the parties directly involved in the communications to have access to information and resources on the network. Data encryption, in particular, makes it almost impossible to implement external monitoring, as has been done in the past. Although the monitor can still access the data, it can do no useful interpretation. if only the user portion of the data is encrypted, external monitors can still perform some of their functions, since the protocol headers on which they operate may be left in the clear. But there is incentive to encrypt even the protocol headers, as a deterrence to certain forms of attack, and as this practice grows, external monitoring may become a thing of the past.

In some respects, however, the use of security in networks may make monitoring even more viable. As it is now, physical access to network media must be carefully protected, because anyone capable of connecting a network monitor to the media has essentially unlimited access to all of the information in the network. Imagine the potential risks, for example, of using monitors to troubleshoot a network for a large bank, or one used for military or intelligence purposes. As more and more of our personal data is maintained by computers, and as these computers are more often connected to networks, the damage that can result from unauthorized access to information increases. By integrating network security mechanisms into network monitors, one may be able to prevent the monitor from being used for purposes for which it was not intended.

5.2.2 Directions in implementation technology

We also described in Chapter 3 how the technologies for implementing network monitors have evolved since the inception of computer networks, and how that has influenced the design and applications of monitors. These trends are likely to continue, especially in the following areas.

5.2.2.1 Processors, memory and disks

There does not appear to be any leveling off in developments in processors, memory, and disk technologies. It can be expected that in the near future processors will continue to increase in speed, and memories and disks will continue to increase in capacity. What is in some ways more significant, the cost of these components is continuing downward. What this means for network monitoring is that it will become possible to do more and more at a cost that is not prohibitive, and this will cause monitors to proliferate. Again, as more and more monitor information gets generated by these components, the need for higher-level processing will increase. The compute-intensive processing of monitor information (such as we described in our discussion of a network workload monitor in Section 3.4.4) that is done today on a large system, is likely in the future to be done in real-time by the monitor itself.

Monitors will be able to process and filter large amounts of data, buffered in local memory, and save the results to local disks. The stored information may be forwarded at the most opportune time to a larger management information base. In some cases, the local storage may actually form a part of the distributed management database, which will tie all of the management components together into one comprehensive information network.

5.2.2.2 Software programming

As monitors become more and more powerful, they will run increasingly complex software. Where a monitor today might have a primitive operating system kernel, monitors of the future will most likely run sophisticated, multi-tasking operating systems, with complete file systems and management utilities. This will increase the portability of monitor software, which will become more and more general purpose, and less specialized than it is today. The software will tie together all of the monitors capabilities, and address the issues of managing heterogeneous networks and systems.

5.2.2.3 User interface

The past decade has also seen enormous changes in the way users interact with computer systems. Simple command and forms interfaces have given way to sophisticated graphics and window interfaces. Monitors have not really kept up with these developments. Most monitors today have relatively primitive user interfaces, that share little in common with other computer applications, and require a significant amount of learning. In the future, monitors are likely to follow the trend in all software towards "ease of use". There are several areas in particular where significant improvements are likely:

1. Using a network monitor today frequently requires learning a whole new interface and style of use. As they adopt common operating systems, monitors will also benefit from the use of common user interfaces that are shared across applications. This will make it easier for more people to access monitor information and use it effectively.

2. Graphics user interfaces and "point and click" input will make it possible for the user to deal much more effectively with the large amounts of information that will be generated by network monitors.

3. The monitor information is likely to be integrated with the information base shared with other applications. For example, it will become easy to view monitor information through a spreadsheet application, or incorporate it into a chart or document. Again, this will make monitors more prevalent, and their information more accessible.

5.2.3 The use of "intelligent systems" in network monitoring

We have used the analogy comparing network monitors to the body's nervous system, and we described in Section 1.1 how monitors form part of a feedback system. We have also described how monitor information can be provided to management applications that allow a network administrator to control configuration and behavior of the network. Most of our examples have implied that a human administrator is present to "close" the feedback loop, and translate the monitor information into actions that modify the network state.

For the most part, this is the case in today's networks. Network administrators are highly trained and experienced people, who know how to interpret monitor information and make effective decisions. Unfortunately, people with these skills are rare, and employing them raises the cost of ownership for communications networks significantly. We have reached a point already where this has become a factor in limiting the size of network configurations. What is needed, then, is some way to capture the knowledge possessed by these people, and translate it into an automated control system. Such as system would use monitors to sense the state of the network components, interpret the results, and translate them into actions that would correct faults, improve performance, and so on.

The technology required to achieve this level of automation will most likely come from the field of Artificial Intelligence, in particular from research into Knowledge-Based Systems. It has already been demonstrated that it is possible to build "expert" systems, in which the rules on which decisions are made can be captured once, and executed at will. Such systems are already being put to practical use in a number of areas, including medical, automotive and network diagnostics. They typically "advise" a human user on recommended corrective actions based on a given set of problem symptoms. In many cases, the symptoms are input by the user, but these systems can sometimes accept input from a monitoring device.

We expect this technology to be employed in future networks, allowing monitors to provide information on a routine basis to management applications, which can make decisions and perform actions on the network directly, without human intervention. They can also be designed to involve humans by notifying them when conditions exceed certain predefined thresholds. In this way, the more mundane management tasks can be automated, reserving the time of the skilled human administrators for situations of a more critical nature.

In some cases, this kind of intelligence may be put into the monitors themselves, to help them manage the large amounts of information they will need to process and filter. Hitson, 1988 gave a good discussion on this topic. Knowledge may be required, for example, to help a low-level monitor determine what information is relevant for forwarding to some management application, to avoid flooding the network with useless or redundant data. As we described in the section on Resource Management (Section 4.9), one way of reducing the amount of data that gets forwarded is to raise the "semantic content" of the information. Using built-in "knowledge" about the network state, a monitor might be able to make its own inferences about what information is relevant to its consumers.

For example, consider a monitor whose sole function is to poll certain components in the network at a given interval to test their availability. In a large network, reporting on this state for every component at each recording interval could result in a large amount of information being generated on the network. However, if the monitor is provided with a set of rules it may be able to make certain decisions on its own. It might have a rule that says, "It's ok for component A to be unavailable for periods up to 10 minutes", and another rule that says, "It's not ok for component A to be unavailable if component B is also unavailable." The monitor then, detecting that component A was unavailable, could postpone forwarding that information until either 10 minutes had elapsed, or it recognized that component B had also become unavailable. By the time either of these events happened, it's possible that component A might become available again, and the monitor would not have to report the failure at all. So in the worst case, the monitor would send a single message reporting the failure of component A, and in the best case it would not even send a message. This is in comparison to constantly reporting the state of component A (and all of the other network components) over the network.

It can be seen from this example that the use of Knowledge-Based Systems technology can significantly reduce the amount of information forwarded by a monitor to other monitors, or to management applications. This also tends to simplify the design of management applications and management information bases, by allowing them to focus on only the essential information that couldn't be filtered at the lower level.

5.2.4 The impact of standards development on monitors

In Chapter 2, we described some of the standards that are most likely to influence the development of network monitors. For the most part, these standards have emerged only over the past decade. While it is unfortunate that there is no one common standard as yet, the standards that we do have represent a major step forward from the time when every network was different, and there were no shared tools. We are only starting to see a significant number of products being produced that conform to one or more of these standards. As more and more products emerge, the standards will take on greater significance, and achieve greater momentum. There will become increasing incentives for future products to conform.

Having the products based on standards means that the job of the end user, the ultimate systems integrator, becomes much easier. They can freely buy products from various vendors with some assurance that the result will function correctly. Thus, they can purchase each component of the network based on specific cost/performance ratios for that component (or other factors, such as ease of use or serviceability), without worrying about whether it will work with other components or not. This is especially useful, since it is unlikely that any one vendor will excel in making all of the network components, especially given that there is such a variety of components in a modern network.

With regard to network monitoring, this "mix and match" approach may be especially useful. There will no doubt be a wide range of management applications available, providing both off-the-shelf and customized solutions. The standardization of the protocols and information formats used by network monitors will make it possible to develop portable applications that are independent of any specific monitoring hardware. This will also allow the implementation of the monitors to evolve to take advantage of new developments in technology without affecting existing management applications.

5.2.5 Integration of network and system management

The other trend that is likely to affect the use of monitors is the integration of network management and system administration. In the past, these two areas were largely unrelated, and were often handled by different groups, with different skill sets, using different tools. A systems administrator, for example, might be skilled in configuring an operating system for optimal performance under a given load, installing software, and performing file backups, while a network administrator might be skilled in planning routing hierarchies, managing the network address space, and solving problems in loss of connectivity. There was very little crossover between these two areas of expertise.

Increasingly, however, systems are attached to networks, and tools are being developed to manage them remotely. As this tendency to distributed management grows, the distinctions between network management and system administration are fading. Who is responsible, for example, if there is a failure while a file backup is being performed over the network to a remote disk? Who is responsible for setting up the appropriate access controls on a system to allow resources to be accessed from other systems? The distinction between these two fields is becoming blurred, and continuing to separate them only makes things more difficult to administer properly.

Network monitors can contribute a lot to the effective management of systems. They can make it feasible to centralize the administration of a number of systems by a smaller management group. For example, one of the concerns of system managers is protecting systems against attack from unauthorized use. A system manager will often check the system parameters on a regular basis to detect signs that the system might have been attacked, or form a preventive standpoint, to insure that the system security hasn't been compromised in some way that would make such an attack possible.

This function could largely be replaced by a security monitor that periodically checks the system configuration against some prescribed set of rules. It can detect when passwords change, what accounts are active, what privileges are required for performing certain operations, etc. If any of these factors changes in a way that puts the system in violation of security policy (as described in the rules), the security monitor can immediately notify a central administration that there is a problem.

There are many other aspects of system behavior that can be monitored in this way. Monitors can track the amount of free disk space, the availability of shared queues, the state of devices such as disks and printers, and so on. By automating these functions, providing local, intelligent monitors, and distributing monitor information over the network the number of people required to manage systems in a large network can be greatly reduced. This usage of monitors also creates opportunities for automating system management in the same way we have described for network management applications.

Appendix A - An ASN.1 Primer

The formal definition of the management information model, the MIB and the management protocol must be in terms of a specification language. Specifying protocol messages and the datatypes of the parameters is analogous to defining a programming interface. For the purpose of our discussion, although we will not get into the formal details of the protocol, it is beneficial to be exposed to some examples of these specifications while trying to understand the concepts.

One such specification language of particular interest is ASN.1, short for Abstract Syntax Notation One. This notation is used to specify both the TCP/IP Internet management protocol, as well as the ISO CMIP management protocol. When these protocols are discussed in the text, some examples are given using ASN.1 to illustrate the concepts. Here, we give a very brief overview of ASN.1.

ASN.1 was first defined in CCITT X.409 (CCITT, 1984) in 1984, as part of the series of *Recommendations for Message Handling Systems*. X.409 consists logically of two parts: one is the definition of a *standard abstract notation* and the other is a *standard representation* for datatypes. The former standard is named ASN.1, and the latter BER, short for *Basic Encoding Rules*. Both ASN.1 and BER also became ISO standards by 1987, published as IS 8824 and IS 8825 respectively.

The encoding rules deal with how the abstract notation is actually represented in protocol messages on the wire. Physical details, such as the size of various datatypes, and the endianness, are decided and represented by the encoding rules. This aspect is not important for understanding the concepts of network management protocols, and thus we will not get into any more details of the encoding rules. A good exposition can be found in Rose, 1990.

ASN.1 NOTATION

Before we begin, it is useful to understand that a module of ASN.1 definition uses four kinds of tokens, as characterized by Rose, 1990.

1. **words**: which consist of uppercase and lower-case letters, digits, and hyphens (a **word** must start with a letter). There are some conventions for using uppercase letters:

    a. If the entire **word** is uppercase, then it is a *keyword,* either reserved by ASN.1 or defined as an ASN.1 *macro.*

    b. If the first letter of the **word** is uppercase, then the word is the name of a *type* Most often a type's name begins with an upper-case letter only; for example, DistinguishedName. Some of the most primitive types, such as BOOLEAN,

168   APPENDIX A

   INTEGER and REAL are spelt completed in upper-case. In this regard, convention is not very consistent.

   c. Other **words** are used to label *variables,* or *instances.*

2. **numbers**: which consist of digits.
3. **strings**: which are of three forms
   a. "character strings"   - character string in double quotes
   b. '0123456789ABCDEF'H   - hex string in single quote ending with H
   c. '01'B   - bit string in single quote ending with B
4. **punctuations**: for example:
   a. ::= is used for assignment
   b. -- is used to start a comment

The rest of the **punctuations** are very natural and will be introduced in examples later.

DATATYPES

The basic purpose of ASN.1 is to define datatypes. The notion of datatypes here is the same as that in programming languages. Programming languages all have some *built-in* basic datatypes (such as integers, real numbers and text strings), and notations for constructing more complicated datatypes, or records, that consist of fields of other datatypes. ASN.1 currently defines the following primitive datatypes:

- **BOOLEAN**: has two values, TRUE or FALSE
- **INTEGER**: is any cardinal number of unbounded precision
- **ENUMERATED**: specifies a subset of integer for the purpose of identification
- **REAL**: specified in terms of a *mantissa*, a *base*, and an *exponent*, again of arbitrary precision. The mantissa and exponent can take any value and the base is either 2 or 10. The value of the real number is (mantissa * base^{exponent}).
- **BIT STRING**; consists of zero or more bits.
- **OCTET STRING**: consists of zero or more octets, each taking a value between 0 and 255.
- **NumericString**: is a subset of OctetString, consisting only of digits (0-9) and spaces.
- **PrintableString**: is also a subset of OctetString, consisting of uppercase and lower-case letters, digits, punctuation marks, and spaces.
- **IA5String**: is also a subset of OctetString, consisting of characters from the CCITT International Alphabet number 5 (which is ASCII).

- **CharacterString**: are various additional character sets defined by the ISO and CCITT standards. The mapping between an octet value and a symbol is best shown by a table. Since we do not need to go into this level of detail, we refer the reader to IS 8824 for the actual definitions.
- **TeletexString**: (see Character String)
- **VideotexString**: (see Character String)
- **GraphicsString**: (see Character String)
- **VisibleString**: (see Character String)
- **GeneralString**: (see Character String)
- **GeneralizedTime**: consists of the data, expressed as a four-digit year, two-digit month, and two-digit day; time, expressed in hours and minutes, optionally with seconds and fractional seconds of arbitrary precision; and an optional indicator of the relation of this time to Coordinated Universal Time (UTC). An example is "19910606192007.1234567Z".
- **UTCTime**: consists of the date, expressed as a two-digit year, two-digit month, and two-digit day; time, expressed with a resolution up to one second; and optionally an indicator of the relation of this time to UTC. An example is "910606192007-0600".
- **OBJECT IDENTIFIER**: is a very important datatype, used for uniquely labeling various objects, types, definitions, etc. Its data structure is a sequence of non-negative integer values. The first two components are bounded by convention. Although any value satisfying the above description is an OBJECT IDENTIFIER, its use for uniquely labeling objects is administered by a hierarchical registration authority structure. If we visualize the space of object identifiers as a tree, then each internal node can be considered as labeling a registration authority and each leaf node as labeling a unique object. The structure of the registration authority is discussed more fully in Chapter 2.
- **ObjectDescriptor**: is a text string that also references an object. There is no registration process for these strings, thus they cannot be guaranteed to be unique. It can be used as a user-friendly way of naming and describing an object.
- **NULL**: is a special datatype/value that indicates the lack of any value present.
- **EXTERNAL**: is a datatype that is not defined in the current module (body of ASN.1 definitions). This is a convenient meta-type for allowing datatypes that are not easily expressible in ASN.1, but possibly specified in another notation.
- **ANY**: is another meta-type to denote the union of all datatypes defined using ASN.1. This allows leaving certain datatypes undefined at the present time, or left as "private" definitions.

The ASN.1 notation for defining types is simply:

NameOfType ::= TYPE

The following are examples of the data type definitions:

```
MessageSize ::= INTEGER

AuthenticationLevel ::=
    ENUMERATED
    {
            none (0),
            weak (20),
            strong (80)
    }
```

CONSTRUCTION OF DATATYPES

A few *construction* types are used to define more elaborate datatypes.

- **SEQUENCE** or **SEQUENCE OF**: is an ordered set of primitive types and/or other constructed types. For example:

```
Interrupt-Request ::=
    SEQUENCE
    {
            fatal-error    BOOLEAN,
            message PrintableString
    }
```

When the datatype is defined as a sequence of zero or more elements of the same type, then SEQUENCE OF is used:

```
RoutingTable ::=
    SEQUENCE OF RoutingEntry
```

where RoutingEntry is another constructed type.

- **SET** or **SET OF**: is an unordered set of primitive or constructed types. For example:

```
AdminDescriptor ::=
    SET
    {
            name    PrintableString,
            mailbox MailAddress
    }
```

Similarly, SET OF is used to define a set of zero of more elements of the same type:

```
AdmGroup ::=
    SET OF AdminDescriptor
```

- **CHOICE**: is a data structure that a set of member types; and an instance of this datatype is one of the member types. For example:

```
TimeOfDay ::=
    CHOICE
    {
            actual-value    UTCTime,
            not-available   NULL
    }
```

TAGS AND CLASSES OF DATATYPES

The ASN.1 datatypes are *tagged*, or assigned labels for their identification and encoding in protocols. The datatypes are classified by a two level scheme. At the first level, four classes of datatypes are defined:

1. Universal
2. Application
3. Context-Specific
4. Private

The *Universal* class consists of the set of basic datatypes defined by the standard that is applicable to all user-defined modules. The primitive types and constructor types defined in the last subsections all belong to this class. The set of all *Universal* class types is shown in Table 1:

Universal Tag	ASN.1 Type
1	BOOLEAN
2	INTEGER
3	BIT STRING
4	OCTET STRING
5	NULL
6	OBJECT IDENTIFIER
7	ObjectDescriptor
8	EXTERNAL
9	REAL
10	ENUMERATED
12-15	reserved
16	SEQUENCE, SEQUENCE OF
17	SET, SET OF
18	NumericString
19	PrintableString
20	TeletexString
21	VideotexString

22	IA5String
23	UTCTime
24	GeneralizedTime
25	GraphicsString
26	VisibleString
27	GeneralString
28	CharacterString
29...	reserved

Table 1 - ASN.1 Universal Tags

Note, the type ANY, and the constructor type CHOICE, are not given tags. This is because when they are encoded in protocols, a selection of a specific datatype is always made in their place; hence there is no need to have tags for them. The other three classes are used for datatypes defined in addition to these *Universal* types.

The types tagged as *Application* class are applicable to a given ASN.1 module. For example, one may define a datatype called Priority for some electronic mail application; yet in a different application context, the datatype Priority can also be defined as a data structure for scheduling processes in an operating system.

The third class, *Context,* is necessary for constructed datatypes. When we introduced constructed types earlier, we avoided the following problem:

```
AmbiguousDefinition ::=
    SEQUENCE
    {
        alpha    INTEGER OPTIONAL,
        beta     INTEGER OPTIONAL
    }
```

In this example, since both the member datatypes in the sequence are optional, when only one value is present in an instance it is not clear whether it is `alpha` or `beta`. The solution is to tag the members of a sequence, set or choice so that this ambiguity is eliminated. The tagged version of the above definition would now look like this:

```
ClearDefinition ::=
    SEQUENCE
    {
        alpha [0]    INTEGER OPTIONAL,
        beta  [1]    INTEGER OPTIONAL
    }
```

It is a common practice to always include context tags when using SEQUENCE, SET and CHOICE to avoid possible ambiguity. It should be realized, however, these context tags carry with them additional encoding overheads and they ought to be only used when necessary to maximize encoding efficiency.

The fourth class, *Private,* is used for definitions of types unique within an enterprise. This allows another way to tag datatypes without global coordination.

The notation for specifying the tag was given for the case of the *Context* class. For the *Universal, Application* and *Private* classes, the convention is to apply the tag to the beginning of datatype definition, as shown by the following examples:

```
IA5String ::=
    [UNIVERSAL 22]
            IMPLICIT OCTET STRING
Priority ::=
    [APPLICATION 7]
            ENUMERATED
            {
                    normal (0),
                    non-urgent (1),
                    urgent (2)
            }
JobCode ::=
    [PRIVATE 0]
            ENUMERATED
            {
                    president (0),
                    vice-president (1),
                    worker (2)
            }
```

Note, IMPLICIT is another keyword. It can be used whenever more than one definition of a encoded in the protocol to save room. In the above example, defining IA5String as UNIVERSAL 22 is already explicit enough, and it is not necessary to say the datatype is also an OCTET STRING.

VALUES

As in programming languages, ASN.1 also defines how values are specified. The specification of values in the language is for the purpose of defining a type and an instance of a type; it should not be confused with how these values are encoded when they are transferred in the protocols.

For the purpose of our discussions, we only need to describe how the values of the most basic types are specified. We have already touched upon how string values are denoted as either a character string, a hex string or a bit string. Other commonly used values are:

> **BOOLEAN** - TRUE, FALSE
> **INTEGER** - numeric digits (without quotes)

174 APPENDIX A

The rule for specifying values for a constructed datatype is to recursively give each field's type and value. For example, a value of the previously defined type Interrupt-Request might be:

```
{
        fatal-error     TRUE,
        message         "disk crash"
}
```

MODULES

Now we have reviewed the basic elements of ASN.1 sufficiently to summarize how a body of ASN.1 definitions are put together as a *module*. The syntax for a module is as follows:

```
\modulename DEFINITIONS ::=
    BEGIN
            \externalreferences
            \declarations
    END
```

The token `\modulename` is a place-holder for the name of the module, which has two components:

- the textual name of a module
- an Object Identifier assigned to the module

For example, consider a module called `InformationFramework` whose name is as follows:

```
InformationFramework                        (textual name)
{
        joint-iso-ccitt ds(5)
        modules(1)
        informationFramework(1)
}
(ObjectIdentifier)
```

The token `\externalreferences` is a placeholder for the various definitions exported and imported by this module. This import and export facility, similar to those in most programming languages, is very useful for modularizing the definitions of an otherwise large module. For example, the `\externalreferences` for `InformationFramework` may look like this:

```
EXPORTS
    Attribute, AttributeType, AttributeValue
```

```
IMPORTS
    selectedAttributeTypes
        FROM UsefulDefinitions
        {
                joint-iso-ccitt ds(5)
                modules(1)
                usefulDefinitions(0)
        }
```

Finally the token \declarations is the place-holder for the actual datatype defined in this module. The notation for this has previously been illustrated in the explanation of datatypes.

MACROS

ASN.1 also provides a facility, *macros*, to allow the basic syntax described thus far to be extended. Although this *macro* facility is useful for making simple extensions to ASN.1 to make the language more flexible, the facility also makes it difficult to build ASN.1 compilers[1]. Currently, extensions to ASN.1 are being designed to replace the need for *macros*.

Macros are an integral part of many existing ASN.1 definitions. Its notation is as follows:

\macroname MACRO ::=
       BEGIN
              TYPE NOTATION ::= \typesyntax
              VALUE NOTATION ::= \valuesyntax
              \syntaxdefinitions
       END

The token \macroname is the place-holder for a textual name of a *macro*. Then the TYPE NOTATION part defines the syntactical extensions. Each instance of a *macro* always has a value associated with it, as expressed by \valuesyntax. Then, any additional syntax definitions to support what is defined in \typesyntax and \valuesyntax follow. An example is as follows:

```
OBJECT-TYPE MACRO ::=
    BEGIN
            TYPE NOTATION ::=
                    "SYNTAX" type (TYPE ObjectSyntax)
                    "ACCESS" Access
                    "STATUS" Status
            VALUE NOTATION ::=
```

---

[1] see an interesting discussion on this in a "soapbox" in Rose, 1990.

APPENDIX A

```
                        value (VALUE OBJECT IDENTIFIER)
            Access ::= "read-only" | "write-only" |
                       "not-accessible"
            Status ::= "mandatory" | "obsolete" |
                       "optional"
    END
ObjectSyntax ::=
    CHOICE
    {
            number  INTEGER,
            string  OCTET STRING,
            object  OBJECT IDENTIFIER,
            empty   NULL
    }
```

This example is used in the text in the description of how managed objects are defined in the SNMP protocol.

Appendix B - ISO OSI Standards

This appendix lists the ISO OSI standards documents that are referenced in this book.

ISO Document	ISO Status[1]	CCITT Reference	Name
- Overview, Services and Protocol -			
7498-4	IS	X.700	Management Framework
9595	IS	X.710	Common Management Information Service (CMIS)
9596-1	IS	X.711	Common Management Information Protocol (CMIP)
9596-2	DIS		PICS Proforma
10040	IS	X.701	Systems Management Overview (SMO)
- Systems Management -			
10164-1	IS	X.730	Object Management
10164-2	IS	X.731	State Management
10164-3	IS	X.732	Objects and Attributes for Representing Relationships
10164-4	IS	X.733	Alarm Reporting
10164-5	IS	X.734	Event Report Management
10164-6	IS	X.735	Log Control
10164-7	IS	X.736	Security Alarm Reporting
10164-8	DIS	X.740	Security Audit Trail
10164-9	DIS	X.741	Objects and Attributes for Access Control
10164-10	CD	X.742	Accounting Meter
10164-11	DIS	X.739	Workload Monitoring
10164-12	DIS	X.745	Test Management
10164-13	DIS	X.738	Summarization
10164-14	WD	X.737	Confidence and Diagnostic Test Classes
- Structure of Management Information (SMI) -			
10165-1	IS	X.720	Management Information Model
10165-2	IS	X.721	Definition of Management Information
10165-4	IS	X.722	Guidelines for the Definition of Managed Objects

[1] IS = International Standard; DIS = Draft International Standard; CD = Committee Draft; WD = Working Draft.

10165-5	CD	X.723	Generic Managed Objects
10165-6	CD	X.724	Requirements and Guidelines for Conformance Statement Proformas associated with Management Information
10733	DIS		Elements of Management Information Related to OSI Network Layer Standards
10737	DIS		Elements of Management Information Related to OSI Transport

- International Standardized Profiles -

11183-1	ISP	Specification of ACSE, Presentation and Session Protocols for the use by ROSE and CMISE
11183-2	ISP	Enhanced Management Communications
11183-3	ISP	Basic Management Communications

- ASN.1 and BER -

8824	IS	X.409	Abstract Syntax Notation One
8825	IS	X.409	Basic Encoding Rules

Appendix C - Internet Standards

This appendix lists the Internet RFCs that are referenced in this book.

RFC791   Postel, J.B. (1981) Internet Protocol.

RFC793   Postel, J. B. (1981) Transmission Control Protocol.

RFC854   Postel, J. B. & Reynolds, J. K. (1983) Telnet Protocol specification.

RFC959   Postel, J. B. & Reynolds, J. K. (1985) File Transfer Protocol.

RFC1028   Davin, J., Case, J. D., Fedor, M., & Schoffstall, M. L. (1987) Simple Gateway Monitoring Protocol.

RFC1034   Mockapetris, P.V. (1987) Domain names - concepts and facilities.

RFC1035   Mockapetris, P.V. (1987) Domain names - implementation and specification.

RFC1052   Cerf, V. (1988) IAB recommendations for the development of Internet network management standards.

RFC1101   Mockapetris, P.V. (1989) DNS encoding of network names and other types.

RFC1109   Cerf, V. (1989) Report of the second Ad Hoc Network Management Review Group.

RFC1147   Stine, R. H. (ed) (1990) FYI on a network management tool catalog: Tools for monitoring and debugging TCP/IP internets and interconnected devices.

RFC1155   Rose, M. T. & McCloghrie, K. (1990) Structure and identification of management information for TCP/IP-based internets.

RFC1156   McCloghrie, K. & Rose, M. T. (1990) Management Information Base for network management of TCP/IP-based internets.

RFC1157   Case, J. D., Fedor, M., Schoffstall, M. L., & Davin, C. (1990) Simple Network Management Protocol (SNMP).

RFC1158 McCloghrie, K. & Rose, M. T. (eds) (1990) Management Information Base for network management of TCP/IP-based internets: MIB-II.

RFC1160 Cerf, V. (1990) Internet Activities Board.

RFC1187 Rose, M.T., McCloghrie, K., & Davin, J. R. (1990) Bulk table retrieval with the SNMP.

RFC1189 Warrier, U. S., Besaw, L., Labarre, L. & Handspicker, B. D. (1990) Common Management Information Services and Protocols for the Internet (CMOT and CMIP).

RFC1212 Rose, M.T. & McCloghrie, K. (eds) (1991) Concise MIB definitions.

RFC1213 replaces RFC1158.

RFC1214 LaBarre, L. (ed) (1991) OSI internet management: Management Information Base.

RFC1215 Rose, M.T. (ed) (1991) Convention for defining traps for use with the SNMP.

RFC1224 Steinberg, L. (1991) Techniques for managing asynchronously generated alerts.

RFC1227 Rose, M.T. (1991) SNMP MUX protocol and MIB.

RFC1228 Carpenter, G. & Wijnen, B. (1991) SNMP-DPI: Simple Network Management Protocol Distributed Program Interface.

RFC1229 McCloghrie, K. (ed) (1991) Extensions to the generic-interface MIB.

RFC1230 McCloghrie, K. & Fox, R. (1991) IEEE 802.4 Token Bus MIB.

RFC1231 McCloghrie, K., Fox, R. & Decker, E. (1991) IEEE 802.5 Token Ring MIB.

RFC1232 Baker, F. & Kolb, C.P. (eds) (1991) Definitions of managed objects for the DS1 Interface type.

RFC1233 Cox, T. A. & Tesink, K., (eds) (1991) Definitions of managed objects for the DS3 Interface type.

RFC1238 Satz, G. (1991) CLNS MIB for use with Connectionless Network Protocol

(ISO 8473) and End System to Intermediate System (ISO 9542).

RFC1239 Reynolds, J. K. (1991) Reassignment of experimental MIBs to standard MIBs.

RFC1243 Waldbusser, S. (ed) (1991) Appletalk Management Information Base.

RFC1250 Postel, J. B. (ed) (1991) IAB official protocol standards.

RFC1253 Baker, F. & Coltun, R. (1991) OSPF version 2: Management Information Base.

RFC1269 Willis, S. & Burruss, J. W. (1991) Definitions of managed objects for the Border Gateway Protocol.

RFC1270 Kastenholz, F., (ed) (1991) SNMP communications services.

RFC1271 Waldbusser, S. (1991) Remote network monitoring Management Information Base.

RFC1283 Rose, M. T. (1991) SNMP over OSI.

RFC1284 Cook, J., (ed) (1991) Definitions of managed objects for the Ethernet-like interface types.

RFC1285 Case, J. D., (1992) FDDI Management Information Base.

RFC1286 Decker, E., Langille, P., Rijsinghani, A., & McCloghrie, K., (1991) Definitions of managed objects for bridges.

RFC1289 Saperia, J., (1991) DECnet phase IV MIB extensions.

RFC1303 McCloghrie, K. & Rose, M., (1992) A Convention for Describing SNMP-based Agents.

RFC1304 Cox, T. & Tesink, K., (eds) (1992) Definitions of Managed Objects for the SIP Interface Type.

Abbreviations

AFNOR	Association Francais de Normalisation. French ISO member body
AM	Access Module
ANSI	American National Standards Institute, US ISO member body
AOW	Asian and Oceanian OSI Workshop
API	Application Programming Interface. Language/subroutine call
ASN.1	Abstract Syntax Notation One
BER	Basic Encoding Rules
BSI	British Standards Institute. UK ISO member body.
CCITT	International Telegraph & Telephone Consultative Committee (of ITU)
CD	Committee Draft (ISO)
CMIP	Common Management Information Protocol (ISO 9596)
CMIS	Common Management Information Service (ISO 9595)
CP	Control Point
CPMS	Control Point Management Service
CSMA/CD	Carrier Sense Multi-Access with Collision Detection
CPU	Central Processing Unit
DARPA	Defense Advanced Research Projects Agency
DIS	Draft International Standard (ISO)
DME	Distributed Management Environment (from OSF)
DNA	Digital Network Architecture
DN	Distinguished Name
DNS	Domain Name Service
DOD	Department of Defense
EMA	Enterprise Management Architecture
EWOS	European Workshop for OSI
FDDI	Fiber Distributed Data Interface
FIPS	Federal Information Processing Standard (US Government)
FM	Function Module
GDMO	Guidelines for the Definition of Managed Objects
GOSIP	Government OSI Profile
IAB	Internet Activity Board, also known as Internet Architecture Board
IEC	International Electrotechnical Commission (electrical standards focus)
IEEE	Institute of Electrical and Electronics Engineers (professional organization)
IETF	Internet Engineering Task Force
IP	Internet Protocol
IRTF	Internet Research Task Force
IS	International Standard (ISO)
ISO	International Organization for Standardization
ISP	International Standardized Profiles

IT	Information Technology
JTC1	Joint Technical Committee No. 1 (ISO/IEC focus for IT stds)
LAN	Local Area Network
LMS	Local Management services
MAC	Media Access Control
MAN	Management Event Notification protocol
MIB	Management Information Base
MICE	Management Information Control Exchange protocol
MOCS	Managed Object Conformance Statement
MS	Management Service
NCL	Network Command Language
NCP	Network Control Program
NICE	Network Information Control and Exchange protocol.
NIST	National Institute of Standards and Technology (US)
NMF	Network Management Forum
NMVT	Network Management Vector Transport
OID	Object Identifier
OIW	OSI Implementors Workshop (US, administered by NIST)
OSF	Open Software Foundation
OSI	Open System Interconnection (ISO 7498)
PM	Presentation Module
PU	Physical Unit
PUMS	Physical Unit Management Service
RDN	Relative Distinguished Name
RFC	Request For Comment
RISC	Reduced Instruction Set Computer
ROSE	Remote Operations Service Element (ISO 9072)
RPC	Remote Procedure Call
RTM	Response Time Monitoring
RU	Request-Response Unit
SAW	Session AWareness data
SDO	Standards Development Organization
SGFS	Special Group on Functional Standards (or ISPs); part of JTC1
SMI	Structure of Management Information
SNA	System Network Architecture (IBM's networking architecture)
SNMP	Simple Network Management Protocol
TCP/IP	Transmission control protocol, Internet protocol:
TCC	Telecommunication Technology Committee (Japan)
UDP	Universal Datagram Protocol
VTAM	Virtual Telecommunications Access Method
WAN	Wide Area Network

Glossary

Abstract Syntax Notation One (ASN.1) - The language specified by ISO standard 8824 for defining the *Management Information Base* in the *Open Systems Interconnection* (OSI).

Access Module (AM) - In Digital's *Enterprise Management Architecture (EMA)*, a component of the Director that provides access to a particular class of managed objects.

Accounting management - The function of recording the usage of network resources in order to control the operational cost of the network.

Agent - In the object-oriented model of network management, a component that performs actions on the behalf of one or more managed objects.

Alarm reporting - Sending to the attention of network managers the more critical errors detected by network fault management.

AppleTalk - The network architecture developed by Apple Computer Corporation.

Application layer - Layer 7 of the *Open Systems Reference Model,* that provides services that may be useful to a large number of user applications, such as file transfer and mail.

Application workload - A measurement of the relative amount network usage imposed by various network applications.

ARPANET - The operational computer network connecting many research institutions, that was created by the *U.S. Defense Advanced Research Projects Agency (DARPA),* and which evolved into the *Internet* network.

Assignment - see *Registration.*

Authentication - A service is that permits the identity of a given principal to be determined reliably.

Authorization - A service through which access to resources can be restricted to only selected principals.

Availability - A measure of the degree to which the resources in a computer network can be accessed when they are actually needed.

Basic Encoding Rules (BER) - The representation specified by ISO standard 8825 for datatypes in management protocol messages in the *Open Systems Interconnection (OSI)*.

Bridge - A network component that can be used to connect two media of the same type, and which provides some filtering of messages transmitted between the two network segments.

Broadcast protocol - A protocol in which a message from a single source is delivered by the network to all connected systems.

Capacity planning - An aspect of configuration management that involves determining the collective traffic load for all network components, and projecting future resource needs.

Carrier Sense Multi-Access with Collision Detection (CSMA/CD) - A form of Local Area Network physical layer protocol that permits multiple End Systems to share the same physical media by allowing them to detect whether or not the media is already in use when they attempt to transmit, so they can delay transmission until it is available.

Common Management Information Protocol (CMIP) - The protocol specified by ISO standard 9596 for implementing the *Common Management Information Services* in the *Open Systems Interconnection (OSI)*.

Common Management Information Service (CMIS) - The abstract procedural interface specified by ISO standard 9595 for a set of network management functions for the *Open Systems Interconnection (OSI)*.

Compression - The process of reducing the size of encoded data without a loss of information, for more efficient transmission on a network.

Configuration management - Initializing and connecting the network components to provide the network services. Configuration management includes assigning names and addresses to the network components and correctly setting the parameters that control the routine operation of the network.

Confirmed request - In the *Common Management Information Protocol*, a type of service in which a request is followed by a response.

Congestion avoidance - A scheme that prevents network congestion by continuously monitoring the network and slowing down the demand as soon as the network resources begin to experience congestion.

Congestion control - A scheme that recovers from network congestion by removing the load and restarting everything very slowly.

GLOSSARY 187

Connection-oriented protocol - A protocol in which the source and destination systems exchange messages in the context of some shared state, that is established prior to any data interchange.

Control Point (CP) - In IBM's *Systems Network Architecture (SNA)*, a monitoring agent that is capable of talking to multiple *Physical Units (PU)*, and which interfaces with the network administrator (operator) who manages the network.

Danger zones - An aspect of fault management involving the monitoring of a network to prevent faults from occurring, in which thresholds are set on the attributes and states of managed objects, and alarms are raised if the thresholds are exceeded.

Data flow - The direction of logical movement of data on a physical link. Data flow can be one of: *simplex*, in which data flows in only one direction on the link; *half-duplex*, in which data flows in both directions on the link, but not at the same time; and *full duplex*, in which data flows in both directions on the link at the same time.

Datalink layer - Layer 2 of the *Open Systems Reference Model,* that provides the transmission of a string of bits, called packets; and performs error detection and correction functions to ensure a packet contains the same information received as sent.

Datalink monitor - An external monitor that is inserted into the physical link to monitor traffic at the datalink layer.

Datatype conversion - The process of converting transmitted data from one form to another, to accommodate differences between the source and destination systems in a communications interchange.

Director - In Digital's *Enterprise Management Architecture (EMA)*, a component that provides a common framework for management application software.

Directory service - A network service that provides a translation from object names to network addresses, and may store other information about objects that needs to be widely available.

Distinguished Name (DN) - In the *Open Systems Interconnection (OSI)* management information model, the global name of a managed object.

Distributed system - A full network computing environment, comprising the physical components of the network, and the network software, as well as the operating systems and applications residing on End Systems. A distributed system relies on sophisticated network services such as directory services and security services, to provide a network computing environment similar to that of a non-distributed computing system

Encryption - The encoding of transmitted data with secret keys, to protect it from unauthorized access during communications interchanges.

End System - A system connected to a network, that runs the full seven layers of the *Open Systems Reference Model*, and supports the use of network applications.

Enterprise Management Architecture (EMA) - The integrated network and systems management architecture developed by Digital Equipment Corporation.

Entity - In Digital's *Enterprise Management Architecture (EMA)*, a managed object.

Ethernet (IEEE 802.3) - A standard for Local Area Networks that provides 10 Mbit/second communications over a multi-access physical media, based on a Carrier Sense Multi-Access with Collision Detection (CSMA/CD) protocol.

Event-driven access method - A method of access to managed objects in which monitor information is provided whenever the state of the managed object changes, without requiring an explicit request.

Event logging monitor - A monitor that records events (i.e., changes in state) of network components, network software and/or network applications.

External monitoring agent - A monitoring agent that is not collocated or integrated with the managed object(s) being monitored.

Fault management - The function of detecting faults in computer networks, as well as isolating, identifying and correcting the causes of the faults.

File transfer - A network application that permits the interchange of data files between systems.

Full interconnection - A physical network topology in which every End System has a direct connection to every other End System.

Function Module (FM) - In Digital's *Enterprise Management Architecture (EMA)*, a component of the Director that is configured to provide a particular value-added function.

Gateway - A network component that can be used to connect two networks of different types, by performing some protocol transformation between the two environments.

Integrated monitoring agent - A monitoring agent that is collocated and integrated with the managed object(s) being monitored.

Interface - In the *Open Systems Reference Model*, the means through which the functions of a given layer access the functions of the layer below.

Intermediate monitoring agent - See *Summarization monitoring agent*.

Intermediate System - A system connected to a network, that runs only the lower layers of the *Open Systems Reference Model,* and supports the routing of messages between End Systems.

International Standards Organization (ISO) - A participatory group of committees set up to establish computing standards for the international community.

Internet Activities Board (IAB) - The coordinating committee that oversees the engineering and management of the *Internet* network.

Internet Engineering Task Force (IETF) - The branch of the *Internet Activities Board (IAB)* responsible for resolving all short-term protocol and architectural issues required to make the *Internet* function effectively.

Internet protocol suite (IP) - The suite of protocols designed for use on the *Internet* network.

Internet Research Task Force (IRTF) - The branch of the *Internet Activities Board (IAB)* responsible for longer-term research, and for developing new technologies for the *Internet* network.

LAN traffic monitor - An external monitor that is attached to a multi-access media to monitor traffic at the datalink layer. LAN traffic monitors are typically passive, in that they do not interfere with normal transmissions on the media.

Load balancing - The use of monitor information to distribute the workload of a given application or applications among a set of available End Systems, such that optimal performance is achieved overall.

Local Area Network (LAN) - A shared, high-speed, multi-access network spanning a limited geographical area.

Local Management Services (LMS) - In IBM's *Systems Network Architecture,* a component of a *Physical Unit (PU)* that acts as a management agent for the *node.*

Managed object - Any entity in a computing network with state that requires management in the form of installation, configuration, fault detection, accounting, etc.

Registration of managed objects - The process of ensuring the unique assignment of object identifiers through an assignment authority.

Management agent - An agent in a computer network that provides access to monitor information, and control of managed objects.

Management application - An application that coordinates the activities of one or more management agents, and makes them accessible to network administrators.

Management Event Notification (MEN) - In Digital's *Digital Network Architecture (DNA)*, the event-driven method of access to managed objects.

Management framework - An operating environment for the development and deployment of management applications.

Management Information Base (MIB) - In the *Open Systems Interconnection (OSI)*, the set of managed objects, when defined formally using a management information model.

Management Information Control Exchange (MICE) - In Digital's *Digital Network Architecture (DNA)*, the polled method of access to managed objects.

Management information model - The information model for managed objects that describes how each item of information accessible through a monitoring agent is identified. The management information model also defines the syntax of each item, as well as its semantic relationship to other items.

Management protocol - A network protocol designed specifically for the purpose of allowing management agents to monitor and control managed objects.

Management Service Request-response Units (RU) - In IBM's *Systems Network Architecture (SNA)*, the encoding of messages in the request/response flow.

Media Access Control (MAC) - A function of the datalink layer when interfacing to multi-access media.

Monitoring agent - An agent in a computer network that monitors one or more managed objects, and provides monitor information to management agents.

Multicast protocol - A protocol in which a message from a single source is delivered by the network to multiple connected systems.

Netview - The network management architecture developed by IBM.

Network address - The unique address by which each End System in a network can be located.

Network element - In the *Internet* network management model, a managed object.

Network Information Control and Exchange (NICE) - The network management protocol used in the Phase IV version of Digital's *Digital Network Architecture (DNA)*.

Network layer - Layer 3 of the *Open Systems Reference Model,* that controls how packets are routed through a network to reach a destination End System. The network layer also controls the rate at which the network accepts packets, to avoid and recover from congestion..

Network management station - In the *Internet* network management model, a management agent.

Network Management Vector Transport (NMVT) - In IBM's *Systems Network Architecture (SNA)*, the application protocol used between a *Control Point (CP)* and a *Physical Unit (PU)*.

Networking software - The software in an End System or Intermediate System that implements the layers of the *Open Systems Reference Model*.

Network Command Language (NCL) - In the Phase V version of Digital's *Digital Network Architecture (DNA)*, a command language utility for performing network management operations.

Network Control Program (NCP) - In IBM's *Systems Network Architecture (SNA)*, a networking program that runs in a network controller, for the purpose of off-loading the host; In the Phase IV version Digital's *Digital Network Architecture (DNA)*, a command language utility for performing network management operations.

Node - In IBM's *Systems Network Architecture (SNA)*, an End System.

Non-confirmed request - In the *Common Management Information Protocol*, a type of service in which a request is not followed by a response.

Object hierarchy - The classification of managed objects into a hierarchical structure, that facilitates the management and scalability of the network.

Object identifier - A name or value that uniquely identifies each managed object in a network.

Object instances - One instance of an object of a given type.

Object types - The abstract definition of a class of objects with the same set of attributes.

Open Systems Interconnection (OSI) - The suite of networking standards developed by the *International Standards Organization (ISO)* to enable the deployment of global networks.

Open Systems Reference Model - The architectural model on which the *Open Systems Interconnection (OSI)* standards are based.

Performance management - The function of tuning and sizing a network to ensure optimal performance with the available network resources.

Physical layer - Layer 1 of the *Open Systems Reference Model*, that provides the transmission of bits from one system to another.

Physical medium - The actual wires, cables and other physical components that provide the infrastructure on which computer networks are built.

Physical Unit (PU) - In IBM's *Systems Network Architecture (SNA)*, a monitoring agent.

Physical Unit Management Services (PUMS) - In IBM's *Systems Network Architecture (SNA)*, a component of a *Physical Unit (PU)* that implements the protocols for interacting with *Control Points (CP)* on behalf of the *Local Management Services (LMS)*.

Point-to-point connection - A direct connection between two End Systems in a network.

Polled access method - A method of access to managed objects in which monitor information is provided only in response to a specific request.

Presentation Module (PM) - In Digital's *Enterprise Management Architecture (EMA)*, a component of the Director that provides the interface to the user.

Principal - An entity in a network that might be the source or destination of an information interchange. Principals can include both human users of the network, as well as components, such as software applications, that might act as agents for human users.

Property inheritance - The ability of a managed object to take on the attributes of some other object.

Recommendations for Message Handling Systems - A set of standards for computer networking developed by the *CCITT*, which includes X.409 (ASN.1 and BER).

Reduced Instruction Set Computer (RISC) - A computer with a small, simplified set of instructions, which is able to execute primitive operations at very high speeds.

Relative Distinguished Name (DN) - In the *Open Systems Interconnection (OSI)* management information model, a component of the global name of a managed object.

Remote Procedure Call (RPC) - A method of designing and implementing network protocols using high-level language tools.

Repeater - A network component that can be used to connect two media of the same type, with no filtering of messages transmitted between the two network segments.

Request For Comment (RFC) - The process employed by the *Internet* for proposing and soliciting input on new network protocol standards.

Request/Reply flow - In IBM's *Systems Network Architecture (SNA)*, the polled method of access to managed objects.

Resource brokering - The use of monitor information to enable applications to select among a set of available End Systems, based on the availability of a variety of resources on those systems.

Resource management - A service that facilitates the management of shared resources in a distributed computing environment, and enables resource brokering in network applications.

Routing - The forwarding, by an Intermediate System, of messages transmitted between End Systems.

Security management - The function of auditing network operations to prevent or detect unauthorized access to shared resources.

Session layer - Layer 5 of the *Open Systems Reference Model,* that assists applications in negotiating the establishment of connections, which may involve locating the destination application, and ensuring that the initiator is authentic and has the access rights to establish a connection.

Simple Gateway Management Protocol (SGMP) - A request-response protocol for managing gateways in the *Internet*.

Simple Network Management Protocol (SNMP) - The protocol used for accessing managed objects in the *Internet*.

Structure of Management Information (SMI) - The structure specified by ISO standard 10165 for defining the relationships among managed objects.

Subnetwork - A portion of a network comprised of connections between Intermediate Systems, that enables a larger number of End Systems to interoperate as if they were fully connected.

Summarization monitoring agent - A monitoring agent that collects information about managed objects from other monitoring agents and aggregates the information for management applications.

Systems Network Architecture (SNA) - The network architecture developed by IBM.

Terminal server - A network component that allows terminal devices to be connected to a network, and acts as a gateway between the terminals and other resources in the network.

Timestamping - The function of marking the time at which specific events occurred, and recording these as part of the monitor information so the correct sequence of events can later be determined.

Token Bus (IEEE 802.4) - A standard for Local Area Networks that describes the Medium Access Control sublayer and Physical layer functions for a bus-structured LAN using a token passing protocol..

Token Ring (IEEE 802.5) - A standard for Local Area Networks that describes the Medium Access Control sublayer and Physical layer functions for a ring-structured LAN using a token passing protocol..

Transaction processing - A special form of reliable communications in which multiple operations can be performed atomically - either all operations complete, or they are all rejected.

Transport layer - Layer 4 of the *Open Systems Reference Model,* that fragments large messages into smaller packets as required by the lower layers, and ensures the reliable delivery of the packets in the correct order. Another function of this layer is to ensure that packets are sent at a rate the receiving End System and application can cope with. At the receiving End System, the transport layer reassembles the packets into messages and delivers them to the next higher layer.

Unsolicited flow - In IBM's *Systems Network Architecture (SNA),* the event-driven method of access to managed objects.

User interface - The means through which an end user accesses management applications.

Virtual Terminal Access Method (VTAM) - In IBM's *Systems Network Architecture (SNA),* the networking program that runs in the host, and provides access to the network to applications.

Wide Area Network (WAN) - The interconnection of network systems using point-to-point links, typically spanning a wide geographical area.

Workload monitor - A monitor that measures the workload imposed on the network by applications.

Trademarks

The following are believed to be trademarks and are acknolwedged as such:

AppleTalk, Macintosh, the Apple logo	Apple Computer, Inc.,
DEC, the DIGITAL logo, DECnet, DECnet/OSI, Digital Network Architecture, EMA, DECmcc	Digital Equipment Corporation
Ethernet	Digital Equipment Corporation, Intel and Xerox
IBM, the IBM logo, NetView, NetView/PC, VTAM, NCP, NMVT	International Business Machines
LANalyzer	Excelan, Incorporated
The Sniffer	Network General Corporation
UNIX	A.T.&T. (Bell Laboratories)
X Window System	Massachusetts Institute of Technology

References

Abramson, N. (1970) The ALOHA System - Another Alternative for Computer Communications, *Proceedings of the Fall Joint Computer Conference.*

Apple Computer Inc. (1985) *Inside Macintosh, Volume II,* Addison-Wesley.

Baiardi, F., de Francesco, N., Matteoli, E., Stefanini, S. & Vaglini, G. (1983) Development of a Debugger for a Concurrent Language, *Proceedings of the ACM SIGSOFT/SIGPLAN Software Engineering Symposium on High-Level Debugging.*

Bates, P. C. & Wileden, J. C. (1983) An Approach to High-Level Debugging of Distributed Systems, *Proceedings of the ACM SigSoft/SigPlan Software Engineering Symposium on High-Level Debugging.*

Bates, P. C. (1989) *EBBA Modeling Tool / Event Definition Language*, COINS Technical Report 89-09, University of Massachusetts.

Bei, J. N. (1985) *Communication Graph Display System: On the Use of Computer Graphics to Debug Distributed Software*, PhD. thesis, Department of Computer Science, University of Waterloo.

Bertsekas, D. & Gallager, R. (1987) *Data Networks,* Prentice-Hall.

Bhatt, G. D. & Ramanujan, R. G. (1987) An Instrumented Testbed for Real-Time Distributed Systems Development, *Proceedings of the 8th IEEE Real-Time Systems Symposium.*

Hitson, B.. (1988) Knowledge-based monitoring and control: an approach to understanding the behavior of TCP/IP network protocols, *Proceedings of ACM SigComm 88 Symposium.*

Caceres, R.., Danzig, P. B., Jamin, S. & Mitzel, D. J. (1991) Characteristics of Wide-Area TCP/IP Conversations, *Proceedings of the 1991 ACM SigComm Conference.*

CCITT (1984) *Message Handling Systems: Presentation Transfer Syntax and Notation. International Telegraph and Telephone Consultative Committee,* Recommendation X.409.

Chiu, D. M. & Sudama, R. (1988) A Case Study of DECnet Applications and Protocol Performance, *Proceedings of the 1988 ACM SigMetrics Conference.*

Chiu, D. M. & Sudama, R. (1989) Studying the User and Application Behavior of a

REFERENCES

Large Network, *Proceedings of IEEE workshop on the Future Trend of Distributed Computing Systems in the '90s.*

Comer, D. (1988) *Internetworking with TCP/IP: Principles, Protocols, and Architecture,* Prentice-Hall.

Digital Equipment Corporation, Intel Corporation, & Xerox Corporation (1980) *The Ethernet: A Local Area Network Data Link Layer and Physical Layer Specification.*

Digital Equipment Corporation, (1987) *DECnet Digital Network Architecture General Description,* EK-DNAPV-GD

Digital Equipment Corporation, (1989) *Enterprise Management Architecture General Description,* EK-DEMARGD.

Excelan Inc., (1986) *LANalyzer EX 5000E Ethernet Network Analyser User Manual,* San Jose, California.

Fehskens, L. (1989) An Architectural Strategy for Enterprise Management, *Integrated Network Management, 1: Proceedings of the IFIP TC6/WG6.6 Symposium on Integrated Network Management,* edited by Meandzija, B. & Westcott, J. pp 41-60.

Franta, W. R. & Chlamtac, I. (1981) *Local Networks,* Lexington Books, Lexington, Massachusetts.

GarciaMolina, H., Germano, F. & Kohler, W. H. (1981) Debugging a Distributed Computing System, *Digital Equipment Corporation, Technical Report TR-118.*

Gupta, N. K. & Sevior, R. E. (1984) An Expert System Approach to Real-time System Debugging, *Proceedings of the First Conference on Artificial Intelligence Applications,* CS Press, 336-343.

Hawe, W. R., Kirby, A. & Stewart, B. (1984) Transparent Interconnection of Local Networks with Bridges, *Journal of Telecommunication Networks,* **3**, No. 2, pp116-130.

International Business Machines, (1975) *IBM System Network Architecture - General Information,* IBM System Development Division, Publication Center, P.O.Box 12195, Research Triangle Park, North Carolina.

International Business Machines, (1987) *System Network Architecture - Format and Protocol Reference Manual: Management Services,* SC30-3346-1, IBM System Development Division, Publication Center, P.O.Box 12195, Research Triangle Park, North Carolina.

International Business Machines, (1989) *Planning and Reference for NetView, Network*

Control Program, Virtual Telecommunications Access Method, SC31-6811-0, IBM System Development Division, Publication Center, P.O.Box 12195, Research Triangle Park, North Carolina.

Jaffe, J. A. (1979) Parallel Computation: Synchronization, Scheduling and Schemes, *PhD. thesis, Massachusetts Institute of Technology, MIT/LCS TR-231.*

Jain, R. & Routhier, R. (1986) Packet Trains - Measurements and a New Model for Computer Network Traffic, *IEEE Journal on Selected Areas in Communications, SAC*-**4**, *No. 6*

Lamport, L. (1978) Time, Clocks and the Ordering of Events in a Distributed System, *Communications of the ACM,* **21** No. 7.

Lampson, B. W. & Redell D. D. (1980) Experiences With Processes and Monitors in Mesa, *Communications of the ACM,* **23** *No. 2.*

LaPelle, N., Seger, M. and Sylor, M. (1986) The Evolution of Network Management Products, *Digital Technical Journal,* **1**, No. 3, pp 117-128.

Macrander, C. M. (1984) *Development of a Control Process for the Berkley UNIX Distributed Programs Monitor,* Master's thesis, UCB/CSD 84/216, University of California, Berkley.

Martin, J. & Leben, J. (1992) *DECnet Phase V - An OSI Implementation,* Digital Press.

Maxion, R. A. (1986) Distributed Diagnostic Performance Reporting and Analysis, *Proceedings of the IEEE International Conference on Computer Design.*

McDaniel, G. (1977) METRIC: A Kernel Instrumentation System for Distributed Environments, *Proceedings of the 6th Symposium on Operating System Principles.*

Metcalfe, R. M. & Boggs, D. R. (1976) Ethernet: Distributed Packet Switching for Local Computer Networks, *Communications of the ACM,* **19**, No. 7, pp 395-404.

Miller, B. P., Secherest, S. & Macrander, C. (1984) *A Distributed Program Monitor for Berkley Unix,* Technical Report UCB/CSD 84/201, University of California, Berkley, also in *Software Practice and Experience,* John Wiley & Son.

Miller, B. P. (1985a) *DPM: A Measurement System for Distributed Programs,* TR-592, Computer Sciences Department, University of Wisconsin.

Miller, B. P. (1985b) *Parallelism in Distributed Programs: Measurement and Prediction,* Technical Report, Computer Sciences Department, University of Wisconsin-Madison.

Miller, B. P. & Yang, C.-Q., (1987) IPS: An Interactive and Automatic Performance Measurement Tool for Parallel and Distributed Programs, *Proceedings of the 7th International Conference on Distributed Computing Systems.*

Network General Corporation, (1986) *The Sniffer: Operation and Reference Manual,* Sunnyvale, California.

Paxson, V. (1991) *Measurements and Models of Wide Area TCP Conversations,* Report LBL-30840, Lawrence Livermore Laboratories.

Rose, M. (1990) *The Open Book: A Practical Perspective on OSI,* Prentice Hall.

Rose, M. (1991a) *The Simple Book: An Introduction to Management of TCP/IP-based Internets,* Prentice Hall.

Schiefler, R. W. & Gettys, J. (1990) *X Window System, Second Edition,* Digital Press.

Schiffenbauer, R. D. (1981) *Interactive Debugging in a Distributed Computational Environment,* MIT/LCS TR-264, Laboratory of Computer Science, Massachusetts Institute of Technology.

Shoch, J. F. & Hupp, J. A. (1980) Measured Performance of the Ethernet Local Network, *Communications of the ACM,* **23** *No. 12,* 711-721.

Shurtleff, D. & Strutt, C. (1990) Extensibility of an Enterprise Management Director, *Network management and Control,* edited by Kershenbaum et al. Plenum Press.

Sidhu, G. S., Andrews, R. F. & Oppenheimer, A. B. (1990) *Inside AppleTalk, Second Edition,* Addison-Wesley.

Soha, M. (1987) A Distributed Approach to LAN Monitoring Using Intelligent High Performance Monitors, *IEEE Network Magazine,* **1,** No. 3, pp 13-21.

Stankovic, J. A. (1980) Debugging Commands for a Distributed Processing System, *Proceedings of COMPCON.*

Sudama, R. & Chiu, D. M. (1990) Experiences of Designing a Sophisticated Network Monitor, *Software Practice and Experience,* **20** *(6),* 555-570.

Svobodova, L., Liskov, B. & Clark, D. (1979) *Distributed Computer Systems: Structure and Semantics,* MIT/LCS TR-215 Massachusetts Institute of Technology.

Schwartz, M. (1987) *Telecommunications Networks: Protocols, Modeling and Analysis,* Addison-Wesley.

Sylor, M. (1988) Managing DECnet Phase V: The Entity Model, *IEEE Networks,* 30-36.

Sylor, M. (1991) DECnet/OSI Phase V Network Management, *Integrated Network Management, II*, edited by Krishnan and Zimmer, Elsevier Science Publishers.

Tanenbaum, A. (1981) *Computer Networks: Toward Distributed Processing Systems*, Prentice-Hall.

Tokuda, H., Kotera, M. & Mercer, C. W. (1988) *A Real-Time Monitor for a Distributed Real-Time Operating System*, CMU-CS-88-179, Computer Science Department, Carnegie-Mellon University.

Zimmerman, H. (1980) OSI Reference Model - The ISO Model of Architecture for Open Systems Interconnection, *IEEE Trans. on Communications*, **COM-4**, No. 4, pp 425-432.

Index

A

Abstract Syntax Notation One (ASN.1), *43*, 44, 52, 54, 84, *167*
    datatypes, *168*, 171
    macro, 167
    macros, *175*
    modules, *174*
    values, *173*
Access Module (AM), *86*
accounting
    for network usage, 32, 34, 125, 149
accounting management, *34*, 36, 73, 100, 114, 122, 127, 137, *149*
Agent, 85, *86*
alarm reporting, *143*
AppleTalk, 26, *27*, 51, 56
ARPANET, *47*
assignment, *43*
attribute group, *65*
authentication, 33, 138, *147*, *161*
authorization, 138, *148*, *161*
availability
    of name services, 42
    of networks, 28, 32, 33, 40, 123, 146, 164
    of objects, 42
    of resources, 153, 165

B

Basic Encoding Rules (BER), *167*
bridge, 111, 134, *146*
broadcast protocol, 25, 85

C

capacity planning, 123
Carrier Sense Multi-Access with Collision Detection (CSMA/CD), *130*. *See also* Ethernet
Common Management Information Protocol (CMIP), *46*, *59*
Common Management Information Service (CMIS), *63*, 64, 73
compression, 24
configuration management, 33, 36, 62, 73, 100, 109, 111, 112, 113, 122, 127, 128, 130, *144*
confirmed request, *64*
congestion avoidance, *130*
congestion control, *130*
connection-oriented protocol, 27, 100, 114, 117, 165
connectionless protocol, 27
Control Point (CP), 73, *76*

D

danger zones, *144*
data flow
    full-duplex, *102*, *187*
    half-duplex, *102*, *187*
    simplex, *102*, *187*
datalink monitor, *101*
datatype conversion, 24, 139
debugging, 127, *138*, 158
DECnet, *46*, *83*, 100
    OSI, *83*, 86
Defense Advanced Research Projects Agency (DARPA), 27, *47*, *185*
descriptor, *66*
Digital Network Architecture (DNA), *26*, 27, 36, 83
    CMIP, *84*
Director, *84*, 85, *86*
directory service, *42*
    Domain Name Service (DNS), *45*
    X.500, 27, *45*, 64
Distinguished Name (DN), *72*
distributed system, *28*, 131, 147

E

encryption, 24, 33, 138, *148*, *161*
End System, *19*, 20, 24, 27, 29, 93, 95, 96, 99, 106, 110, 111, 113, 140, 142, 148, 151, 158, 189, 193
Enterprise Management Architecture (EMA), *84*, 85, 86
Entity, 84, *85*
  Global, *86*
Ethernet (IEEE 802.3), 24, 116, 121, *130*, 133. *See also* Local Area Network (LAN)
event logging monitor, *105*
event traces, 141
external monitor, *40*

F

fault management, *32*, 34, 36, 109, 127, *143*, 144
file transfer, 24, 27, *28*, 134
flow
  request/reply, *78*
  unsolicited, *78*
framework
  for management applications, *127*
  information, *85*
  OSI management, *32*, 61, 160
full interconnection, *20*
Function Module (FM), *86*

G

gateway, 47, 51, 75, 134

I

inheritance
  class, *65*
  multiple, *65*
  property, 29, 85, *153*
interface, *23*, 63, 99, 110, 186

interface24, 127
Intermediate System, *20*, 24, 29, 99, 159
International Standards Organization (ISO), *22*, 44, 45, *63*, 64, 84, 167, 169
  in DECnet, *84*
Internet, *27*, 46, *47*, 53, 58, 185
  Protocol (IP), *47*
Internet Activities Board (IAB), *47*, *48*
Internet Engineering Task Force (IETF), *47*
Internet protocol suite (TCP/IP), *27*, 36, 43, 45, *48*, 51, 56, 100, 112, 167
Internet Research Task Force (IRTF), *48*

L

LAN traffic monitor, *108*, 145, 150
layer, *23*, 27, 29, 45, 51, 90, 91, 99, 106, 114
  application, *24*, *100*
  data link, *24*, *99*
  network, *24*, 27, *99*, 119, 145
  physical, *24*
  presentation, *24*
  session, *24*, 27, *100*, 150
  transport, *24*, *100*
load balancing, 100, *151*
Local Area Network (LAN), *26*, 27, 30, 32, 41, 93, 96, 101, 108, 111, 112, 113, 114, 115, 126, 132, 137, 144, 145, 146, 148, 150, 160. *See also* Ethernet, Token Ring, Token Bus
Local Management Services (LMS), *76*

M

mail, 17, 24, *28*, 172
  X.400, *27*
managed object class, *64*
managed objects
  registration of, *43*
management agent, 18, 29

INDEX 205

management application, *32*, *36*, 37, 41, 73, 89, 91, 92, 96, 99, 101, *127*, 157, 163, 165, 166
    as Control Point (in SNA), 76
    as director (in EMA), 84, *85*, 86
    as external monitor, *40*
    as network management stations (in IP), *51*
    design of, 164
    frameworks, *127*
    method of access, *40*
    protocols, 38, 85
Management Event Notification (MEN), *85*
Management Information Base
    in OSI, 61
Management Information Base (MIB), 29, 36, *43*, 47, 99, 167
    in Appletalk, *56*
    in OSI, *63*
    in TCP/IP, *56*, 58
Management Information Control Exchange (MICE), *85*
management information model, 36, *42*, 43, 45, 46, 52, 167
    in EMA, *85*
    in OSI, 63, *64*, 177
    in SNA, *81*
    in TCP/IP, *52*, 56
management protocol, 36, 40, *45*, 144, 145
    access methods in, *41*
    and information models, *42*
    and object names, *41*
    definition of, *167*
    standards for, *46*, 50, 53, 84. *See also* Digital Network Architecture (DNA); Open Systems Interconnect (OSI); Simple Network Management Protocol (SNMP)
Management Service Request-response Units (RU), *78*

Media Access Control (MAC), *24*, *43*
monitoring agent, 18, 29, *36*, 37, 38
    addressing, *41*
    as agent (in EMA), *85*
    as management agent (in IP), *51*
    as Physical Unit (in SNA), *76*, *187*
    characterization of, *90*, 99
    examples of, *100*
    external, *30*, *37*, 40, 92, 95, 96, 97, 98, 99, 140
    functions of, *89*
    integrated, *30*, *91*, 92, 99, 140
    intermediate, *37*, *193*
    methods of access, *40*, 51, 64, 85, 159
        event-driven, 36, *41*, 52, 64, 74, 78, 85, 144, 157
        polled, 36, *40*, 41, 52, 78, 85, 144, 157
    summarization, *37*
multicast protocol, 26

N

name bindings, *70*
Netview, *73*
network address, 27, 28, 33, 36, *41*, 84, 86, 104, 107, 110, 186
    registration of, *43*, 45
Network Command Language (NCL), *86*
Network Control Program (NCP), 73, 86
network element, *51*
Network Information Control and Exchange (NICE), *84*
network management station, *51*
Network Management Vector Transport (NMVT), *74*, 78
networking software, *19*, 22, 27, 91, 99, 127, 128
node, *76*, *86*
non-confirmed request, *64*

O

object hierarchy, 29, 41, *54*, 64, 85, 86
    containment, *70*, 153
object identifier, 52, 53, 57, *66*
    datatype, in ASN.1, *44*, *169*
    hierarchy of, *54*
    registration of, *44*
    tag, in ASN.1, *171*
object instances, 52, *56*, *64*, *86*
object types, 43, *52*, 53, 54, 56, 57, 64
    constructed, *55*
Open Systems Interconnection (OSI), *22*, 27, 32, 36, 43, 84, 85, 100, 112, 114, 160
    reference model, *22*, 23, 29, 45, *61*, *62*, *73*, 90, *130*

P

packages, *65*
    conditional, *65*
performance
    of accounting applications, 150
    of applications, 92, 126, 131, 138, 140, 148, 151, 155, 189
    of distributed systems, 28
    of external monitoring agents, 95
    of LAN traffic monitors, 110
    of network protocols, 129, *131*
    of networks, 26, 32, 33, 95, 96, 99, 130, 137, 143, 145, 163, 164
    of operating systems, 165
    of workload monitors, 116, *121*
performance management, *33*, 36, 40, *145*
physical medium, *19*, 24, 25, 30, 99, 102, 108
    multi-access, *24*, 27, 32, 43, 108, 130, 146
Physical Unit (PU), *76*
Physical Unit Management Services (PUMS), *76*
point-to-point connection, *26*, 93, 96, 101, *102*
Presentation Module (PM), *86*

R

Recommendations for Message Handling Systems, *167*. See also X.409
Reduced Instruction Set Computer (RISC), *97*
Relative Distinguished Name (RDN), *72*
Remote Procedure Call (RPC), 91, 139, 140, 159
repeater, 111
Request For Comment (RFC), *48*, 54, 56, 57
resource brokering, *152*
resource management, 144, *152*, 163
routing, *20*, 24, 26, 57, 100, 119, 134, 145, 146, 165

S

security
    of applications, 138
    of distributed systems, 28, 147
    of monitoring agents, 99
    of networks, 32, 33, 95, 127, 147, *160*
    of operating systems, 165
security management, 18, *33*, 36, *147*
Simple Gateway Management Protocol (SGMP), 47, *50*
Simple Network Management Protocol (SNMP), *46*, *47*, *50*, *51*, 52, 56, 58, 63, 64, 75, 176
specialization, *65*
standard abstract notation, *167*
standard representation, *167*
Structure of Management Information (SMI), 61, 85, 177
subnetwork, *26*
Subordinate Entity Class, *86*

Systems Network Architecture (SNA), *26*, 36, 46, *73*

T

terminal, 27, *28*, 126, 134
    server, 51, 131
time synchronization, *107*
timestamping, *107*
Token Bus (IEEE 802.4), 50, *130*. *See also* Local Area Network (LAN)
Token Ring (IEEE 802.5), 50, *130*. *See also* Local Area Network (LAN)
transaction processing, 17, 27, *28*, 36

U

user interface, 29, 36, 74, 76, 86, 96, 104, 110, 128, 139, *162*, 187, 192

V

Virtual Terminal Access Method (VTAM), *73*

W

Wide Area Network (WAN), 96
workload
    of applications, 100, 114, 151, 189
workload monitor, *114*, 161

X

X.409. *See* Recommendations for Message Handling Systems